The Goo

Adventures in and around my kitchen

The Good Table

Valentine Warner

With photographs by Jonathan Lovekin

MITCHELL BEAZLEY

The Good Table by Valentine Warner

Dedicated to Minnie Iris Wilmer Warner. The last thing I used to think about before sleep, and the first on waking, was breakfast. Now it is you, little apple of my eye.

First published in Great Britain in 2011 by Mitchell Beazley, an imprint of Octopus Publishing Group Limited, Endeavour House, 189 Shaftesbury Avenue, London, WC2H 8JY. www.octopusbooks.co.uk

An Hachette UK Company www.hachette.co.uk

ISBN: 978 1 84533 540 3

A CIP record for this book is available from the British Library.

Set in Georgia.

Printed and bound in China.

Commissioning Editor | Becca Spry
Senior Editor | Leanne Bryan
Photographer | Jonathan Lovekin
Art Director, Designer and Jacket Designer | Pene Parker
Editorial Director | Tracey Smith
Copy-editor | Hattie Ellis
Home Economist | Justine Pattison
Stylist | Sarah O'Keefe
Illustrator | Valentine Warner
Proofreader | Jo Richardson
Indexer | Isobel McLean
Production Manager | Peter Hunt

Contents

Introduction

'What does *The Good Table* mean?', my publisher asked me again and again throughout the tussles to give this book a title. 'People will think it's a carpentry book', she said, or 'It sounds too old-fashioned, a thing of pounds, ounces and lampreys', was her other strategy. I resisted the urge to look pleased at the latter remark.

Clinging on fiercely, in the end I won only through the deployment of staring silences and an infuriating habit of telling her that a lot of people she had never met thought it a fine name for a cookbook.

The 'Good Table' as an approach is my heart on a plate, a badge, so to speak, that I have carried around for a long time, my attitude to the stove.

The 'Good Table' as an object is, of course, the kitchen table, that four-legged friend – strong, sturdy, simple in design, functional, worn by many hands and awarded with wine-stain rosettes, faded with vinegar and hot water, while the wood remains well treated with fat and oil spilt through accident, speed or generosity.

If there's one piece of furniture that represents the centre of the home, the passion, interaction, survival and joy of family life, surely it is the table at which we prepare food, sit and eat (although it may be argued that today it is the sofa!). I enjoy the fact that so often those who enter my house gravitate straight to the kitchen, bypassing the sitting room, and I know this happens in many more houses than my own. I like to think this reassurance that the kitchen offers is an evolutionary hangover from time spent huddled around the fire telling stories and eating together.

Sharing food and drink is not just a practicality but a deep display of affection and love. It implies that we want those we give it to to prosper and survive. Busy hands reaching, cutlery scraping to the warming volume of voices, it makes me smile to know that it is good food and drink that create a bonhomie like no other, feeding our minds as much as our stomachs.

For me, this wooden surface is the earth gone flat again, as many of the recipes cooked or served on my kitchen table were brought home from overseas. Although this rectangle of marks, dents and cuts shows no discernible timeline, it is an epicurean map of my life, appetites, attempts, puzzled failures and the pleasures I have enjoyed alone or shared with others. It is a workhorse whose back has been loaded with books, birds and animals, moss-footed mushrooms, strange bottles, the cheap and the dear. The very fact that it is made of wood represents the inextricable link between food and nature that I feel is so important.

Of course, a 'Good Table' doesn't always mean the one in our kitchen. It is any surface where good food has been prepared and eaten; it could be the sea wall where a memorable fish and chips was devoured with greasy fingers.

For me, it can be the large river stone on which I cleaned chicken guts in the Indian jungle. It's the wonky plastic garden furniture of a Spanish roadside bar where I enjoyed a steak that tasted of bull sweat; the sun-dappled picnic cloth displaying a ransacked hamper. It is a French market, full of jostling baskets and tomato-squeezing locals, the stalls boasting plucked chickens, heads and feet left on, fabulous bread and honking cheeses. All represent places, people and information exchanged, that have helped me eat better or find something new.

Laid out like a town banquet in a Spanish square, the 'Good Table' seats many. Friends, chefs, authors, farmers, home cooks, stall owners, fishermen, knife-makers, waiters, raconteurs, in fact anyone who has shared something with me that I have kept, have all influenced my 'Good Table'. It stretches the globe and, as long as there is no one way to cook a dish, its place settings are endless.

I do not believe a plate of food to be simply a list of ingredients, a set of instructions resulting in a dish, but rather a plate seasoned with mood, stories, memories, lives, geography and natural history; sourced, then prepared and eaten with all senses firing. Rising to the nose in the fragrant steam are the sum parts of everything that contributed to the plate. See any dish prepared with love, however humble, then surely it is preceded by centuries of trying to make it as delicious as possible. The more we know about our food, the more we know about life – and I see that as a good thing.

When trying to define my feelings about the British food scene today, my brain feels as messy with conflicting thoughts as the table linen after a dinner in a Chinese restaurant. On the one hand we are increasingly squeamish in our tastes, while at the same time we greedily gobble up cuisines from all over the world. Despite the towers of cookbooks, hours of food telly, food festivals bubbling up like mushrooms and acres of farmers' markets boasting chutney galore, in the home we still seem to be witnessing the disappearance of ingredients and cooking skills faster than ever. It seems sometimes that that our appetites are satisfied on a diet of telly programmes and the photos in cookbooks, but the baton is not carried on when it comes to shopping and cooking. So often I hear 'I don't have the time to cook.' We all have the time to cook. Perhaps it's more that we have forgotten what to cook. Literally, in minutes, a splendid grilled black bream (*see* page 120) or Cauliflower with Curry Leaves and Tomatoes (*see* page 205) can be made from scratch. A dizzying buffet of salads, omelettes, soups, grilled dishes and the poached are at hand for those with little time; convenient maybe, but primarily invented because the few ingredients and steps involved were all that was needed to make them delicious. For those with more time, cooking can provide the very meditation needed as respite from the humdrum of everyday worries and frenetic modern life.

I appreciate that supermarkets are here to stay; it is how the nation is fed. I use them sometimes. I still feel, however, that the more we suckle from the teat of convenience in the orchards of aisles 1–26, the more boring our fridges and subsequently our food becomes. We have a blindingly bright array of produce and culinary traditions in this multicultural Britain, and in order that they remain an inheritance, we need to cook.

Not so long ago it was essential to know the rhythms and offerings of our fields, woods, streams, rivers, hills and seas, as for most of us, who rarely travelled at all, they supplemented the table and often ensured the survival of our families. Although arguably not necessary now, surely knowledge as valuable as this – with all the wonderful secrets, delights and variety we have learnt, tweaked, recorded and tasted – is better remembered than forgotten? It gives us increasingly important choices to act on and a healthy pride. Food and cooking, apart from being expected to keep us alive, are such large parts of who we British are as a nation and what made us so. What's more, knowing about food is certainly kinder to the purse, while still giving greater variety on the table.

I like to think of my plate as an environment. If making something Indian, for example, and ghee is not close to hand, then use butter (the most similar ingredient) rather than olive oil, which has no place in a curry. Of course to balance this, cooking is a constant journey of surprise and discovery, and I would also wholly advocate not being a slave to a recipe, but I like my food to have a sense of roots; a kind of doffing of the hat to all that came before. I prefer my steak and onion pudding (*see* page 57) to be served with violent English mustard and my *Lapin à la moutarde* (*see* page 76) with a bronchial clearing dollop of Dijon. Call me boring, but I don't want mango in a crumble, yet mixed with condensed milk and ice it teleports me straight to Delhi.

The rhythms of nature too dictate my menu and it is precisely because the pigeon likes to raid the pea plant or blackcurrant bush that these ingredients sit cheerily alongside it on a plate. A pig snuffling in its pen close to the salty shore you may find surprisingly delicious when served with the clams hidden in the sand nearby (*see* page 38). Cooking like this also helps build a food logic, a language with the cuisine with which you have decided to engage. An egg pickled in balsamic vinegar would surely be a wrong turn – show me an Italian pub.

This idea of geography, people and produce brings into play the enjoyable pursuit of cooking and eating seasonally. Sometimes I cannot resist reaching for a pineapple, aubergine or chipotle chile, but on the whole, eating this way is a gentle dictatorship I happily follow. Autumn and winter are for the friendship of roots, the iron strike of brassicas and fat shellfish. A berry pavlova in December to me is as unwanted as a suet pudding in summer; a time for the click of salad tongs and that wonderful ingredient – wood smoke. Greeting produce seasonally not only makes the year a succession of treats but feeds us the very things we need according to the time of year and subsequent climate. There are some recipes in this book that, although foreign, are seasonal in that they use ingredients that grow both here and in the country from which the dish originated.

Seasonality is a game to be played when out shopping; it demands the cook be adventurous, trying to find multiple ways to romance the ingredients until the affair is over. It engages the cook to steam, roast, fry, dry, cure, pickle, bake or purée the ingredient to the utmost point of its capabilities, while also helping to avoid becoming bored of any one ingredient. Especially in the case of vegetables, it can open up a realisation that no meat or fish need necessarily lay alongside them. It also makes clear definitions between varieties of a particular ingredient. Take venison, for example; which venison? In the UK there are six species of deer living in the wild, but all have different seasons and a very different taste; seasonality will hopefully prompt you to find out which one you are eating or prefer.

Here I would like to make a quick point on foraging, which takes up a small part of this book. Our lands and waters have plenty of wild ingredients to offer us, lifting their skirts to reveal an abundance of goodies as the calendar pages turn. Understandably, not everyone wants to trundle the grassy paths, bucket in hand, with eyes to the ground as if looking for a dropped mobile, but for me, foraging is just another kind of shopping that can increase options with a kaleidoscope of seaweed, shrimps, mushrooms, elderflowers, sorrel, blackberries, cockles, damsons; the list is endless. This free larder features heavily in the markets, restaurants and households of Europe, and that is partly why I enjoy the food of these countries so much; these ingredients contribute to a way of life that comes with an expertise, anticipation and passion. But for a squeeze of lemon or a knob of butter, a meal thrown together from the wild places (and not so wild places, for that matter) is a truly satisfying one that comes with a glowing feeling of self-sufficiency. On the subject of shooting and fishing, although I find the death of any animal a sad thing, leaving a gap on the branch or in the grass or river, meat is meat and whether farmed or wild requires premeditated killing. The respect is shown in a quick death, the quarry then cooked with care, love and appreciation. The UK has very strict and rigorous hunting seasons in order that we retain healthy stocks of these beasts, birds and fish that may end up on our plates. Certainly, their provenance is second to none, which is more than I can say for a sad-looking mackerel that will pass its sell-by date or a hunk of beef that never ate an interesting plant in its life. Foraging, hunting and fishing all conjure up the old spirits, the not-forgotten country lore that never really left our bones or blood but may lie there asleep. To go on a walk and return home with food is a part of cooking that allows me to stay in touch with and enjoy the very things modern life seems to steamroll with voracity.

In this book, I felt it was important to include some of the very ingredients that I fear may disappear, things that make the 'Good Table' better. Lots of foods have vanished from our tables since World War II and the geared-up mechanisation of food production, and this is a shame, as many of them are cheap and certainly delicious. Maybe 15 long years of rationing saw to it that rabbit stew or turnips became associated with hard times and the need to banish difficult memories bred a picky dislike that became inherited by the next generations. Personally, I love the calming smell of rabbit stew or a bowl of gooseberries and cream.

Take the quince, for example. It cannot be grabbed from the barrow, tossed in the air and then scrunched with a big, juicy bite. No, it is obstinate and hard, its juice withering the mouth dry, and it requires cooking. Once tackled though, its secret is unlocked. There, bathed in a deep bronze syrup, is a joyous fruit quite unlike anything a cooked apple or pear can confess. It is not a convenient ingredient, but what's the rush?

In fact, take russet apples too, which, because of their sandpaper texture, are unlikely to be found in a supermarket. What a shame; they may be ugly but they taste good; they do not fit into the categories of big, red and shiny, but they beat a lot of our daily apples hands down. What of ox cheek, lovage and swede? The 'Good Table' positively invites you to find friendship with these once-loved joys.

Is eating a plate of herring milts (*see* page 279) any more odd than eating crisped hairy pig skin with a pint? Buy that unknown fish from the boat in the harbour or that local cheese when on holiday, as the minute you do, a step has been taken away from the usual. Everything is accessible; it may just take a while to find, even months. Don't necessarily search it out, just happen to remember it as, once eaten, it has been tried and the seed may take root. Take chances; reach for an ugly celeriac over a potato or buy a megrim instead of the farmed salmon.

Regarding fish, there are some very serious worldwide concerns about overfishing that are now very much on the public eye. In the case of quotas resulting in *discard,* (fresh fish being thrown back overboard, dead) the practice is unacceptable, wasteful and demonstrates no respect for life taken. In short, the ongoing debate is in favour of fewer fishing days with all fish landed for sale. When choosing, do not only look at the eye of the fish, but also into the eyes of the fishmonger and ask questions, as although certain fisheries have been emptied, others may sustain healthy stocks of the particular fish you want to buy.

Where and how fish have been caught are of prime importance. Read labels and make your decision accordingly. There is plenty of information online (please excuse the unavoidable pun) through organisations such as the MSC and, while our main target species will go on being landed, there are many alternative fish that, once tried, may become a favourite.

From time to time I'd encourage you to buy things you don't know how to cook. Believe me, I have produced some memorable disasters through inexperience, but the anticipation of the result was fun and I know what not to do next time. Ignore the perfect cooking on telly; failure contributes to success.

This book is about tasting all the time, partly to avoid those failures, but also to see how things change as they metamorphose from kitchen to table. Taste things in their own right as well, raw when possible. Bite everything except the passer-by on the street so that each new taste can be credited with its own merits. A plate of food may look all well and pretty, but the taste may remain a dud because sneak previews were not taken along the way.

I think that's about enough. If you enjoy this book and find yourself using it regularly, distance yourself each time from measurements, adding more of whatever you think the dish would be better with. Cover the pages in smears and try something again if you felt it didn't work. Be adaptable about timing in the knowledge that one woman's oven is another man's incinerator, and taste all the time. Cook with love, shop like a European and don't ignore the knobbly veg. Scrape the mould off the chutney, don't forget to honour the things at the back of the fridge; and above all remember that this book is, in a sense, no longer mine but rather yours.

Meat

Moussaka

Serves 6

White sauce

50g butter
3 heaped tablespoons plain flour
500ml cows', sheep's or goats' milk
100g feta cheese
flaked sea salt
½ teaspoon grated nutmeg
2 free-range egg yolks

Lamb mince

2 tablespoons olive oil
2 medium white onions,
    finely chopped
2 teaspoons dried oregano
1½ level teaspoons ground cinnamon
1 teaspoon caster sugar
6 garlic cloves, finely chopped
750g minced lamb
150ml dry white wine
3 heaped tablespoons tomato purée
2 teaspoons flaked sea salt
black pepper

Aubergines and potatoes

2 medium aubergines (about 600g)
2 teaspoons flaked sea salt
    (or just 1 teaspoon if using fine salt)
2 teaspoons olive oil for each slice of
    aubergine, plus extra for sautéing
2 medium potatoes, peeled and very
    finely sliced

To serve

spinach
tomato, olive and onion salad

There was once – sadly she is gone – a food writer, well known in the Seventies, called Marika Hanbury-Tenison. I always thought this friend of my mother's was called Moussaka Hanbury-Tenison, which did seem very odd to me. But then grown-ups were strange.

I really like Greece, with the unmistakable smell of its arid coastal mountains thick with parched herbs, the squint white walls, sugar-lump houses and cold amber retsina. Greek food, though, gets a tepid reception from many. This is a shame as, when off the beaten track, you find all variety of tender kid-goat, octopus salad and flaky pastries stuffed with crude cheese and herbs, which make the menu feel less limited. If you find yourself always eating the usual suspects, hire a moped and follow the dustier routes. Even so, I like the Greek staples, and moussaka with its spiced sweet mince, faintly tangy white top and olive oil-rich aubergines takes me back to long lazy lunches on Crete.

First make the white sauce. Melt the butter in a saucepan over a gentle heat and sprinkle in the flour. Cook together, stirring constantly with a whisk, for 30 seconds or so. Start adding the milk bit by bit, still stirring. The mixture will clag up at first, then loosen as you add more milk. Crumble in the feta and gently whisk until it has melted. Season with salt and the nutmeg. Take the saucepan off the heat and allow to cool. When at room temperature, beat in both egg yolks.

While the sauce cools, start the mince. Heat the oil in a large frying pan over a medium heat, then sauté the onion with the oregano, cinnamon and sugar until soft and golden but not burnt (about 10 minutes). Add the garlic in the last 2 minutes of cooking. Next, tip in the lamb and fry it, taking care to break it up and stir out any clumps, for 10 minutes or so until browned and loose. Tip in the wine and add the tomato purée, then season with the salt and a good grinding of black pepper. Keep cooking, on a lower heat, until any obvious liquid has evaporated but the mince still appears moist. Check the seasoning and put the mince to one side.

Preheat the oven to 170°C fan/190°C/Gas 5. While the mince cooks, prepare the aubergines. Heat a large frying pan with a generous teaspoon of oil in it. Slice the aubergines to about the thickness of two stacked £1 coins. Salt them on both sides and rub a teaspoon of oil on both sides of each slice. Fry the slices in batches, each slice lying flat in one layer, fairly hard over a medium heat for about 8 minutes, turning once or twice. They should be streaked deep golden brown and be soft to the prod of a knife. Drain the slices of oil on some doubled kitchen paper. Repeat until all the aubergine is cooked.

Cover the bottom of a round oven dish approximately 27cm in diameter with the mince. Lay over the aubergine slices, overlapping. Gently press everything down. Put the potato in a layer on top. Cover with the white sauce and smooth.

Bake for 45 minutes–1 hour. The top should be a rich golden brown. Eat outside with spinach and a tomato, olive and onion salad.

Pot leg of lamb with white wine & vegetables

Serves 6

a half leg of lamb (about 1.3kg)
flaked sea salt
3 tablespoons light olive oil
1 garlic bulb
3 sprigs of rosemary
6 banana shallots
3 celery sticks
2 medium fennel bulbs
12 baby turnips
6 medium carrots, scrubbed
2 sprigs of thyme
2 large bay leaves
6 peppercorns
650ml Mâcon, or other dry
   white wine
150ml water
2 tablespoons chopped tarragon
   and flat-leaf parsley (optional)

To serve

French bread or boiled
   waxy potatoes
Dijon mustard

So often joints of meat are automatically roasted just because they are joints, with little or no thought of poaching them instead. Gently bubbling a leg of lamb in a pot, surrounded by vegetables, produces a very clean-feeling meal, bathed in a delightful liquor and tasting delicately of the sum parts. Since this dish is so uncomplicated and honest in its style, I like to carve the meat with my large penknife while finishing off a pre-lunch pastis.

Preheat the oven to 180°C fan/200°C/Gas 6. Salt the lamb generously all over. Heat the oil in a large, flameproof casserole, getting it nice and hot. Cut the whole bulb of garlic through the middle horizontally. (Try to keep both pieces in tact so you don't have to chase lots of pieces around the pot when frying.) Lower the garlic into the casserole, cut-side down, and fry gently until dark golden. Take the garlic out and lower in the lamb – if the oil is hot enough, it should sizzle immediately – then add the rosemary. Really take time to brown the lamb properly all over, as this will add a greater depth of flavour to the sauce. If the rosemary begins to singe, this is quite alright, but don't burn it.

While the meat colours, peel the shallots, taking great care to keep them whole by cutting only the whiskers off the root end. De-string the celery by snapping the wide end slightly up from the bottom; pull it away from you and the string should come away with the small piece of flesh. Chop the celery sticks into thirds. Cut off any unsightly or damaged areas of the fennel and quarter, leaving any little bit of green feather at the top. Trim the turnips, leaving each one with a tiny green top. Trim the carrots, leaving a small green tuft and the whisker on the bottom. Tie the thyme sprigs up in the bay leaves with a little kitchen string. Place the vegetables and garlic around the lamb, pop in the bouquet garni with the peppercorns and pour over the white wine, followed by the water.

Bring the liquid up to a gentle simmer, place the lid on the casserole and transfer it to the oven. Cook the lamb for 1–1¼ hours, by which time it should be niccly pink near the bone. Remove the lamb from the pot and leave to stand for 10 minutes or so covered by foil and a tea towel before carving.

Serve the meat surrounded by the vegetables with a good bowl of the juice nearby to pour over. A scattering of finely chopped tarragon and parsley over the top would be a good idea. Excellent crispy chewy French bread or smallish boiled waxy potatoes go nicely with this, and pokey Dijon mustard is a necessity.

Harira

Serves 4

300g vine tomatoes, or the same
    weight of canned tomatoes
2 tablespoons olive oil
175g trimmed lamb neck fillet,
    cut into very small morsels
a small bunch of coriander,
    very finely chopped
1 large thumb-sized piece of root
    ginger, peeled and grated
2 young celery sticks, very finely
    chopped
1 small onion, finely chopped
1 good teaspoon plain flour, sifted
2 teaspoons tomato purée
a small pinch of saffron threads
flaked sea salt and black pepper
600ml water
2/3 × 400g can chickpeas, drained
1 vermicelli nest

To serve

a little lemon juice
a little olive oil
ground cumin (optional)
warm white rolls (optional)

This lamb, chickpea and tomato soup is a Moroccan staple eaten at dinner when breaking the fasting day during Ramadan.

I used to eat this soup probably twice a week, served up by my neighbour Ibrahim from his battered mobile food stall parked permanently on the Golborne Road in West London. He pulls a small crowd most days and I recommend a trip there, as the chat is jolly, the food delicious and his tiny prices virtually unchanged for as long as I lived there. He is closed Thursday, Sunday and for Ramadan. I made my own *harira* when Ibrahim was away and here is my version. Even though recipes evolve, different from mother to mother, he has told me never to put turmeric or cumin in the pot. So I won't, although he did let me add cumin from the row of condiments on the front of his stall to finish the dish.

If using fresh, cut the cores from the tomatoes and criss-cross the bottoms. Put them in a bowl and cover with just-boiled water. After a minute, tip away the water and then peel the tomatoes, discarding the skin. Heat the oil in a medium saucepan until hot. Add the lamb to the oil and fry it briskly for about 3 minutes until browned. Lower the heat and add the coriander, ginger, celery and onion. Introduce the flour and then cook everything for 3 minutes, stirring regularly, until the onion has softened a little but not coloured.

While the vegetables cook, roughly but finely chop all the tomatoes, then add them to the saucepan with the tomato purée, saffron, 2 teaspoons salt and a good grinding of black pepper. (Be careful with the saffron, as it is popularly and wrongly thought to be just used for its colour when the good stuff in fact has a strong iodine-like taste.) Add the water and chickpeas and gently simmer for 30 minutes, with a lid on.

Break up the vermicelli in your hands and drop it in the soup to cook for a further 5–10 minutes. Stir the soup and you will see that the flour and starch from the vermicelli have thickened it slightly. Check the seasoning and serve hot in bowls, having passed over them a little lemon juice and oil.

Some like to add a dusting of cumin on top but, as Ibrahim says, not in the cooking. Warm white rolls are also good with *harira*.

Seared lamb neck fillet with garlic sauce

Serves 2

2 thick lamb neck fillets
(about 250–300g each)
2 good tablespoons finely chopped
thyme leaves
2 good tablespoons finely chopped
rosemary leaves
flaked sea salt and black pepper
a little olive oil

Garlic sauce

2 large garlic bulbs
15g butter
150ml white wine
1 teaspoon white wine vinegar
1 teaspoon caster sugar
100ml double cream
flaked sea salt

With its enjoyably high fat content, neck of lamb is a very tender and giving cut, easy to find and good for the purse. No pussyfooting around here: this sauce is exceptionally garlicky, but with that deep, sweet taste that comes from roasting the garlic in the oven. It is essential that the garlic be large, very hard when pinched and with no signs of green shoots sprouting from the cloves, as this gives it an unpleasant taste. I would barely bother laying the table, but eat the moist pink slices pronged on a fork straight from the board and dragged through the velvety sauce. I suppose the addition of a salad would make for a more rounded repast.

Preheat the oven to 180°C fan/200°C/Gas 6. Bake the garlic bulbs on a baking tray for about 30–40 minutes. They should be totally squidgy with a golden sticky ooze beginning to leak from them. Allow the garlic to cool, or bravely attempt to peel them when hot – it is easier to extract the flesh. To do this, flake off the outside skin, separate each clove from the bulb and squeeze the innards into a small saucepan. Mash the roasted garlic with a fork and heat with the butter until it has melted. Now add the wine, vinegar and sugar. Let them simmer away gently until the wine has reduced by two-thirds. Add the cream, bring the sauce up to the faintest bubbling and turn off the heat. Purée the sauce with a stick blender, if you'd like it more refined. Season with salt.

Put a frying pan on a medium heat and let it get very hot. Meanwhile, trim the outside lamb neck of any particularly tough fat or sinew and discard. Mix the thyme and rosemary leaves with a good amount of salt and a very heavy grinding of black pepper. Roll the lamb gently in the seasoned herbs and rub all over with a little oil.

Add the lamb to the hot frying pan, where it should start frying immediately. Brown the fillets on one side, then turn down the heat so that they do not get burnt and cook for another 4 minutes on the same side. Turn over for another 5 minutes. The lamb should be nicely pink inside, but not raw. Allow the lamb to rest for 5 minutes before slicing it on a slant at a half-finger thickness. If you want a cooky's perk, take an end – just the one!

Ghengis' lamb chops

Serves 3–4

1 teaspoon cumin seeds

1½ teaspoons black pepper

3 cloves

¼ star anise

3 large garlic cloves, chopped

1 thumb-sized piece of root ginger,
peeled and roughly chopped

1 level teaspoon ground coriander

4 dessertspoons black vinegar
or brown rice vinegar

2 dessertspoons dark muscovado
sugar

4 dessertspoons thick dark soy sauce

1 finger-length hot dried chile,
deseeded and roughly chopped

1 lemon grass stalk, finely sliced

100ml water

2 × 6-cutlet racks of lamb

This barbecued lamb is of no particular origin: it is an invention of mine that had to have a name. Ghengis Khan came to mind in a notion that, as he ferociously rode over various terrified populations across Asia on tiny Mongolian horses, he must have picked up a few cooking tips and influences along the way.

The taste that the smoke from the charcoal gives makes it an ingredient in itself, so ideally a gas barbecue will not be used. The black vinegar can be bought in any good Asian food shop. As for the dark soy sauce, I like the Golden Boat brand, also found in such shops.

In a little frying pan, gently dry-fry the cumin seeds until toasted and pleasant to the nose. Pound them with a pestle in a mortar with the black pepper, cloves, star anise, garlic, ginger and coriander until you have a fine paste. Scrape into a sealable container large enough to hold the racks of lamb, then mix in the remaining ingredients, apart from the lamb, to make the spicy sauce.

Criss-cross the fat of the lamb with a sharp knife. Roughly scratch the underside. Marinate the lamb in the sealed container in the fridge for at least 8 hours before using, turning the box upside down for half the time.

Load the barbecue with charcoal and, when the embers are glowing orange and grey, cast on the lamb. Grill the racks for about 20 minutes, painting with the sauce and turning occasionally. Take care not to burn them, as the dripping oils from the fat will catch alight. They should be crisp, well coloured and slightly charred on the outside.

On a board, divide the racks of lamb into cutlets; they should be pink inside. Briefly throw them back on the grill. Daub with the sauce and cook for a further 1–2 minutes on each side. Once cooked, leave the cutlets to rest in a warm place and in the meantime boil up the remaining sauce with a splash of water for 5 minutes. Daub the chops on the plate one last time and serve immediately.

Porchetta

Serves about 8

leaves from 1 sprig of rosemary

12 large sage leaves

1 teaspoon flaked sea salt, plus 2
  extra teaspoons for the pork skin

2 teaspoons black pepper

3kg piece of boned pork belly, skin
  left unscored

a little olive oil

150ml water or white wine

Stuffing

1 dessertspoon fennel seeds

1 dessertspoon coriander seeds

3 tablespoons olive oil

2 large onions, very finely chopped

1 large fennel bulb, very finely
  chopped

finely grated zest of 1 unwaxed lemon

9 garlic cloves, finely chopped

12 rashers of pancetta, sliced into
  matchsticks

1 teaspoon flaked sea salt

150ml white wine

200g minced pork

200g pork liver, medium–finely
  but roughly chopped

Late morning on a wet, grey day somewhere outside Bagni di Lucca in Tuscany, I passed what I thought was an ice-cream van and immediately pulled over with pistachio-flavoured thoughts. I dashed across the road to find the counter window filled by a rotund little man in a paper cap, standing behind not sugar cones but the most splendid piece of crisp, red-skinned, stuffed pork. I bought some in bread and ate it in the drizzle on a bridge overlooking a dramatic ravine. I swooned over my first *porchetta* experience. I went back to the green van to find the vendor feverishly cutting little morsels for himself and wiping his fatty fingers on his white apron. I tried to engage him in chat, asking what he'd done to prepare such an excellent sandwich. 'Cooked it', he repeated, while shrugging unhelpfully (though I don't blame him). So here's my version and I'm pretty sure I have remembered most of what I could taste in the stuffing.

Preheat the oven to 170°C fan/190°C/Gas 5. In a large frying pan, dry-fry the seeds for the stuffing over a medium heat, swirling them gently until their toasted fragrance comes to the nose. Do not burn them. Add the oil to the frying pan along with the onion, fennel, lemon zest, garlic, pancetta and salt and fry all together gently, stirring occasionally, for 10 minutes or so over a medium heat. Add the white wine and simmer it away over the next 10 minutes, stirring occasionally, until the contents of the frying pan just begin to catch and colour. Transfer everything to a large mixing bowl and let it cool. Add the mince and liver to the bowl and stir everything together well.

Finely chop the herbs with the salt and mix in the black pepper. Lay the pork on the work surface, skin-side down. Angling a sharp knife between the fat and meat, cut along the length of the loin fillet so you have almost cut it from the fat but not quite. Open out this flap to create room for the stuffing. Season all over with the herby salt and black pepper. Evenly distribute the stuffing down the length of the belly, packing it in tightly and tucking it in against the loin.

Cut ten to twelve lengths of butcher's string (to be honest, domestic string will do), each one long enough to go round the meat once rolled. Roll the meat up, starting with the meaty side, tucking it in tightly as you go. Secure the string at equal intervals all the way down the rolled belly. Put the pork on an oven rack with the open edge facing down. Rub a little oil all over the skin and sprinkle with the remaining salt. Put the joint in the oven with a tray underneath to catch the juices.

Cook the pork for 3 hours, by which time the skin should be very crispy indeed. As it cooks, take the tray from the oven about three times, add a glug of water or wine and scrape up the syrupy juices using a spoon before pouring them into a saucepan for gravy.

Rest the meat for 10 minutes or so. Warm the meat juices and skim off the fat. Cut the string off the meat and carve in very thick pieces (about 3–4cm). Delicious with very fine puréed potatoes and maybe some boiled chard with sweet-and-sour onions, sultanas and pine nuts on top. Alternatively, wedge it into some good Italian bread.

Pork chop with apple & crispy sage

Serves 1

1 pork chop (about 300g)
1 dessert apple (Cox's is ideal)
a little cider vinegar
a little caster sugar
flaked sea salt and black pepper
30g butter
8 large sage leaves

The other morning, I proudly announced to myself: 'I am going to have a pork chop with apples and sage tonight.' With this thought in mind, the day went very well and dinner was excellent. It would take too long to write exactly why pork, apple and sage go so well together. They are just three close and happy friends who have gone through a lot.

Preheat the oven to 200°C fan/220°C/Gas 7. Deeply score through the rind of the chop with a very sharp knife at 2cm intervals all the way along. Peel the apple and cut off two sides as close to the core as possible. (Eat the smaller two uncut sides.) Splash the apple pieces all over with cider vinegar, then scatter a little sugar over them followed by some salt.

Melt the butter in an ovenproof frying pan over a medium–low heat. When it starts to foam, lay in the sage leaves without overlapping. Cook, undisturbed, for a minute or so on both sides, or until crisp, and then transfer to a piece of kitchen paper.

Turn up the heat a little and season the chop well. Lay the apple pieces flat on the chopping board and, keeping them intact at one end, cut them into 5mm slices. Keeping each sliced half together, as if in one piece, transfer them to the frying pan with the chop. Push the apple slices a bit, so that they lean to one side. This will help them catch some good colour. Cook the apple and chop for 2 minutes or so, or until the pork is deep and richly browned, then turn the chop on to its uncooked side, spoon some butter over the apple pieces and put the whole frying pan in the oven for 7–8 minutes, or until the pork is cooked but retains the faintest pinkness.

Put the chop and apples on a plate and pour over a little of the butter from the frying pan. Pile the crispy sage on top and eat with a glass of good cider.

Heaven & earth

Serves 2

1 large Bramley apple, peeled
  and cut into 2cm chunks
1 large baking potato, peeled
  and cut into 2cm chunks
flaked sea salt and black pepper
a splash of sunflower oil
4 good rashers of rindless smoked
  streaky bacon, cut into small pieces
1 medium onion, halved and sliced
2 tablespoons whole milk
30g butter
4 fat slices of a large black pudding,
  or 6 fat slices of a small
  black pudding, skinned
grain mustard, to serve

This fine dish for a wet day was taught to me by Father Rainer Verborg, a monk at Ampleforth Abbey, when I was there for a day's filming. I had never come across the dish before and loved the name's evocative reference to its ingredients. I followed Father Rainer through the orchards and the vision of the back of his black robe speeding purposefully through the damp misty rows of apples has haunted me strangely ever since. Despite this, his cooking and cider were as modest and pleasing as I had hoped, and I left feeling calmer than normal.

Put the apple and potato in a saucepan and cover with cold water. Add a good pinch of salt and bring to the boil. Reduce the heat slightly and simmer for about 15 minutes, or until both the potato and apple are very soft.

Meanwhile, heat the oil in a large, nonstick frying pan. Fry the bacon until the fat melts and the meat begins to crisp. Add the onion to the frying pan and cook together over a medium heat for 10 minutes or so, stirring fairly often, until the onion is softened and coloured a rich golden brown – perhaps even slightly burnt. Four minutes before the end of the cooking time, add the slices of black pudding and cook for a couple of minutes on each side until hot and crispy.

While the pudding fries, drain the cooked potato and apple in a sieve and tip back into the saucepan. Add the milk and butter and mash until absolutely smooth. Season well and cover with a lid.

Spoon the apple mash into the centre of two warmed plates and top with the hot bacon and fried onion and the black pudding. Serve with grain mustard on the side – and cider, of course. Amen!

Cinghiale con ginepro
(Wild boar with juniper)

Serves 4–6

1kg stewing wild boar (shoulder
   or neck, for example)
1 large onion, finely chopped
2 celery sticks, finely chopped
3 large garlic cloves, finely chopped
3 tablespoons tomato purée
1 tablespoon juniper berries,
   lightly bashed
1 bay leaf
4 peppercorns
2 teaspoons dried thyme
1½ teaspoons flaked sea salt
enough good Italian red wine
   to just cover the meat (near
   enough a bottle)
3 tablespoons olive oil
4 slices of white bread, cut crossways
   into 4 triangles
plain boiled potatoes, to serve
   (optional)

The glory of this recipe is that it is all just popped in the pan in its raw state and left to do its work in the oven.

The recipe came about like this. I was invited to Kent in September 2009 to shoot a quarry that has not been seen in the wilds of England for 350 years. Arriving in the wood, I was shown the broken fences, dug-up ground and well-used paths caused by these bristly beasts. This first (unsuccessful) day, I sat up an old painter-and-decorator's scaffold, lashed to a tree, where I stayed alert and stock still, save for the occasional cigarette. Finally, darkness fell and I drove home.

Six months later, on a biting February afternoon, I climbed the frame once more, but this time the tree stumps in my field of view were slathered with black treacle and a few turnips had been tossed here and there. I sat still again, ran out of cigarettes and got very, very cold. I also really needed a wee, which was not helped by the hide wobbling dangerously from side to side in a strong evening wind. Then I heard snorting – some way off – but they did not present themselves. I could no longer see down my rifle scope in pitch-black, and so my hosts suggested we change tactics and go for a drive. At 9.45pm, I turned to one of the guys and said 'I believe they are here, we've tried our best, but I must drive back to London.' At that very moment, some way off, we heard the snap of a stick. We switched on the infra-red lamp and, 200 yards off, there they were: five feral boar snuffling in a woodland clearing. The biggest boar was a 400 pound male – but he was not to be cooky's choice. He had plenty of meat on him, but I'm not interested in trophies; the smaller the boar, the more tender. So although in my sights, they started to trot off even while I was being told 'shoot, shoot!'. But I waited for the leg I had spotted sticking out from behind an oak to present more, and it did. With the quick maths done, there it was, the smallest, at about 150 pounds. SNAP! went the rifle and the young boar went down instantly. So far I have eaten half. I like the idea that country walks are a little more edgy now that boar are back once more.

Preheat the oven to 180°C fan/200°C/Gas 6. Into a heavy casserole, drop all the raw ingredients (bar half the oil and bread) and mix them together thoroughly, then place over the lid. Cook in the oven for approximately 2 hours, or until the meat is tender, removing the lid for the last 30 minutes of cooking to reduce the sauce. If there is lots of fat on the surface, then skim some off.

Just before serving, fry the bread in the rest of the oil until deep golden but retaining a little pliancy in the middle. Drain on kitchen paper and decorate over the stew that has been transferred to a serving dish. Undressed boiled potatoes appear frequently with this dish.

Faggots

Makes 12 faggots

50g butter

1 medium onion, finely chopped

1 tablespoon chopped thyme leaves

12 sage leaves, finely chopped

1 teaspoon ground mace

2 teaspoons black pepper

500g minced pork belly

100g minced bacon

4 lamb's kidneys, rinsed, skinned, cored and finely but roughly chopped

150g pork or lamb's liver, finely but roughly chopped

1 level tablespoon flaked sea salt (½ tablespoon if using fine salt)

100g coarse white breadcrumbs, made from stale bread

100ml whole milk

200g beef caul

Gravy

2 large onions, finely sliced

1 tablespoon soft dark brown sugar

2 tablespoons malt vinegar

1½ level tablespoons plain flour

500ml good dark beef stock, or a can of consommé mixed with water

flaked sea salt and black pepper

To serve

good mash

cooked frozen peas

English mustard

Faggots remind me of the less-comfortable pubs that are better for it: hard, dark-wood bench seating, whitewashed walls and a low ceiling, a small crackling fire and the low murmur of locals leaning against the bar. I come alone and like a corner table and a pint of bitter with a pickled egg (*see* page 259). The faggots are quietly set down as I read the paper and I'll probably have to ask for some mustard. Lunch will bring a quiet smile and then it's back out into the drizzle. I like the old things.

Melt 30g of the butter in a frying pan and in it sweat the onion with the thyme, sage and spices over a medium–low heat for about 15 minutes, or until very soft. Add the mixture to the meats and salt in a big bowl, and mix all together well, then add the breadcrumbs and milk. Get your hands in there and squish the mixture through them until it is really well combined. Take a little of the raw mixture and fry it to see how it tastes; correct the seasoning accordingly.

Tenderly open up the caul and hold it up to the light to see where any holes might be (to avoid when assembling the faggots), then spread it out on the work surface. Take an open fistful of the mixture and place it on the caul so that you can cut a sheet around it to the size of two-thirds of a piece of A5 paper. Fold the caul over the top of the meats as if you were wrapping up treasured possessions in a handkerchief. All the corners should overlap and the meats be tightly surrounded. Turn the faggot over. Repeat until all are done.

Heat some more butter in a frying pan over a medium–high heat and put the faggots in, fold-side down. Briskly fry until brown, taking care not to burn them. Turn over and gently fry on the other side. They should not open, but if they do, place a plate over the top of the batch to secure the folds. Repeat until all are good and brown. Transfer them to a board.

In the same frying pan, fry the onions in the leftover faggot fat over a medium–low heat for 30 minutes or so until richly coloured. Meanwhile, preheat the oven to 160°C fan/180°C/Gas 4. Add the brown sugar and malt vinegar to the frying pan and cook until the vinegar has evaporated completely. Then sprinkle in the flour and cook gently, stirring, for a further minute or so. The flour must not burn. Start adding the beef stock or canned consommé, bit by bit, stirring constantly. Taste for seasoning, remembering that the faggots are highly seasoned.

Place the faggots in a good-sized, shallow casserole and cover with the gravy, then the lid. Bake gently for 1½ hours. For the last 20 minutes, remove the lid. What else could you serve it with but some good mash and some frozen peas? Oh! And, of course, some pokey English mustard.

Toad in the hole

Serves 3–4

2 tablespoons sunflower oil
6–8 good meaty pork sausages
tomato ketchup, to serve

Batter

115g plain flour
½ teaspoon flaked sea salt
225ml semi-skinned milk
2 large, vibrant-yolked
    free-range eggs

With no mucking around and honest as the day is long, you know where you are when the toad comes out. The excellent batter comes from a long line of tall Pattison women, a fierce tribe from Hertfordshire, and is as reliable as their friendship. The better the eggs, the more your toad batter will have a rich, golden glow.

Preheat the oven to 180°C fan/200°C/Gas 6. To make the batter, put the flour, salt and milk into a food processor bowl and crack in the eggs. Blitz together for 15 seconds or so into a smooth batter, then pour it into a jug and set aside for 30 minutes.

Pour the oil into a large, nonstick, ovenproof frying pan and sizzle the sausages over a medium heat for 6–8 minutes until nicely browned on all sides. Stir the batter well before pouring around the hot sausages and put the frying pan in the oven. Bake for around 35 minutes. By this time, the batter should be very well risen and golden brown.

Remove from the oven – taking care to use an oven cloth, as the handle will be extremely hot. Eat at once, with much blobbing of tomato ketchup.

Note: If you don't have a large frying pan that you can use in the oven, fry the sausages and then transfer to a roasting tin (rather than an ovenproof dish, as the heat will conduct better through the metal and should result in a lighter batter). Tip in the sausage fat and pop in the oven for a couple of minutes to heat up before adding the batter. Whether you add the batter to the frying pan or the roasting tin, the sausages and fat must be hot to help the batter to rise well.

Pork neck with clams
& Jerusalem artichokes

Serves 4

1kg live fat palourde clams,
  well scrubbed

a little olive oil

1kg rindless pork neck or shoulder,
  in one piece

1 large glass white wine or water
  (about 200ml)

6 Jerusalem artichokes

3 large banana shallots, finely sliced

3 garlic cloves, finely sliced

2 big bay leaves

flaked sea salt and black pepper

a fistful of finely chopped
  curly-leaf parsley

1 lemon, halved

This recipe is the child of some defrosted pork neck, borderline clams and slightly wizened artichokes, but it proved to be so good that I now cook it regularly. You could also use pork shoulder. You do not want the pork rind in this dish, but reserve it, as it is useful in many other dishes – boil it until it is soft, then fry it hard and mix with capers, finely chopped shallot and a fresh dressing and serve it with salad leaves, or just poach it and eat it warm with capers.

Preheat the oven to 160°C fan/180°C/Gas 4. Rinse the clams under the tap in a colander. Tap any that are open on the edge of your sink. If they are alive, they will close; if not, they are no more, so throw them out. Some of them may be stuck tight with mud, ready to ambush your dish with silt, but if you shake them vigorously in the colander under running water, they should come open and you can get rid of them.

Choose a heavy, flameproof casserole and in it heat a good splash of oil. Brown the pork briskly until well coloured all over. Take care not to burn the oil and fat. Remove the pork and all but 1 tablespoon of the fat, tip in the clams with the wine or water and cover with a lid. After 2 minutes, turn off the heat and remove the clams to a bowl with a slotted spoon, leaving the juice in the pot. Allow the clams to cool, then refrigerate, uncovered.

Peel the artichokes and quarter them lengthways. Scatter the shallots and garlic into the clam juice. Add the artichokes and bay leaves and then nestle the pork among its companions. Add a generous pinch of salt, and don't be shy with the black pepper. Cover again and place in the oven.

After 2 hours, lift the pot from the oven, then add the clams, putting the lid back on for a further 4 minutes, or for just enough time to heat them in the steam. When done, remove the pork to a carving board. Throw the finely chopped parsley into the pot and squeeze in the juice from one lemon half. Mix thoroughly. Remove any clams that have failed to open. Carve the pork thickly and take to the table on a serving plate, surrounded with the artichokes all scattered with the clams and juices. The first time I ate this, additional vegetables seemed unnecessary. Serve with the remaining lemon half cut into wedges.

Chorizo in cider

Serves 4

250g chorizo, cut diagonally
    into 2.5cm pieces
a little olive oil
100ml dry cider
2 bay leaves
4 black peppercorns
a little cider vinegar
crusty bread, to serve

This is such simple and tasty fare that when I eat it with honest bread and a penknife, it has me fantasising that I'm a travelling labourer and this is payment for a morning of apple picking somewhere hot, dry and far from London. When choosing chorizo, I always seem to go for the ones shaped like croquet hoops, as they seem to be nicer than the straight ones. Go for a proper cider, made from pressed fresh apples, not concentrate.

Fry the chorizo gently for 4 minutes or so with a little oil until well coloured but not burnt. Pour over the cider, add the bay leaves and peppercorns, sharpen with a little splash of cider vinegar and simmer until the liquid has reduced by half.

Serve in a small bowl, using your penknife or cocktail sticks to stab the meat, with crusty bread to soak up the rich, smoky juice.

Boiled smoked ham with saupiquet sauce

Serves 6–8

a piece of barrel-shaped smoked
    gammon (about 1kg)
1 onion, peeled
1 celery stick, cut into 3 short lengths
1 carrot, cut into 3 short lengths
10 black peppercorns

Saupiquet sauce

1 medium banana shallot,
    finely chopped
2 garlic cloves, finely chopped
½ teaspoon caster sugar
200ml white Burgundy,
    or other dry white wine
4 tablespoons white wine vinegar
8 juniper berries, lightly bashed
1 teaspoon thyme leaves
40g butter
25g plain flour
300ml ham stock
100ml double cream
flaked sea salt and black pepper

I once worked for a French chef whose tantrums were simply intolerable. His food, though, was so delicious that it dissipated my constant urge to leave his employ (well, for 6 months). Saupiquet sauce, a sweet-and-sour white wine cream sauce, was one of his specialities, made to a particularly extravagant recipe using *Beaumes de Venise* and egg yolks. I have gone back to its simpler origins and am using the stock from the ham, a traditional meat to eat with this sauce. Should your sauce be for chicken, use chicken stock instead.

Place the gammon in a good-sized flameproof casserole or saucepan with the vegetables and peppercorns and fill it with cold water until it comes over the top of the meat. Bring up to a gentle simmer and cook for approximately 1 hour, lid on, until totally tender yet carvable without falling apart.

About 40 minutes before the ham is ready, put the shallot, garlic, sugar, white wine, vinegar, juniper berries and thyme into a separate saucepan and simmer rapidly until you are left with about 2 tablespoons of reduced liquid, then turn off the heat.

Melt the butter in another saucepan over a medium heat and scatter in the flour, then whisk it in for around 30 seconds to cook out the taste. Pour in the wine reduction through a sieve, then rescue the berries and drop them in the sauce. The mixture will clag up at first. Slowly add ladlefuls of ham stock, whisking all the time. Once the stock has been added, let the sauce bubble gently for 10 minutes in order to slightly thicken.

Pour in the cream and bring the sauce to the faintest simmer (do not allow it to boil), then turn off the heat. Check the seasoning (although the ham stock in the sauce should mean it does not require the addition of too much extra salt). If the sauce is ready a little before the meat, turn off the heat and warm it again when needed.

Remove the meat from the stock to a board and carve thickly. Serve on boiled Puy lentils with carrots, or in the Burgundian way, with simple boiled potatoes.

Cumberland sauce

Serves 4–6

2 medium unwaxed oranges

1 unwaxed lemon

2 tablespoons red wine vinegar

2 level teaspoons English
mustard powder

300ml port

1 bay leaf

3 black peppercorns

1 thumb-sized piece of root ginger,
peeled

4 tablespoons redcurrant jelly

Cumberland sauce is great tipped over large, succulent slices of hot ham and, confused together with the gravy on your plate, is also good with goose or turkey. Christmas just isn't Christmas without it, enough so that I once took a jar to India with me as a reminder of home for the festive day. Sadly, I left it in a hotel room and wondered what the finder must have thought of it.

Use a potato peeler to cut the zest from the oranges and lemon in long pieces. Make little piles and shred them as thinly as you can into slivers about 6cm long. Put them in a small saucepan and cover with cold water. Bring to the boil and cook for about 5 minutes. This will remove any wax and also reduce the skin's bitterness. Tip away the water, leaving the zest in the saucepan. Squeeze over the juices from the oranges and lemon, avoiding the pips falling in. Add the vinegar, mustard powder, port, bay leaf and peppercorns.

Next slice the ginger thinly using a knife or a potato peeler. Stack up the pieces and shred into long slivers as thin as the citrus zest. Put the saucepan back on the heat and add the ginger and redcurrant jelly, breaking it up with a whisk and stirring until dissolved.

Bring the liquid to a medium simmer and reduce until syrupy over about 15 minutes, or until it is the consistency of a runnier cough mixture. Transfer to a bowl, allow to cool and serve with Christmas lunch. You can keep it in the fridge in a jar with a lid on for a couple of weeks. It is great incorporated into a vinaigrette for a warm green bean and duck salad.

Osso bucco

Serves 2–4

2 tablespoons olive oil

½ garlic bulb (cut in half
   horizontally), skin left on

2 sprigs of rosemary

2 tablespoons plain flour

1 teaspoon flaked sea salt

4 pieces of veal shin with large
   marrow area (about 800g)

2 large banana shallots,
   finely chopped

1 medium carrot, finely grated

400g tomatoes

200ml dry white wine

1 heaped tablespoon tomato purée

black pepper

Gremolata

3 tablespoons finely chopped
   flat-leaf parsley

finely grated zest of ½ large
   unwaxed lemon

1 large garlic clove, finely chopped

Fiddling out the marrow from any shin bone is a delight I go about with the concentration of a chimp at a termite mound. Veal is a particular favourite and something that is at last back on the British plate, due to the kinder practices of British rose veal farming.

I am constantly reminded of the joys of Italian cooking when just a few ingredients come together with such effect – and this is a great dish to use up the abundant tomatoes of late summer, by which time the bull calves have suckled on the milk of sunny grasses. Reheated and eaten the day after it is made, the flavour improves, as with all stews.

Preheat the oven to 170°C fan/190°C/Gas 5. Pour the oil into a heavy-based medium-sized, flameproof casserole and fry the garlic bulb half with the rosemary until faintly coloured.

Mix the flour with the salt and powder each side of the veal pieces by pressing them in the seasoned flour. Fry with the garlic and rosemary for 3–4 minutes on each side until well coloured, taking care not to burn the oil or garlic (remove it and the rosemary, if needs be). Remove the veal from the casserole and put to one side, then turn down the heat and sauté the shallots with the carrot, garlic and rosemary. Cook until tender but not coloured. Return the veal to the pan.

In the meantime, cut the cores from the tomatoes and score a criss-cross in their bottoms. Cover with just-boiled water for 1 minute, then remove them and peel off their skins. Quarter and remove the seeds – press the juice from these, through a sieve, over the veal. Finely chop the tomato flesh. Pour the wine over the veal, then add the tomato flesh and tomato purée and bring the liquid to a simmer. Add a grinding of black pepper. Darken the scene with a lid and place the casserole in the oven. Cook for 1½ hours, or until the meat comes away from the bone with only the littlest prompting. If the sauce appears too thick, you might need to add 100ml of water at this stage.

While the casserole does its work, make the gremolata. Combine the parsley with the lemon zest and garlic.

Once the veal is plated, scatter the gremolata on top and serve immediately.

Fegato alla Veneziana

Serves 2

75g butter
2 medium onions, halved
   and quite finely sliced
50ml white wine
1 dessertspoon good white
   wine vinegar, plus extra if you like
1 heaped tablespoon plain flour
500g calves' liver, sliced across
   in 5mm-wide slivers
1 tablespoon olive oil
flaked sea salt and black pepper
1 tablespoon finely chopped
   curly-leaf parsley
soft polenta, to serve

Sometimes I like liver in one elegant slice lying near some fried courgettes on a white plate, but other times I want it all cut up, smothered in rich onions and served with soft polenta on a chipped brown plate. Read on if you agree.

Melt the butter in a large frying pan, add the onions and cook over a medium–low heat for about 30 minutes, stirring regularly, until they are totally soft and beginning to colour. Pour in the wine and vinegar and let the mixture simmer away, stirring every now and then, until the consistency of the onions is creamy (2–3 minutes). Transfer to a plate and wipe the pan clean with kitchen paper.

Put the flour on a plate and roll the liver in it until lightly coated. Heat the oil in the frying pan over a high heat and put the liver in the pan – it should sizzle immediately if you have got the oil hot enough. Fry it hard, for approximately 3 minutes, so that it becomes richly coloured, but taking care not to burn the oil. Season the liver generously while it fries and give it a couple of shakes or stirs – but not too many, as you want it to get some colour. Reintroduce the onions and toss all together until hot. Check the seasoning. Serve sprinkled all over with the parsley and seasoned with a little more vinegar should you desire it. The time-honoured accompaniment is soft polenta.

Veal with Taleggio & Parma ham

Serves 1

70g white breadcrumbs,
  made from stale bread
½ teaspoon flaked sea salt
1 free-range egg
a drop of whole milk
1 good tablespoon plain flour
2 veal escalopes (about 75g each),
  beaten to about 3mm thickness
2 slices of Parma ham
black pepper
40g Taleggio cheese, rind removed,
  cut into wafer-thin slices
40g butter
12 sage leaves

To serve

lemon wedge(s)
steamed chard or spinach

I rarely eat this sort of thing, but I really enjoy it when I remember to. It reminds me of pleasantly over-familiar Italian waiters and the white paper tablecloths that I so love doodling on over lunch.

Place the breadcrumbs on a plate and mix in the salt. In a bowl, beat the egg with the milk. Sift the flour on to another plate. Arrange these in a row: flour, egg, crumbs.

Take the veal escalopes and lay a piece of Parma ham on each. Grind a little black pepper over one of them, then add two wafer-thin slices of the cheese, laid side-by-side and covering the ham. Lay over the other piece of veal, Parma ham side-down, making a sandwich. Press down lightly so that everything is stuck together.

Gently introduce both sides to the floured plate (make sure the thin sides are floured too, and gently pat off any excess). Next take it to the bowl with the egg, dipping both sides, and finally to the seasoned breadcrumbs. Make sure that the crumbing is all over and around.

Melt the butter in a frying pan over a medium heat. When it's foaming, lower in the veal and fry for about 3 minutes on each side, or until the breadcrumbs are a rich gold. Add the sage leaves when you turn the veal, making sure they are not on top of each other. It's important to regulate the heat so that the cheese inside has a chance to melt and the veal cook, rather than just the crumbs on the outside.

Serve with the crispy sage, the butter from the frying pan and a good wedge of lemon. Steamed chard or spinach would be the correct accompaniment.

Carne con chile

Serves 6–8

5 ancho chiles
200ml hot water
4 tablespoons cider vinegar
   or lime juice
4 chipotle chiles (smoked jalapeños)
40g lard
2 medium red onions, finely chopped
a fistful of coriander stalks
   (about 10g), roughly chopped
1 teaspoon cumin seeds
½ teaspoon ground cinnamon
½ teaspoon ground cloves
1 level teaspoon ground white pepper
1 teaspoon dried oregano
4 small garlic cloves, finely sliced
500g beef tomatoes (about 2 or 3)
2 teaspoons soft light brown sugar
1½ teaspoons flaked sea salt
1kg chuck steak, cut into very large
   square chunks
1 teaspoon cocoa powder
150ml soured cream

To serve

Frijoles de la Olla (*see* page 199)
warmed soft corn tortillas

I was staying in a hotel in Mexico that had a fixed price for everything, including not only the booze but a cringe-making stage show from the staff every night. The one good thing about the place – apart from an interesting array of colourful lizards around the pool – was the carne con chile. I wrote the recipe on the inside of a cigarette packet, which subsequently got a little wet and smudged, but what I could read is in here. I prefer the reverse wording, carne con chile, or meat with chile. It sounds as if you've got subtler spicing that suits the beef, rather than the firey, wet mince that I associate with British pubs.

Rip up the ancho chiles and put them in a dry frying pan over a medium–low heat. Tumble and toss them often, as they must not burn but rather toast, and no smoke should be seen coming from them or the frying pan is far too hot. They will change from a red colour to take on a more tobacco hue and their smell will give a rich, full, nutty headiness – really get your nose right down into them to check. All this will take about 5 attentive minutes. Take the frying pan off the heat, pour over the water and vinegar or lime juice and crumble in the chipotle chiles. Leave the chiles to soak for 30 minutes.

Preheat the oven to 150°C fan/170°C/Gas 3½. Melt the lard in a heavy flameproof casserole and in it fry the onions with the coriander stalks, spices and oregano over a medium heat, stirring occasionally, until the onion is golden and soft, adding the garlic for the last 2 minutes. Remove from the heat.

Cut the cores from the tomatoes and slash a criss-cross in the bottoms with a knife. Steep the tomatoes in just-boiled water and leave them there for a minute or so. Discard the water, peel the tomatoes and quarter. Take out the pulp and put it in a sieve over a blender. Use a spoon to push through the juice from the seeds, then chuck the seeds. Put the tomato flesh into the blender. Drop in the chipotle chiles and their soaking liquid. Blitz everything until totally smooth. Press the liquid through a clean sieve into a bowl, leaving behind only the finely ground chile skin. Pour the bowlful back into the blender and add the cooked onions and garlic along with the sugar and salt. Blitz again.

Put the beef in the casserole and pour over the chile purée. Stir well.

Cook in the oven for 2 hours until very soft and tender. Transfer the dish to the hob over a low heat and stir in the cocoa powder. Cook gently for a couple of minutes.

Stir in the soured cream and serve with *Frijoles de la Olla* (*see* page 199), soft warmed corn tortillas and cold beer with fresh lime juice squeezed into it.

Steak haché, straw potatoes & sharp salad

Serves 1

40g butter

a splash of olive oil

½ large banana shallot,
  finely chopped

225g lean minced beef

1 good teaspoon Dijon mustard

1 free-range egg yolk

1 level teaspoon tomato ketchup

a good dash of Worcestershire sauce

flaked sea salt and black pepper

Straw potatoes

1 medium potato

sunflower oil or light olive oil,
  for frying

flaked sea salt

Sharp salad

1 teaspoon Dijon mustard

1½ teaspoons red wine vinegar

½ teaspoon caster sugar

½ small hard garlic clove with no
  green shoot, very finely chopped

2 tablespoons olive oil

a handful of flat-leaf parsley leaves

a handful of tarragon leaves

½ large banana shallot, finely sliced

1 heaped teaspoon baby capers,
  well rinsed

Somewhere between steak tartare and a breadless burger, and very much a lunchtime dish, I only really ever eat this when visiting Paris. It's also my habit to eat it outside when the weather is a bit too cold for such behaviour, wearing a scarf and some leather shoes and reading a book. You may very well stroll past and mutter 'ponce', but I like these fleeting moments of Frenchness. Do as you will, but this is more for those who prefer their burger rare.

To make the steak haché, heat 20g of the butter and the oil in a small, nonstick frying pan and gently fry the shallot until very soft but not coloured, stirring regularly. Tip into a bowl with the beef, mustard, egg yolk, tomato ketchup and Worcestershire sauce. Season with a good bit of salt and an enthusiastic grinding of black pepper and then mix all together well until thoroughly combined. Eat a little raw to test the mix. Adjust the seasoning if needs be.

Peel and finely slice the potato lengthways to the thickness of a £1 coin. Make two piles of potato and slice them lengthways again, as straw-thin as you possibly can. Wash away the starch by running the potato in a sieve under cold water and leave it to drip dry for 10 minutes, tumbling it a little if it helps get rid of more water.

Heat a heavy-based saucepan filled with 2cm oil until a piece of the potato dropped into the oil frizzles immediately. Alternatively, heat your fryer to 180°C. If using a saucepan, turn the handle inwards towards the wall so as to help avoid a hideous accident. Now drop in all the potato and let it fry for around 8 minutes, until the chips are deep golden. As they form tangled clumps while cooking, roughly comb them apart with two forks. When done, lift them out and drain them on a plate covered in kitchen paper and allow to cool to room temperature. It is imperative they be fried until totally crisp.

Heat the remaining butter in a frying pan over a medium–high heat. Form the mince mixture into a thick, rugby-ball shape, around the same size as the palm of your hand. Cook in the frying pan for 3 minutes on each side until nicely browned on the outside but reddish pink and juicy within.

While the steak is cooking, make the salad. Whisk the mustard, vinegar, sugar and garlic together in a small bowl. Gradually add the oil, whisking constantly until the dressing is glossy and emulsified. Toss the herbs, shallot and baby capers with the amount of vinaigrette required.

Serve the steak haché with the sharp salad, a little pile of the straw fries and, needless to say, a small glass of red wine.

Raw dressed beef fillet with green olives & walnuts

Serves 4

175g beef fillet, trimmed
10 good green olives, pitted
  and roughly chopped
8 good-quality walnuts, halved
½ medium unwaxed lemon
1 dessertspoon walnut oil
1 dessertspoon olive oil
flaked sea salt and black pepper
a pinch of dried chile flakes
leaves from 2 sprigs of marjoram

I'm a huge fan of raw beef and this is one of my favourite preparations. Quick to prepare, it makes an excellent starter for guests.

Cut the beef in slices approximately 5mm wide and lay a few between two large sheets of baking paper. Beat out each slice paper-thin (about 1mm) with a rolling pin. Gently peel each slice from the paper and lay the slices over one large plate, or as four single servings.

Scatter the olives over the beef followed by the walnuts. Finely grate over the zest of the lemon half. Squeeze over the lemon juice, then splash over the oils before scattering generously with flaked sea salt and the dried chile flakes. Follow with a little black pepper and a scattering of the marjoram. Eat immediately.

Pickled onion, steak & ale pudding

Serves 5–6

750g braising beef

3 tablespoons plain flour

1½ teaspoons flaked sea salt

1 teaspoon black pepper

40g dripping or lard

1 medium onion, finely chopped

500ml real ale

4–5 sprigs of thyme

1 bay leaf

1 tablespoon dark
   muscovado sugar

350ml beef stock, or canned
   consommé

1 tablespoon tomato purée

butter, for greasing

150g baby pickled onions, drained

mustard, to serve (optional)

Suet pastry

400g self-raising flour, plus extra
   for dusting

200g shredded suet

½ teaspoon flaked sea salt

This pudding is a delicious beast, a gutsy hero. Were it a person it would, no doubt, be the local thick-wristed, silent giant who whops cricket balls from the village green to kingdom come. Be the first to boldly venture into the pudding: it is most satisfying to see the steam swirling up and saucy meats spilling forth, and you cannot but think: corrrr! Visit a good butcher for the meat. It should be well fatted and not like the supermarket lean braising steak that magically transforms into shoe leather.

Preheat the oven to 170°C fan/190°C/Gas 5. Trim the beef of any tough bits of gristle but leave the fat. Cut the beef into cubes (roughly 3cm) and put in a large, strong plastic bag. Add the flour, a good pinch of flaked sea salt and a good grinding of black pepper. Tie the end in a knot and shake wildly until the beef is well coated in the seasoned flour.

Heat 25g of the dripping or lard in a large frying pan and fry the beef over a high heat in two batches until well browned all over, adding an extra 10g of fat when the frying pan appears dry. Transfer the beef to a flameproof casserole as it is browned. Return the frying pan to the heat and drop in the onion with a little extra fat if needs be. Cook over a medium–low heat for 5 minutes, or until softened, stirring often. Stir into the pot with the beef.

Deglaze the frying pan with half the ale, bringing it to the boil while stirring to lift all the sediment from the bottom of the frying pan. Pour over the beef and onion. Strip the thyme leaves from the stalks and add with the bay leaf, sugar, beef stock or consommé, tomato purée and the rest of the ale. Grind all over with a heavy bombardment of black pepper. Bring to a healthy simmer, then cover and cook in the oven for 1 hour. Remove the lid and continue cooking for a further 30–40 minutes, stirring once or twice. After this time, the beef should be almost tender and the sauce thick. Remove from the oven, taste for seasoning and then leave to go cold.

Butter a 1.75-litre pudding basin. Sift the flour into a large bowl and stir in the suet and salt. Gradually stir in enough water to make a very soft, slightly tacky, spongy dough – you'll need around 300ml. Turn out on to a floured work surface and bring the dough together to form a ball. Remove just under a third of the dough to make a lid for the pudding. Roll out the rest 1 cm thick and use a plate as a guide to cut out a round roughly 27cm across, using a dusting of flour here and there to prevent sticking issues. Line the basin with the pastry level resting at around 3cm under the top edge of the dish. This is important, as you must allow for the pudding to rise. Be careful with the pastry; if ripped, the gravy will snake out and create a mess. Trim neatly to make a flat edge on which to fix the lid.

Stir the pickled onions into the beef mixture and spoon into the lined basin. Brush the top edge of the pastry with water. Roll the remaining pastry into a circle just large enough to sit snugly on top of the pastry edge and place over the filling. Press the edges well together to seal. Tear a large sheet of baking

» paper that amply overlaps the rim of the basin and over this lay a similar-sized sheet of foil. Keeping the two together, fold a pleat in the middle, as this will allow for the pudding to expand. Tie both tightly in place with a long piece of string just under the outside lip of the basin. Create a carrying handle by taking the excess string over the top of the basin and tying it to the string on the other side. This will help you lift the pudding once it's cooked. Trim the baking paper and foil.

Place the pudding basin on an upturned saucer or small trivet in a deep saucepan and add enough just-boiled water to come halfway up the side of the basin after its placed inside. (Alternatively, cook in a hob-top steamer.) Cover the saucepan with a tight-fitting lid and place over a medium heat. Allow the pud to steam in simmering water for 2½ hours, adding more water when necessary.

Remove the saucepan from the heat and carefully lift the basin from the water. Stand for 5 minutes. Cut off the string, foil and baking paper. Loosen the side of the pudding with a blunt-ended knife and invert the pudding carefully on to a warm serving plate large enough for the filling to ooze into. Attack this meat stronghold with spoons, knives, forks and mustard reinforcements.

Bollito misto

Serves 6

700g fatty beef brisket

1 whole veal tongue

500g piece of unsliced streaky
  smoked bacon

2½ litres water

3 small onions, peeled and halved

6 medium carrots, scrubbed

1 celery heart (the bottom part
  of a celery)

2 medium fennel bulbs, trimmed
  and halved, with the root keeping
  the segments intact

2 cloves

2 large bay leaves

4 black peppercorns

½ small cinnamon stick

2 large chicken breasts

2 whole chicken legs

4 *frutta di mostarda*, roughly
  chopped, to serve

Fennel aïoli

2 free-range egg yolks

6 good medium garlic cloves, peeled

juice of ½ small lemon

200ml light olive oil

flaked sea salt

Salsa verde

4 tablespoons finely chopped basil

2 tablespoons finely chopped
  young curly-leaf parsley

4 mint leaves, finely chopped

2 tablespoons baby capers,
  well rinsed

½ medium banana shallot,
  finely chopped

2 teaspoons red wine vinegar

5 anchovies in oil, drained and
  finely chopped

about 4 tablespoons olive oil

flaked sea salt

A selection of meats poached very slowly in their own clear, clean broth and surrounded by happy vegetables, this dish is a northern Italian delight, as enjoyable on a warm sunny day as on a cold one. It is also one of my favourites. The Italian simply translates as 'mixed boiled' and that is exactly what it is: mixed boiled meats, in this case beef brisket, chicken, bacon and tongue. I met with a resounding NO! from my publisher when I wanted to dedicate a whole recipe to poached tongue, so I've slipped it in here. If you are shy of cooking a whole one, but want to try it nonetheless, bravely add pre-cooked and pressed slices at the end. But do try some, as it is tender and giving. Bear in mind that a whole tongue might need pre-ordering from a butcher. I've used veal tongue, which is smaller than the more usual ox tongue and has a more delicate taste as well as taking less time to cook. Eat the *Bollito Misto* with the chopped-up condiment *frutta di mostarda* (fruit preserved in wine and mustard syrup) when you can find them. Otherwise, I like mine with aïoli and a salsa verde.

Submerge the brisket, tongue and bacon in the water in a large pot with all the vegetables and aromatics (the cloves, bay leaves, peppercorns and cinnamon). Bring to a trembling simmer, skim, then cover. Remember the lid will increase the temperature inside the pot, so regulate the heat after a few minutes. Throughout the cooking, skim the stock and do not let it boil, or it will become cloudy and greasy. The brisket will need cooking for a minimum of 3 hours, and checked every 15 minutes thereafter until tender.

Remove the vegetables from the stock after 90 minutes and set aside. After approximately 2 hours of the cooking time, lift the bacon and tongue from the pot. Put the bacon to one side. Peel the tongue while it is hot, as the skin is easier to remove then. To do this, put it on a chopping board with the smooth side up. Make a slit lengthways from the top to the bottom, down the centre – the cut should be literally skin deep – and then peel and cut away the skin and any unsightly bits underneath the tongue, including the stem at the base.

For the last 40 minutes of cooking the brisket, add the chicken pieces. Once the brisket is nearly tender, return the tongue, bacon and vegetables to the pot for the final 20 minutes of cooking, reserving half a fennel bulb.

Towards the end of the cooking time, make the aïoli. Blitz the yolks, garlic, lemon juice and reserved fennel in a food processor while slowly adding the oil. If the mixture appears too thick before the oil has been used up, add a drop of warm water to loosen it. Doctor the acidity and seasoning at the end.

For the salsa verde, mix together the basil, parsley, mint, capers, shallot, vinegar and anchovies. Add just enough oil to loosen the mix, then season.

When the meats have cooked remove them to a board and cut into 5mm–1cm-thick slices. Cut the celery heart into six, the rest of the fennel bulbs into four and the half leftover from the aïoli into two. Leave the onions in two. Serve the meats and vegetables either in the broth or on a separate plate with the broth in bowls as a starter or beside the main event. Eat with the roughly chopped mustard fruits, aïoli and salsa verde in combinations that suit your desired mouthful.

Braised ox cheek with flageolet beans & turnips

Serves 4–6

8 medium–small banana shallots,
    peeled carefully to keep whole

2 tablespoons olive oil, plus a little
    used for oiling and frying

flaked sea salt

1 garlic bulb

1 tablespoon red wine vinegar

2 teaspoons caster sugar

2 tablespoons plain flour

1.2kg ox cheek, trimmed

25g butter

250ml red wine, such as
    a Côtes du Rhône

415ml can consommé

1 bay leaf

2 good sprigs of thyme

8 black peppercorns

2 tablespoons tomato purée

3–4 medium turnips, or the equivalent
    weight of baby turnips

400g can flageolet beans

2–3 tablespoons finely chopped
    curly-leaf parsley

good bread, to serve (optional)

This dish came about on Exmoor in a kitchen so overrun with mice that before we found their hole blocked with salami and whole packets of biscuits, we thought that spectral forces were at work. They took what little dinner option there was, including a particularly runny Camembert I had specially brought from London. I drove into the strange local town just before closing and got what I could. Then I also found a couple of cans of flageolet beans that had been rolling about in the car boot for a year. Anyway, thanks to the mice, we had this.

Don't be put off by the word 'cheek' and just think 'beef', as this cut is ever so tasty, very inexpensive and delicious. It is also lenient on distracted cooks; even when accidentally forgotten, it simply becomes even more tender, when other things would be horribly overcooked (though there is a point of no return, of course!).

More often found in local butchers, there is one daring supermarket, Waitrose, displaying ox cheek in a 'Forgotten Cuts' range. And that is the point for me; forgotten, maybe, but certainly not gone. So I beg you to try ox cheek and champion its happy return. A kilogram of cheek may seem a lot for 4–6 people, but it does shrink a fair amount once cooked.

Chuck the shallots in a bowl with a couple of tablespoons of oil and mix them around with a good scattering of salt until evenly oiled. Get a frying pan good and hot and toss in the shallots. They should start to fry swiftly and the aim is to get them nice and richly coloured all over. Let them get on with it, giving the frying pan the occasional jostle every now and then so as not to let them burn on any one side. This should take about 8 minutes. While the shallots cook, separate the garlic bulb into cloves and peel them all, then toss them in the oily bowl.

Splash the vinegar over the shallots and let it burn off completely before adding the garlic cloves and evenly scattering over the sugar. Keep all cooking together for approximately 3 minutes more, swirling them around more frequently than before. You want the sugar to caramelise and colour the contents richly but not burn. Put the shallots and garlic on a plate to one side.

Mix together the flour with a generous amount of salt. Chop the ox cheek into big chunks comparable to dividing your fist into four. Roll the cheek chunks in the seasoned flour. Superficially wipe out the frying pan and get the butter and a little oil nice and hot but not smoking. Add the ox cheek to the pan where it should sizzle immediately. Don't crowd the pan; fry the meat in batches if necessary, as this will allow it to colour better. After 10 minutes or so, when the chunks are deeply browned all over, remove the ox cheek to a heavy, flameproof casserole. Pour the wine into the frying pan and bring it up to a simmer while scraping at any tasty sticky stuff from the meat with a spoon, then take off the heat. Tuck the shallots and garlic between the meat pieces and then pour in the canned consommé. Tie the bay leaf around the

» thyme with a little kitchen string and pop this bouquet garni in with the peppercorns too. Squeeze or splat in the tomato purée here and there between the meat. Ensure the meat is submerged under the liquid.

Bring the pan up to a gentle yet brisk simmer (a kind of plup, plup, plup), replace the lid and leave the ox cheek to braise for approximately 2 hours. When probed with a knife it should be beginning to feel quite tender. At this point peel the turnips, divide them into six, and add to the pan with the flageolet beans, drained of three-quarters of their juice. Check to see if a little more water is needed to cook the turnips, but add sparingly if so. Run a spoon around the inside edge of the pan to get any delicious sticky residue back into the stew. Replace the lid and cook for a further 40 minutes until the turnips are soft and the sauce is the consistency of gravy.

Scatter all over with the chopped parsley and eat as it is, or with good bread, if you like. It does not need any extra vegetables.

Rabbit with prunes in red wine

Serves 2

3 tablespoons olive oil
1 fresh wild rabbit, jointed into eight
1 garlic bulb, cut in half horizontally
leaves from 3 long sprigs of rosemary
200g smoked bacon lardons
1 large onion, finely chopped
4 canned anchovies in oil, drained
    and roughly chopped
75cl bottle red wine
a large handful of pitted
    no-soak prunes
a 5cm strip of lemon rind
flaked sea salt and black pepper
a splash of freshly squeezed
    lemon juice
mashed potato, to serve

This is a favourite of mine, with the strong flavours perfect for grassy wild rabbit. When buying rabbit, try to choose a young one, preferably head-shot with a rifle as the meat will be much less damaged.

Preheat the oven to 160°C fan/180°C/Gas 4. Heat the oil in a large, flameproof casserole and add the rabbit, garlic (cut-side down) and rosemary leaves. Fry over a medium–high heat, turning occasionally, until the rabbit is well browned on all sides. Do not allow the garlic to burn or the sauce will taste bitter.

Remove the rabbit from the casserole with tongs and put to one side. Add the bacon to the pan. Fry over a high heat until browned on all sides. Throw in the onion and anchovies and fry together for a couple of minutes until the onion colours, stirring.

Return the rabbit to the pan and immediately pour over the wine. Plop in the prunes and lemon rind, and bring to a simmer. Season with plenty of black pepper, cover with a lid and cook in the oven for about 2¼ hours, or until the rabbit meat is meltingly tender but remains on the bone. If the sauce is too watery, remove the rabbit to a plate and thicken the sauce by reducing it over a high heat. Return the rabbit to the pot, then stir in a splash of lemon juice and season to taste. Serve immediately with good loose mashed potato.

Rabbit & pickled walnut terrine

Serves 6

150g very fatty pork belly (weight
  once rind has been removed),
  roughly chopped
2 young rabbits (or 1 large adult rabbit
  if young ones are not available), liver,
  kidneys and heart reserved if possible,
  or 6 rabbit portions
50g butter, softened, plus extra
  for greasing
1 medium onion, finely chopped
2 garlic cloves, finely chopped
8 large sage leaves, finely shredded
3 tablespoons medium sherry
flaked sea salt and black pepper
a grating of nutmeg
10 pickled walnuts, well drained
  (you may need more), sliced into coins
3 tablespoons finely chopped
  curly-leaf parsley
300g rindless unsmoked streaky
  bacon rashers
hot buttered toast, to serve

Terrines are handy to have around for those moments when distraction
can only be overcome with buttered toast and a snoop into the fridge.
If you feel skint, wild rabbit is pocket-friendly. Small, young rabbits –
the best ones to eat – are born through most of the year, but you will not
find them at the butchers. Should you find them elsewhere, it might interest
you to know that the correct term for baby or bunny rabbits is 'kittens',
although I imagine 'Kitten and Pickled Walnut Terrine' might have the
RSPCA storming your kitchen.
The sexually mature rabbits, which you will certainly find on the counter,
are better eaten in the autumn through to mid-spring, as their taste becomes
inferior when they start doing what we all know rabbits love doing.

Put the pork belly in a food processor and blitz to to a medium-smooth
consistency (too smooth and the texture becomes dull). Put the rabbit on a
board and remove as much of the meat as possible from the bone with a small,
sharp knife – you should have around 450g. Put it (and the liver, kidneys
and heart, if using) in a food processor with the chopped pork belly. Blend to
medium-smooth again. You may need to remove the lid and push the mixture
down a couple of times with a spatula. Flop the mixture into a large bowl.

Preheat the oven to 160°C fan/180°C/Gas 4. Melt the butter in a frying pan
and cook the onion and garlic with the shredded sage over a medium–low
heat until the onion is soft. Add the sherry and cook until it has evaporated.
Tip the onion mixture into the meat and stir together with a generous amount
of salt, lots of black pepper and the nutmeg. (It is worth noting here that a lot
of seasoning is needed to really bring out the taste of the terrine, as so many
of them look good enough to eat but are bland in the mouth. Fry a little of the
mix before cooking just to check the seasoning.) Slice the pickled walnuts and
toss them very gently with the chopped parsley.

Line a 1.2-litre terrine, pudding basin or ovenproof dish with three or four
sheets of clingfilm, leaving some overhanging the edge. Stretch each rasher
of bacon on a board with the back of a knife to really flatten it out. This cuts
down considerably on the number of rashers you will need and prevents the
bacon overpowering the terrine. Now use them to line the terrine or dish,
allowing the rashers to overlap slightly and leaving an overhang along the
outside of the terrine. Put a third of the rabbit mixture into the terrine dish
and then pave with half the walnuts, laying the discs flat-side down and side
by side. Build up with another third of the rabbit, then the rest of the walnuts
and finally rabbit again. Use the overhanging bacon to cover the terrine,
working from one side to the other alternately, down the length of the dish.
Cover with the overhanging clingfilm and a lid, or tight-fitting foil.

Put the terrine in a small roasting tin. Add around 2cm of just-boiled
water to the tin and carefully place it in the centre of the oven. Bake for
35–40 minutes. The terrine is ready when a clean metal skewer inserted
into the centre and left for the count of 10 feels very warm – but not hot –
when pressed against your lip.

» Lift the terrine carefully from the water, remove the lid (or foil) and cover the surface with a new quadruple-folded piece of foil. Place a heavy weight down the centre of the terrine to press it – if using a round pudding basin, put a snug-fitting saucer on top before weighting (it may take longer to cool in a pudding basin, so use the skewer method to check). Cool for an hour, then transfer to the fridge and leave for several hours, or overnight. Turn out and serve at room temperature in thick slices, with plenty of hot buttered toast.

Lapin à la moutarde
(Rabbit in mustard sauce)

Serves 4

75g butter

2 medium–large banana shallots,
   very finely chopped

1 teaspoon dried thyme

ground white pepper

3 garlic cloves, finely chopped

3 tablespoons plain flour

1 teaspoon flaked sea salt

a little olive oil

1 large farmed rabbit, jointed into
   7 pieces (2 front legs, 2 back legs,
   2 saddles and the fillet above the
   upper ribs), liver, kidneys and heart
   reserved if possible

1½ tablespoons white wine vinegar
   or tarragon vinegar

300ml white wine

100ml water

2 heaped dessertspoons
   Dijon mustard

1 heaped dessertspoon
   wholegrain mustard

150ml double cream

sautéed potatoes, to serve

I've eaten a lot of rabbit in my time. I hope that, when I enter the next life, I don't have cohorts of bristling bunnies, all twinkling coal-black eyes and blank expressions, slowly advancing towards me. I sincerely hope my respect was shown in my careful preparation of them for the table. When I see a rabbit, I not only see a plate of food but also an opportunity to cook it in a totally different way from the last time. I think on rabbits a lot and happen to draw them on everything.

Treated modestly with vinegar onions or bacon, rabbit is a humble joy, but tempted with the classic French treatment of *Lapin à la Moutarde*, I realise I do have a favourite way. In France, you are more likely to find a farmed rabbit upon your plate than a wild one, and this dish is always made with the big farmed ones. Although their taste lacks the grassy attitude of the wild bunny, the meat is still subtly pleasant, very tender and can be eaten all year round.

Preheat the oven to 170°C fan/190°C/Gas 5. Melt 25g of the butter over a gentle heat in a flameproof casserole. Add the shallots, thyme (rub this through your fingers so that it becomes dust-like) and a little white pepper. Cook the shallots until they are soft and a little golden. Add the garlic and cook it for a couple of minutes, but no more; if it burns, it will taint the taste of the sauce. Turn off the heat.

Sift the flour on to a plate and mix in the salt with your fingertips. In a large frying pan, heat the remaining butter over a medium heat with a little oil. Roll the rabbit pieces (and the liver, kidneys and heart, if using) in the flour and, once the butter is foaming, brown them fairly swiftly in the frying pan, cooking in batches, if needs be, as the pieces will colour better when given space. Once sizzling, leave the rabbit pieces alone, resisting the urge to prod and fiddle, as they will colour better without harassment. By all means check them for turning, but as little as possible. The rabbit will take about 3–4 minutes to colour on each side. Do not burn the rabbit or the butter.

Remove the rabbit pieces to the casserole and lay them on top of the fried shallots. Tip any obvious fat from the frying pan whilst leaving all the lovely brown bits in the bottom. Keeping the empty pan on the heat, splash in the vinegar and a little of the wine. This will help lift any of the tasty scrapings from the bottom of the pan. Distress any obstinate bits with a spoon. Pour the sauce over the rabbit and follow it with the remainder of the wine and the water.

Place the lid on the casserole and transfer it to the oven. Cook the rabbit for 1 hour. The meat should be tender to a poke with a knife, but should not come away from the bone. If it is not ready, return it to the oven for intervals of 10 minutes until it is. At this point add the mustards to the juice between the pieces of rabbit in the pot. Follow with the cream and gently swirl or stir all together until the juices, cream and mustard have combined well. Turn off the heat as soon as the cream shows early signs of simmering. The sauce should not be thin; reduce carefully if necessary. Adjust the seasoning.

Serve with some good, salty, crispy sautéed potatoes. *Et voilà!*

Venison curry

Serves 4

a large handful of shaved
   dried coconut or 3 tablespoons
   unsweetened desiccated coconut
40g ghee or butter
2 small red onions, finely chopped
1 cinnamon stick (about 4cm long)
6 black peppercorns
2 garlic cloves, finely chopped
1 large thumb-sized piece of root
   ginger, peeled and finely chopped
1 teaspoon flaked sea salt
4 cloves
1 teaspoon fennel seeds
2½ teaspoons hot chile powder
1 teaspoon cayenne pepper
¼ star anise
½ teaspoon cumin seeds
1 teaspoon garam masala
3 tablespoons tomato purée
500g venison fillet (be it red, fallow,
   sika, roe or muntjac), cut into
   medium cubes
300ml coconut water or water
juice of ½ lime
shredded flat-leaf parsley leaves,
   to garnish
rice, paratha or naan bread, to serve

On a trip to Sri Lanka, I stopped for lunch at a lean-to with a couple of grubby plastic chairs and tables set before it. Behind a small gas stove were a scrawny man and his wife. I asked what I could have and the vendor immediately did a bizarre impression of some creature, which I took time to realise was a deer. I gave him a nod and a thumbs up. A little dish arrived with small pieces of the tenderest meat bathed in a sharp, rich red gravy covered with toasted shavings of coconut. It was delicious and unbelievably hot, by which I mean it tore off the lid of my head.

As I chased the last smear across the plate with a kind of sour pancake, the police arrived on the scene and immediately started poking around the couple's field kitchen. One of the officers came up to me and, in English, asked: 'What it is are you having?' 'Lunch', I replied. 'No' he said pointing at the plate, and so I told him, as I had been, that it was 'of the forest', very good too, and he was welcome to join me for lunch.

It turned out that cheffy was also a poacher and I had just unwittingly enjoyed a very small and unfortunately endangered miniature deer. Cook and wife were taken away with a coolbox full of, no doubt, evidence and the policeman demanded I settle the bill with him. I felt a certain sympathy for the cook, as obviously hand-to-mouth applied to not just his job but his whole life, yet as a poacher, surely, it was a bit silly to reveal the true nature of his incriminating ingredients.

The meat was tender because it was cooked very briefly rather than the tenderness that results from a long, slow cook. Therefore, it is essential that you do not overcook the meat. Venison has next to no fat and fillet will seize up suddenly and go past the point of no return. Ghee is Indian clarified butter and is widely available from shops and supermarkets. Coconut water is not the same as the coconut milk found in a can but the water that is in the centre of a fresh coconut.

In a dry frying pan, gently toast the coconut until you notice the first signs of it colouring. Allow to cool.

Melt the ghee or butter in a wok or pan (the lighter and thinner the metal, the better, as it is closer to using Indian cookware such as a balti). Throw in the onions and cook fairly briskly with the cinnamon and peppercorns until softened and deep golden, taking care not to burn them.

Using a pestle and mortar, or blender, crush the garlic, ginger, salt and all the remaining spices into a fine paste and combine with the tomato purée.

Add the curry paste to the onions and fry for 2–3 minutes, stirring often. Do not let it burn. Add the meat and briskly sauté for a couple of minutes. Add the coconut water or water and lime juice and bring to a rapid simmer for 4 minutes, or until you have a thickish gravy. Remove from the heat and scatter with the coconut and parsley. Serve with rice, paratha or naan bread.

Birds

Green & pleasant land chicken salad

Serves 4–6

3 boneless, skinless free-range
   chicken breasts (about 450g)

100ml white wine

200ml cold water

1 small onion, halved

3–4 sprigs of thyme

1 bay leaf

6 black peppercorns

150g French beans
   (about 2 large handfuls)

150g shelled small broad beans

1 small fennel bulb, trimmed

10 radishes, halved lengthways

a small handful of chives, trimmed
   and chopped in half

leaves from 5–6 sprigs of tarragon

20 small lovage leaves

25g raisins

40g flaked almonds

Vinaigrette

1 teaspoon tarragon vinegar

6 tablespoons mayonnaise

3 tablespoons single cream

¼ teaspoon grated nutmeg

¼ teaspoon mustard powder

¼ teaspoon sugar

1 fresh bay leaf, scrumpled

flaked sea salt and black pepper

If at all possible, try and find some lovage for this salad, or plant some yourself – it is very easy to grow. This wonderful English herb is sadly ignored in modern cooking, and should be reinstated. Its slightly curried, aniseed twang is wonderfully intense and also goes well with lamb and all shellfish (and there's a lot to say for it in a jug of Pimms too). Lovage really lifts this whole dish into another dimension; but if you can't get any, it's good anyway.

Put the chicken breasts in a saucepan and pour over the wine. Add the water, onion, thyme, bay leaf and peppercorns. Place over a medium heat, cover and bring to a gentle simmer. Poach the chicken for 10 minutes, or until just cooked through. With a slotted spoon, transfer the chicken to a plate to cool. Strain the liquor through a fine sieve into a clean pan. Bring the stock to the boil and drop in the French beans. Return to the boil and cook these for 5 minutes. Remove them from the pan with a slotted spoon, transfer to a colander and cool under cold water. Drain, then, transfer to your desired serving bowl.

Drop the broad beans into the boiling stock and cook for 2–3 minutes, then transfer to a colander and cool under cold water. Squeeze the broad beans out of their skins and place in the serving bowl.

Cut the fennel into wafer-thin slices. Add to the bowl along with the radishes, chives, tarragon and lovage. Tear the chicken into long shreds and scatter over the salad, along with the raisins and almonds.

In a small bowl, stir together all the dressing ingredients and leave to stand for 15–20 minutes. Drizzle the dressing over the salad and toss lightly just before serving.

Jerk chicken wings

Serves 2

12 chicken wings

2 dessertspoons groundnut oil
  or sunflower oil

2 teaspoons flaked sea salt

Jerk seasoning

1½ Scotch Bonnet chiles, seeds
  left in, finely but roughly chopped

6 large hard garlic cloves, roughly
  chopped

1 large thumb-sized piece of root
  ginger, peeled and coarsely grated

4 teaspoons dried thyme

1¼ teaspoons ground cloves

1 teaspoon ground allspice

1 teaspoon black pepper

⅓ nutmeg, grated

4 tablespoons malt vinegar

2 dessertspoons water

2 tablespoons molasses
  or dark muscovado sugar

Whenever I make this, I cannot help being reminded of the time when I had to read out some creative writing to my school in assembly. The story started with the line 'I woke up with a jerk', at which point everyone erupted into uncontrollable laughter. I did not click and searched the room, red-faced, wondering what I had done.

Living off the Portobello Road in London's Notting Hill Gate, the heart of the British-Caribbean community, I've eaten a lot of jerk chicken. There are particular vendors I seek out over the Notting Hill Carnival, as I prefer jerks with the strong presence of cloves. Above all, I must admit, I like my own. Wings are better than legs, as the marinade really infiltrates the meat. Accompany by grilled corn and some chilled and plentiful Red Stripe.

To make the jerk seasoning, combine the chiles, garlic, ginger, thyme and spices with a pestle and mortar. Scrape the paste into a bowl, then add the vinegar, water and molasses or muscovado sugar. Stir until well combined.

Score the chicken wings deeply with a sharp knife four times on both sides, through to the bone. Put the chicken into a tight-fitting lidded container, pour over the seasoning and seal with the lid. Marinate in the fridge overnight or for the equivalent time, turning the wings once or twice.

Light the barbecue and, when the charcoal glows orange and white, tumble the chicken wings in the oil and cook for 18–20 minutes, seasoning them with the salt, turning occasionally and brushing often with the remaining seasoning until it is all used up. The skin should be well coloured, slightly charred and sticky, and the wings should be cooked through.

Chicken stuffed with pearl barley, livers & walnuts

Serves 6

45g pearl barley
1 bay leaf
85g butter
1 medium onion, finely chopped
1 teaspoon flaked sea salt
black pepper
40g walnuts, roughly chopped
150g chicken livers, plus those from
    the giblet bag, trimmed
zest of 1 unwaxed lemon
5 tablespoons finely chopped
    curly-leaf parsley
1.5kg boned chicken (with giblets)

Jus

a splash of sunflower oil
neck and heart of chicken
½ small brown onion, halved,
    skin left on
1 carrot, scrubbed and quartered
a few stalks of parsley
1 garlic clove
½ teaspoon flaked sea salt
1 bay leaf
600ml water
1 dessertspoon plain flour
a little lemon juice
black pepper

Every now and then I am overcome with an urge to de-bone a fowl. It is a fun sort of surgery, but were I to write instructions for how to do it in my long-winded way, it would take up far too much space. Get your friendly straw-hatted butcher to do it for you instead. Anyway, more enjoyment is to be had later in the carving at the table, with no bones to negotiate. When choosing your walnuts for this stuffing, (a) don't use the ones that have been knocking around in your storecupboard for ages – the oil in them does go off, and (b) my observation is the paler the skin, the less bitter the nut.

Put the pearl barley in a pan, cover with cold water and add the bay leaf. Bring to a simmer and cook for 40 minutes, or until tender. Drain and allow to cool. While the barley cooks, melt 40g of the butter and gently sauté the onion, seasoned with ¼ teaspoon of salt and plenty of black pepper. Add the walnuts and take care to stir everything around every now and then so that the nuts do not burn. When golden and softened, remove the onion mixture to a plate.

Increase the heat to medium and briskly fry the chicken livers, including those from the giblets bag, turning them once so that they colour on the outside and remain pink within (about 2 minutes). Season with a further ¼ teaspoon of salt. Turn the chicken livers on to a board and chop them coarsely. Combine the onion, walnuts and chicken livers with the pearl barley, lemon zest and parsley. Check the seasoning – it should be good and peppery.

Preheat the oven to 170°C fan/190°C/Gas 5. Turn the chicken out on to a board, breast-side down, and open it out fully. Place the stuffing down the centre of the bird, remembering to poke some into the hollow leg cavities. Fold the two sides back over the stuffing so that one overlaps the other. Starting at the breast end and pinching up a seam in your fingers as you go, make a neat suture all the way down the chicken's back using string and a butcher's needle if you have one (if not, make holes with a knife and poke the string through with a chopstick). If your work is a little Dr Frankenstein, don't worry too much. Make sure you have sewn up the holes at each end.

Melt the remaining butter in a large frying pan and, when hot, season the chicken on its breast side with ½ teaspoon of salt and place it this-side down in the butter, where it should sizzle immediately. Cook for 6 minutes until the skin turns a rich golden orange. Flip the bird over on to its surgery side and roast for 40–45 minutes. It should be just cooked and beautifully tender.

Meanwhile, heat the oil in a saucepan and fry the neck and heart from the giblets bag with all the *jus* ingredients apart from the water, flour and lemon juice, until well coloured before pouring in the water. Bring it up to a gentle simmer and cook down by half, skimming where necessary. Turn off the heat.

When the bird is ready, leave it for 10 minutes to rest. Tip away the majority of the fat in the pan, leaving about a dessertspoon's worth within. Put it back over the heat and sift in the flour (sifting isn't necessary so long as you are prepared to chase lumps about the pan or use a sieve). Cook out the flour

» for about 30 seconds or so, really stirring it through any chicken caramel in the bottom of the pan (but do not burn the flour). Strain in the stock through a sieve and bring it up to a healthy simmer, stirring constantly. The flour will thicken the jus slightly. Check the seasoning once more and finish the sauce with a little squeeze of lemon juice to taste and a final grinding of black pepper. Transfer to a warm jug.

Carve the chicken into thick slices across the bird. Serve with the *jus,* and a very wet and creamy mashed potato and green salad.

Chicken stew & dumplings

Serves 4 hungry winter folk

1 medium chicken, jointed into
   8 pieces, carcass reserved and
   the bones cut into 3 for stock
1 large leek, trimmed, cleaned and
   cut into rounds about 5mm thick
2 tablespoons plain flour
2 level teaspoons dried thyme
1 bay leaf
8 black peppercorns
4 carrots, scrubbed and cut into
   1cm rounds
malt vinegar, to serve (optional)

Stock

25g butter
a splash of sunflower oil
2 medium onions, cut in half
   lengthways, root intact and skin left
   on (the skin colours the stock)
1 litre cold water
2 teaspoons flaked sea salt

Dumplings

100g shredded suet
4 tablespoons finely chopped
   flat-leaf parsley
½ teaspoon flaked sea salt
200g self-raising flour
75–100ml water

Sadly, dumplings seem to be fading into food history, found seldomly on the good tables of farm kitchens or hidden pubs in faraway dales. It is time to celebrate them again and let their spongy merits soak up the gravy and extend the bulk. Dumplings, or rats' pillows, as I knew them at school, don't feature in my home until winter has frozen the sticks brittle. They are more comforting than potatoes – a belly-sticking antifreeze for the human engine. Here is a tasty stew with no fancy ingredients. Humble, it is essence of chicken with some fat, green-speckled dumplings on top. A well-deserved cold-comfort saviour.

Start with the stock. Melt the butter with the oil in a large flameproof casserole over a medium heat and fry the chicken bones with the onion halves, flat-side down, for 6 minutes, or until well browned. Transfer the bones and onions to a pan and cover with the water, then add the salt. Bring the pan up to a gentle simmer and cook for 45 minutes, with the lid half on.

While the stock is cooking, fry the chicken joints in the butter and oil in the casserole, skin-side down, fairly briskly for 5 minutes, or until well browned. Turn the joints and briefly brown the other side. Remove them to a plate. Throw the leeks into the butter and chicken fat and fry for 4 minutes or so until browned. Scatter the plain flour and thyme over the leeks and cook out the taste of the flour for 1 minute more. Turn off the heat, drop in the bay leaf and peppercorns and wait for the stock to be finished.

Discard the bones and reserve the onions from the stock. You should be left with 800ml. Get the leeks frying again, then slowly add the stock bit by bit, stirring all the time until all the stock is in. It should thicken nicely. Nestle the chicken, onion and carrots into the gravy. Place on a lid and gently simmer on the stove-top for 40 minutes.

Meanwhile, combine the suet, parsley, salt and self-raising flour in a large bowl. Slowly dribble in the water, working the mixture around the bowl with a spoon until the dough comes together. Lift out the dough on to a work surface and very briefly knead it (do not overwork the mixture or the dumplings will be too dense). Split the dough into 12 bun-shaped dumplings and pop them on top of the stew (if appropriate, tilt the pan and skim off some of the fat first). Replace the lid and cook for a further 20 minutes. Eat with a little malt vinegar splashed over the chicken, if desired.

Coq au vin

Serves 8

600g button onions, skins left on

350g smoked bacon lardons, or piece
  of unsliced streaky smoked bacon
  or rashers

3 tablespoons plain flour

2 teaspoons flaked sea salt

50g butter

olive oil, for frying

8 free-range chicken legs
  (drumstick and thigh)

2 tablespoons red wine vinegar

1 tablespoon caster sugar

2 celery sticks, finely chopped

6 good hard garlic cloves with
  no green shoots, finely sliced

2 teaspoons dried thyme

2 bay leaves

300g small chestnut mushrooms

black pepper

75cl bottle red wine

125ml brandy

small pieces of fried bread, or
  mashed or puréed potato, to serve
  (optional)

I make this with the thighs and legs of good birds, as I don't like the idea of tender breasts overcooking in the sauce – a stew with a comparatively long cooking time just isn't the place for them. This dish would originally have been made with a tougher cockerel, stewed with intense wine, bacon and mushroom flavours to turn it into something deep and inky in flavour, but these birds are hard to come by and the nearest comparison in the UK would be a boiler occasionally found in street markets (if you find one, cut it into eight pieces and use instead of just the chicken legs). Try and see if the butcher will give you unsliced bacon or lardons, as these bigger bits of bacon won't collapse after cooking like the pre-sliced variety. This dish is best prepared the day before eating to make it even more delicious, then reheated.

Preheat the oven to 180°C fan/200°C/Gas 6. Pour some hot water over the onions in a large mixing bowl and leave them for 10 minutes or so, then drain and peel. Be careful to nip off only the smallest bit of root end with a knife, as you want them to stay intact. De-rind the bacon, if necessary, and if it is in one piece cut it into lardons about the length and twice the thickness of the two short pins on a household plug, or chop up thickly if using rashers. Sprinkle the flour over a large plate, scatter in a good amount of salt and mix it all together with your fingertips.

Melt the butter in a large frying pan over a medium heat with a splash of oil (to help prevent the butter burning). Roll the chicken legs in the flour until very well covered. When the butter is foaming, lower in half the chicken legs skin-side down, where they should sizzle immediately. Thoroughly brown them on both sides, turning them over after approximately 5 minutes. Remove the legs to a large bowl and brown the remaining ones. It is important not to burn the butter, as you are going to fry the onions in it, so adjust the heat when necessary.

Add the peeled onions and cook until they are a deep hazelnut colour. Pour over the vinegar and burn it off completely before scattering over the sugar and swirling the onions around until the sugar has caramelised, making them look even darker and more delicious. Put the onions with the chicken legs, without any of the residual fat.

Put a little oil in a large, heavy flameproof casserole and get the bacon frying in it over a medium heat until it too begins to properly colour. This should take about 10 minutes. Add the celery, garlic, thyme and bay leaves to the pan and cook until the celery has softened – a few minutes or so. Lift the bacon and celery into the bowl, leaving the bacon fat in the bottom of the pan. Take the pan off the heat for a while and wipe the mushroom caps with a damp cloth to remove any grit and oomska. Return the pan to the heat and, when hot, throw in the mushrooms. Any liquid must totally evaporate; at this point the mushrooms will begin to colour quite swiftly. Do this in batches, if needs be, adding the tiniest splash of oil each time. When all the mushrooms are coloured, leave a few in the bottom of the pan and put the rest in the onion bowl. The above colouring stages are important, as the ingredients intensify the flavour of the dish.

» Scatter some bacon and onions over the mushrooms and place over half the chicken legs. Scatter in more onions, bacon and mushrooms and then the rest of the chicken. Season heavily with black pepper. Put anything left in the bowl on top of the chicken. Pour over the wine and brandy and bring the contents of the pot to a gentle simmer before placing on the lid and putting it in the oven. Cook for 1¼ hours.

Either serve the dish straight away or, ideally, let it cool and put it in the fridge overnight. This was once served to me in France, decorated with small pieces of golden fried bread – an excellent idea. Mashed or puréed potato is another worthy companion.

Chicken, pea & herb rice

Serves 4

50g butter

1 large onion, finely diced

2 medium carrots, cut into small cubes

2 celery sticks, finely sliced

250g risotto rice or pudding rice

2 garlic cloves, finely chopped

125g frozen peas

juice of ½ lemon

flaked sea salt and black pepper

a good handful of finely chopped dill

a good handful of finely chopped tarragon

a little finely chopped mint

Chicken stock

a good chicken carcass, skin removed, meat reserved and roughly chopped for the rice

1.6 litres water

2 teaspoons flaked sea salt

Rich, sloppy and served in a bowl, this kitchen table supper uses up not only the wreckage of Sunday's roast but also the contents of the pea packet that's been open all year and is spilling into the freezer draw at the merest rustle. This used to be a Warner staple, but my mother has not made it for 20 years – boo hoo! The very memory of it makes me think fondly of family; this is what food does.

The stock must not be made with a chicken carcass that's been roasted with a lemon inside as it will give the liquid an unpleasant bitter taste, even if the lemon has been removed.

For the stock, simmer the chicken carcass in the water with the salt for 45 minutes with no lid. It should be very chickeny when done. Strain, measure out 1 litre, put into a fresh pan and bring to a gentle simmer.

Melt half the butter in a large, heavy saucepan and sauté the onion, carrots and celery over a medium heat for 6 minutes or so, or until the onions are golden. Add the rice and garlic and fry with the vegetables for 2 minutes or so more, stirring often. Add the first ladleful of stock. It should bubble madly; it is imperative that the stock be hot, as if cold it will slow down the cooking and spoil the rice. Feed the rice with stock when it appears to be lacking liquid and stir it often to promote creaminess by coaxing out the rice starch.

Test the rice after about 15 minutes; it should be beginning to tenderise. Add the peas and the cooked chicken meat from the carcass and keep adding stock and stirring (if you have run out of stock, add boiled water). After another 5 minutes you should be nearly there. The rice should be plump yet firm but not chalky in the centre and the consistency of a wettish porridge (it must migrate a little when spooned on to the plate, but not be stiff).

Stir the rest of the (fridge-cold) butter into the rice until it has disappeared and follow it with the lemon juice, bit by bit, until correct. There should be a definite lemoniness, but not so much as to make the rice sour. Stir in a healthy amount of black pepper. Check the seasoning. Stir in the chopped herbs and serve.

Roast duck breast with radishes & broad beans

Serves 2

2 medium duck breasts
1 level tablespoon plain flour,
   seasoned with plenty of salt
1 tablespoon sunflower oil
300g shelled young broad beans
8 long hot radishes, with leaves
1 medium banana shallot,
   finely sliced

Vinaigrette

2 teaspoons Dijon mustard
2 teaspoons tarragon vinegar
1 teaspoon caster sugar
1 fat garlic clove, finely chopped
40ml olive oil
flaked sea salt and black pepper

All weather is nice weather for ducks, whether it's a slow-roasted grease fest for the bitter winter days or fresh, vinegary gizzard and bacon salads for summer lunches and memories of Paris café life. The two rules with duck breast are that, unless poached, it must be nothing less than crispy and it must certainly be pink. The vinaigrette, beans and radishes make this dish surprisingly light.

Set a small, heavy-based frying pan over a medium–low heat.

Put the seasoned flour on a plate. Press the skin side of the duck into the flour, then pat off any excess.

Pour the sunflower oil into the pan to help the breasts get going. Lay them, skin-side down, in the pan, where they should sizzle immediately. Cook for 12 minutes, taking care to regulate the heat if you think they are burning. The skin by this time will be very crispy; turn the breasts over for 3–5 minutes. I like my duck breasts pink in the middle. Move and leave to rest for 5 minutes before carving.

Meanwhile, drop the broad beans in a saucepan of boiling water and boil for 3 minutes. When the beans are done, drain and put in a bowl with the radishes and their leaves (remove any manky parts first) and the sliced shallot.

To make the vinaigrette, stir the mustard, vinegar, sugar and garlic together, then slowly beat in the olive oil with a fork and season. Mix the vinaigrette with the salad.

Slice the duck thickly (about 5mm) on a diagonal. Pour the juices that have leaked from the meat on to the board over the salad. Divide the salad between two plates and lay the slices of duck on top, crispy skin facing the ceiling on each plate. Accompany with a glass of wine – I like Sancerre, maybe with a little splash of *crème de mûre*.

Mallard & cabbage

Serves 4

70g butter, at room temperature

1 red cabbage, cored and finely sliced

12 plump pitted no-soak prunes (and a couple to eat while cooking), roughly chopped

1 bay leaf

6 cloves

flaked sea salt and black pepper

juice of 1 orange

2 tablespoons red wine vinegar

1½ teaspoons soft light brown sugar

2 mallards, at room temperature, giblets removed

Green Split Peas (*see* page 249), to serve

This is one of my favourite dishes. I received a few inflamed letters for parading it on television but not in the accompanying book *What to Eat Now*; it had been jammed into the series at the last minute, when the fine Italian paper was already rushing through the spinning printers. Well, here it is now. I'm happy to see that mallards are appearing more commonly in good butchers and some more adventurous supermarket branches. During the shooting season, I like to stockpile them in the freezer, as every one I sit down to reinforces my fear of running out. I recommend that you serve half a bird per person because they do not have as much meat as might at first appear (although I must admit that I can eat a whole one with ease). After you've tried a mallard, you'll never look upon the village pond in the same way. Although maybe not the wisest recommendation for post-mallard dinner reading, Roald Dahl's *The Magic Finger* is a bizarre and wonderful story for anyone desiring some duck literature.

Preheat the oven to 200°C fan/220°C/Gas 7. Melt 30g of the butter in a large frying pan over a medium heat until it is foaming. In a colander, rinse the cabbage with water. This is purely so that when the water has drained away there will be water droplets to take to the frying pan and soften the cabbage. Drop the cabbage into the frying pan with the prunes, bay leaf, cloves, salt and an enthusiastic grinding of black pepper (when adding the cloves, rub and pinch the crown end to really deploy their full capability). Fry and stir vigorously for 10 minutes or so. Feel free to dribble in a little water if the cabbage appears to burn before loosening up – though a little singeing is fine and tasty too. When the cabbage has softened but retains a slight bite, pour in the orange juice and vinegar. Evaporate the liquid away completely. The acids will have snatched back the vivid colour of the cabbage. Scatter in the sugar and cook, stirring continuously, until you start to smell it caramelising. Taste and rejig the seasoning accordingly.

Allow the mixture to cool a little before spooning it into the empty cavity of the ducks. Pack it in without really forcing it – the cooking time would change if it were too densely packed. There should be some just peeping out of the end. Lay the ducks on a roasting tray with the breasts facing up. Season them liberally before smearing the remaining butter over the mallards. Roast them in the oven, with the stuffed ends facing the door, for 27 minutes.

Remove the birds from the oven and rest them for 5 minutes before carving. Serve the breast on the cabbage that you have spooned out. Both go excellently with my Green Split Peas (*see* page 249), which can be happily cooked in advance and reheated with a splash of water.

Note: The duck flesh should be pinky-purple near the bone when served, as it will be tough, ungiving and no doubt disappointing if overcooked. The little legs can always be put back in the oven if you would like them more done.

Confit duck legs with carrots, spring onions & beetroot relish

Serves 6

8 heaped tablespoons coarse
   rock salt
1 tablespoon juniper berries,
   lightly bashed
2 good handfuls of thyme sprigs
1 garlic bulb, skins left on the cloves,
   cloves roughly chopped
8 good handfuls of rosemary sprigs,
   broken
10 black peppercorns
6 good duck legs from free-range
   farmed ducks
5 × 350g jars duck or goose fat
150ml white Burgundy, or other
   dry white wine

Beetroot relish

2 medium beetroots
2 teaspoons Dijon mustard, plus
   extra to serve
1–1½ tablespoons red wine vinegar
½ teaspoon flaked sea salt, or to taste
black pepper
3–4 tablespoons olive oil

Carrots and spring onions

20 baby carrots, end whisker left on
   and leaves cut away but leaving
   a tiny green quiff
1 tablespoon duck fat from the pot
flaked sea salt and black pepper
16 really good spring onions,
   washed and trimmed

A recipe such as this is a true representation of my attitude to cooking and how I like my food: simple, delicious and colourful where possible.

In a large bowl, throw in the salt and all the aromatics (the juniper berries, thyme, garlic, rosemary and peppercorns). Toss the duck legs in the mixture, really pushing the salt into them. Take a few of the stems that haven't stuck to the duck, some berries, some peppercorns and excess salt in the bowl, and scatter it into the bottom of a lidded container large enough to take all the duck legs. Putthe first three duck legs in the bottom, skin-side up. Scatter over more of the bits and bobs left in the bottom of the bowl on to the duck legs, before placing on the next three duck legs on top. Tip any bits left in the bowl over the top. Put on a lid and wrap the whole box in clingfilm. This is so that when you turn it upside down, you do not cover your fridge in salty juice. Leave the duck legs for 12 hours in the fridge, turning the box upside down halfway through.

In a large saucepan, melt the duck or goose fat. Take each duck leg, brush off any visible salt with your hand and pop it into the pan of fat. Repeat with all the legs. Pick out some berries, peppercorns, garlic, rosemary and thyme, and drop these into the fat as well, taking care not to add residual salt to the duck fat. Add the wine. Cut out a cartouche (a circle of baking paper) that fits neatly into the pan and place over the duck legs. Put a robust kitchen plate on top; this will keep the duck under the oil. Bring the fat up to a gentle, bubbling simmer (plup, plup, plup) and cook like this on the stove-top for 2½–3 hours. You will know when the duck is ready by testing it with a fork; the meat should come away easily from the bone with only the slightest prompting, but should not fall off without.

While the duck cooks, boil the beetroots whole with the skins on. They want to be very tender and will cook in about 1–1¼ hours in a pan with the lid on. Peel off the skins, wearing rubber gloves, and grate them coarsely, while hot, into a bowl. Stir in the Dijon mustard, add the vinegar, salt and black pepper to taste and follow with enough oil to get a consistency that is soft and glossy. By doing this when the beetroot is warm, the flavours really come into their own. Leave to one side.

Poach the carrots in a small saucepan of boiling water for 3 minutes, then drain, reserving the carrot water. Scatter the carrots on the bottom of a large roasting tray, mix them with the duck fat and season. Nestle the duck legs among the carrots. It doesn't matter if some of the carrots sit under the legs.

Preheat the oven to 200°C fan/220°C/Gas 7 half an hour before you plan to use the duck legs. Roast the duck legs for 30 minutes, or until the skin is very crispy and the carrots have taken on colour. About 5 minutes before serving, poach the spring onions in the simmering carrot water for 2 minutes.

To assemble the dish, put the carrots and duck legs on a large platter and intersperse with the spring onions. Eat accompanied with the beetroot relish, some Dijon mustard and a bottle of excellent wine.

Quails with Fino & ham

Serves 3–6 (1 or 2 quails each)

6 quails
2 tablespoons olive oil, plus extra
    for oiling the quails
flaked sea salt
cloves from ½ garlic bulb, peeled
100g jamón (Spanish ham), roughly
    chopped into 1cm-wide ribbons
1 medium onion, finely sliced
4 good bay leaves
1 heaped teaspoon plain flour
250ml Fino sherry
2 tablespoons roughly chopped
    flat-leaf parsley
good bread or sautéed potatoes,
    to serve (optional)

Wild quails taste exceptional, but I also find farmed quails very delectable and this is an Andalucian treatment for their pale, tender meat. Normally the jamón (Spanish ham) in cooked dishes such as this would be off-cuts from the edges of the cured leg. Although bacon could be used as a replacement, it will not deliver that holiday taste. Try to buy sliced off-cuts or a little block of ham for cooking from a Spanish deli. Alternatively, proper slices will give the flavour, but this is a somewhat expensive option. I use Fino in this dish, but any dry sherry would do.

Preheat the oven to 200°C fan/220°C/Gas 7. Use a sharp pair of scissors to cut out the spines of the quails by holding each one cupped in one hand with the back up. (The spines can be used to make a little stock for one person's evening bowl of soup).

Put each quail breast-side up on a chopping board. Put the heel of your hand on the breastbone and squash the bird flat. You should hear the breastbone break. Make sure the quails are dry; if not, wipe off any moisture with kitchen paper. Rub the birds with a little oil and season with salt.

In a shallow metal casserole or an ovenproof frying pan that can borrow a lid, sear the oiled quails over a medium–high heat, browning them all over. This will take around 4 minutes. Do not cook them for too long – this stage should be brief if the pan is hot enough. Remove the birds from the pan to a large plate.

In the same cooking vessel, fry the garlic cloves with the jamón in most of the oil over a medium–high heat until nicely coloured (about 2–3 minutes). Add the onion and bay leaves, then cook for another 7 minutes or so, stirring regularly, until softened (but the onions should not colour). Scatter over the flour and stir it into the onions for 30 seconds or so, to cook out the raw taste.

Add the remaining oil to the casserole or pan then return the quails to it. Stand back and add the Fino. If you are cooking with a gas hob, it is easy to flame them as you do this: tip the pan towards the gas and, as the vapours ignite, swirl the flame around the pan until the fire goes out (but flaming isn't necessary). Immediately transfer the cooking vessel to the oven for 12 minutes.

When it is cooked, remove the birds briefly from the pan. Swirl the sauce to make sure the flour thickens it properly and scatter in the parsley. Put the birds back and serve in the middle of the table, straight from the pan, perhaps with some good bread or sautéed potatoes.

Pot partridges with Savoy cabbage & cider

Serves 6

50g butter

a splash of sunflower oil

6 plump partridges

flaked sea salt and black pepper

1 small Savoy cabbage, trimmed

500g smoked bacon lardons

6 medium carrots, peeled and
    cut into 1cm rounds

2 medium onions, finely chopped

4 cloves

3 sprigs of thyme

½ teaspoon ground mace

300ml cider (*see* recipe introduction)

mash or creamy puréed potatoes,
    to serve

This is a robust, very tasty and simple dish, and a good recipe for guests if you are short of time. Partridge is a bird wisely served if you feel certain folk might be nervous of game; it's 'game for beginners', as the meat is delicate and mild. Please buy French red-legged partridges because the wild English grey partridge is now very rare. As well as this, the Frenchies are not indigenous, so trespassers will be eaten.

Concerning the cider, please choose a good dry or medium old-style variety and not the kind with the orange hue of Tizer that people insist on drinking with ice.

Preheat the oven to 150°C fan/170°C/Gas 3½. Take a large flameproof casserole that will fit the birds snugly and in it melt the butter with the oil over a medium–high heat. When good and hot, lower in half the partridges, well-seasoned with salt. The heat should be such that the birds colour quickly but the butter does not burn. Cook until the birds are richly golden all over, then do the same with the second batch.

While the birds sear, cut the cabbage into six segments, keeping the stem intact so as to hold the leaves together. Lift out the partridges on to a plate, lower the heat and gently fry the lardons, carrots and onions with the cloves, thyme, mace and a really vigorous grinding of black pepper. Cook gently for about 10 minutes, stirring occasionally, until the carrots and lardons have softened but not coloured.

Spoon half the contents of the pan on to a plate. Place the partridges in the casserole, breasts facing up and narrow end inwards. Wedge the cabbage, chisel-edge down, between each partridge and scatter over the reserved carrots and bacon. Pour the cider all over and bring it up to a gentle simmer before placing on a lid and putting the casserole in the oven.

Cook for 50 minutes–1 hour, or until the birds are only just done – faintly pink in the breast and tender. When they are done, sit them in an orderly fashion with the vegetables on a serving platter to rest, with some foil and a dishcloth draped over them to retain the heat. Skim the sauce of any obviously excess fat, then briskly simmer it for 5 minutes before removing the covering from the birds and pouring the gravy over them. Serve with mash or creamy puréed potatoes. Cider may be worth considering over wine as a drink to complement the covey.

Roast pigeon & ale pie

Serves 6

40g butter

350g smoked lardons or bacon
  rashers, chopped

3 medium carrots, peeled and
  roughly chopped (but not too big)

1 large onion, peeled (reserve skin
  and trimmings for stock) and
  finely chopped

1 bay leaf

4 cloves

½ tablespoon chopped thyme leaves
  (reserve stalks for stock)

1 tablespoon malt vinegar

breasts from 6 pigeons, carcasses
  reserved for stock

3 tablespoons plain flour

flaked sea salt

Stock

1 tablespoon sunflower oil

10 black peppercorns

2 teaspoons Worcestershire sauce

flaked sea salt (optional)

Pastry

250g plain flour, plus extra for
  dusting

1 teaspoon crumbled flaked sea salt

125g butter, frozen for at least 1 hour,
  coarsely grated

85–100ml cold water

1 medium free-range egg, beaten

Pigeons remind me of all our seasons, whether cooing me awake on wet spring mornings or slapping away in their arcing displays come summer evenings. They bob and bow over the fallen grains of the autumn and clatter from bare winter branches in great whooshing flocks at the slightest cough. And I think as I look up at them: what a very British bird you are! And when looking down upon the spoon breaking through the crust of the pie, I think: how totally delicious you are! Pigeons make good eating all year round. For this dish, have the butcher remove the pigeon breasts and legs from the carcasses, making sure you keep these for making the stock.

To make the stock, start by chopping the reserved pigeon carcasses into three with a large, heavy knife. Heat the oil in a large saucepan over a medium heat. Throw in the carcasses and brown them well, then pour in enough water to cover the bones (about 1.25 litres). Add the peppercorns, skin and trimmings from the onion and the stripped stalks from the thyme you will use in the pie filling. Bring to a gentle simmer and cook for an hour with the lid off (after this time you would be hard pushed to extract any more flavour from the bones). Strain the stock into a bowl, then return it to the saucepan and reduce it to 500ml. Season it with the Worcestershire sauce and salt, if needed, then leave it to cool. The stock should be delicious in its own right.

While the stock is doing its thing, make the pastry. Mix the flour and salt in a large bowl and stir in the butter with a round-bladed knife. Slowly add enough of the water to bring the mixture together into a soft dough. Turn out on to a floured work surface and knead very lightly. Form into a flattish ball and wrap in baking paper. Chill in the fridge for 30 minutes.

Meanwhile, make the pie filling. Take a large frying pan and drop in 25g of the butter. When it has melted, add the bacon, carrots and onion with the bay leaf, cloves and thyme leaves. Cook all together over a medium–low heat, stirring occasionally, until the carrots and onion have become tender (about 15 minutes). Add the vinegar and cook until it has evaporated. Put the contents of the pan in a bowl to one side. Wipe out the pan with kitchen paper.

Preheat the oven to 180°C fan/200°C/Gas 6. Pull the skin from the pigeon breasts and discard, then chop the breasts into large chunks, about three pieces per breast. (The size is important as, chopped smaller, they would overcook by the time the pastry is done and will be tasty but tough.) Sift the flour into a mixing bowl and add some salt, combining everything together briefly. Toss the pigeon pieces in the seasoned flour until well covered.

Melt the remaining butter in a large frying pan and when it is smoking fry the pigeon bits hard, for no more than 2 minutes, tossing regularly so as to brown the pieces evenly on all sides. Again they need to colour fast so as not to spend too much time in the pan, so really make sure the pan and butter are truly hot. Combine the pigeon pieces with the carrot, bacon and onion. Place a pie bird in the middle of a 1.25-litre pie dish. Add the filling; it should come slightly above the level of the rim to prevent the pastry from sagging. Pour over the cooled stock so that it comes up to just below the rim of the dish.

» Take the pastry from the fridge about 15 minutes before using it. Roll it out on a floured work surface to slightly thicker than a £1 coin and 5cm larger than the pie dish. Brush the rim of the dish with beaten egg. Cut two or three 2cm-wide strips from around the edge of the pastry and press these on to the rim all the way around. Brush with more egg and carefully lift the remaining pastry over a rolling pin and on to the pie dish, making a small slit with the point of a knife to allow the pie funnel to pass through the pastry. Press the edges to seal, then trim neatly. Crimp the edge, if you like, to give the pie a decorative finish. Glaze with more egg. Bake the pie on a baking tray until its roof is dark golden brown and the filling is hot (about 30–35 minutes).

Tandoori partridge

Serves 4

4 partridges

Marinade

2 teaspoons ground cumin
2 teaspoons turmeric
1½ teaspoons ground coriander
½ teaspoon ground cinnamon
a good grating of nutmeg
6 cloves
seeds from 10 green cardamom pods
1 tablespoon cayenne pepper
2 teaspoons flaked sea salt
1 thumb-sized piece of root ginger,
   peeled and roughly chopped
4 garlic cloves, peeled
½ small onion, roughly chopped
250g full-fat yoghurt
juice of ½ lemon
red food colouring paste (optional)

To serve

lemon wedges
chopped iceberg lettuce
sliced red onion
naan bread

The partridge season starts in early September, when you can see some excellent weather for barbecues (although having said that, I light them all year round and put a big coat on, if needs be). Ideally, the partridge will be grilled over charcoal, as this is the closest thing to a tandoor (Indian clay oven), but a gas barbecue will suffice. Use a preheated griddle pan to cook the partridge if you don't have access to a barbecue.

This recipe is not an attempt to transform the usual chicken tandoori into something quirky. In India there are various francolins (or teetars as they are known locally) that are close relations of the partridges found in the UK, and these are no strangers to a dusting with spices.

It is important that powdered spices are as fresh as possible. Kept all higgledy-piggledy in a dusty box with the lids half off, they will very quickly lose their individuality. Using a pestle and mortar and whole spices makes spice-grinding a more personal experience. If doing so, estimate the amount you need to replicate the spoonfuls of the pre-ground powders. Excuse the food dye but I like the restaurant red.

To make the marinade, put the spices, salt, ginger, garlic and onion in a blender and blitz until as smooth as possible. Turn the paste out into a large bowl, then stir in the yoghurt and lemon juice. Stir in the food colouring paste, if using. (Ideally, use colouring paste designed for cake decorating, as liquid food colouring won't tint the marinade sufficiently.)

Remove the skin from the partridges and cut each bird in half, first along and through the breastbone and then the spine. Score the thighs and breasts lightly several times with a sharp knife. Drop the halved partridges into the tandoori marinade and turn them over until all are well coated. Cover the bowl with clingfilm and leave to marinate in the fridge for at least 3 hours.

About 45 minutes before serving, light a small charcoal barbecue and let the flames die down to hot coals. Take the tandoori pieces out of the marinade and tap off the excess. Put the birds on the barbecue and cook for 6–8 minutes on each side, or until the meat is nicely charred but tender and cooked through (take care not to overcook them so that they become dry). Serve with lemon wedges, iceberg lettuce, red onion and naan bread.

Fish & shellfish

Rosti with salmon eggs, dill & crème fraîche

Serves 1

40g butter
2 medium waxy potatoes,
    such as Duke of York
1 heaped teaspoon plain flour
black pepper
½–1 teaspoon flaked sea salt
a small bunch of dill
½ small red onion
a little crème fraîche
50g salmon eggs
½ lemon, cut into wedges

I am increasingly obsessed with the Scandinavian approach to cooking and this dish uses a lot of its kitchen regulars. Nothing short of outrageously good, it makes a superb Sunday brunch for one, or cut it up and serve with ice-cold vodka as a very good little pre-dinner snack.

Melt the butter in a small saucepan over a low heat, taking special care not to let it burn. You will see small white islands of milk solids rising to the top after a couple of minutes. Carefully skim these off and discard. Pour the golden butterfat into a mixing bowl, while at the same time trying to leave any residual white water that lurks below the butterfat in the saucepan.

Peel and shred the potatoes on the larger setting of a grater. Give the gratings a good squeeze to get rid of the initial starchy water (there is no need to strangle them). Add the potato to the butter in the bowl and sift over the flour. Grind in a heavy bombardment of black pepper and then a bit more. Add the salt and use your fingers to mix everything together very thoroughly. If the potato appears to discolour as it oxidises, this is normal, but the aim should be to cook it sooner after grating rather than later.

Heat a large, nonstick frying pan to a medium heat, place all the rosti mixture in the centre of the pan and spread it out to the edge with the back of a spoon. It needs to be pressed flat and spread out really thinly and evenly, but without holes. It will look rather like the inside surface of a fibreglass boat. If you have too much mixture, take a little out, as it should be crispy, not cakey. The rosti should gently sizzle away for about 8–10 minutes on each side. Lift an edge and have a peek; if it is golden brown, flip it over with a big spatula or your fingers (it can be handled fairly robustly, as the starch has glued it together well) and fry the other side. The whole thing can take 16–22 minutes. It wants to be deep orange, browny-gold and very crisp, but with a slight squidge. I regulate the cooking with occasional flipping and heat control.

While your rosti fries, strip the dill feathers from the stalks and roughly chop them, then finely dice the onion. When the rosti is ready, lay it on some baking paper on a plate. Working clockwise around the edge, and in no particular order, dollop the crème fraîche and salmon eggs in separate piles, followed by the dill, onion and lemon wedges. What you do after that is up to you.

Pickled herrings

Makes 2 × 500g jars

6 whole medium herrings,
   scaled, gutted, filleted and
   pin-boned
3 tablespoons flaked sea salt

Marinade

8 juniper berries
2 teaspoons coriander seeds
1 teaspoon caraway or dill seeds
2 teaspoons fennel seeds
1 teaspoon mustard seeds
10 black peppercorns
500ml white wine vinegar
200g caster sugar
4 small bay leaves
2 small carrots, peeled
1 medium white onion,
   very finely sliced

To serve

crusty rye bread
a little cold butter
a scraping of hot horseradish

A silver tide of pickled herrings is shoaled up in my fridge and, when there are none of my own left, I will take a pot from a shop shelf, open it immediately and pay for the empty jar with the rest of my purchases. Odd moments have seen me crouching on a kitchen stool, chin back, while attempting to gulp the fish down whole. I need them. I like my cure quite sweet in taste, so cut back on the sugar as you see fit.

To sterilise the jars, preheat the oven to 160°C fan/180°C/Gas 4. Wash the jars and lids really well and put them on a baking tray in the oven for 10 minutes.

Put a clean cloth on the kitchen table and lay out the fillets in close rows, skin-side down. Evenly scatter over the salt and leave them for 1½ hours.

To make the marinade, crush the juniper berries and coriander seeds a little under a knife, as this will help them release their taste. Tip all the spices into a medium pan and warm them over a low heat until their smell comes to the nose. Do not burn them. Pour in the vinegar and sugar. Scrumple the bay leaves to help them release their aroma, and then add them to the pan. Continue to simmer gently to melt the sugar as you prepare the carrots.

If you like, use a canelle knife to cut four equally spaced grooves down the entire length of each carrot. (This is not obligatory, but will give a pretty flower pattern to each sliced piece.) Slice them as close to paper-thin as you can and add to the pot with the onion. Bring it all up to the boil, then reduce the heat and simmer gently for 5 minutes. Leave to cool completely. If the liquid is applied to the fish hot, they will cook rather pickle and all hands would be lost.

When their time is up, put the herrings in a colander and rinse well under cold water. Pat the fillets dry with kitchen paper. Cut each fillet in half at a diagonal angle. Sprinkle some of the marinade into the base of the two sterilised jars and scatter with a few pieces of the fish. It's nice if the silvery sides press against the glass, as this is what you will see when opening the fridge or when the jar is placed on the table. Add a little onion and carrot. Continue layering the jars, fairly dividing the bay leaves between them, until the top of each jar is reached. Make sure that the pickling liquor completely covers the fish and goes to just under the brim of each jar.

Cover tightly and chill in the fridge for at least two days before serving. Eat them before and they will not have had time to soften and mature; open a tin of pâté instead. They will store well in the fridge for 1 month, but should be eaten within a week once opened. (This is why it is better to make them in smaller jars rather than a single big one.)

Serve with good rye bread, cold butter and hot horseradish, making sure each loaded morsel is quivering with the onion and carrot.

Trout & Pernod pie

Serves 6

a little olive oil
1 whole large trout (about 1kg),
 or 2 whole small trout (about
 500g each), gutted and degilled

Rough puff pastry

225g strong white flour, plus
 extra for dusting
a good pinch of fine sea salt
185g butter, chilled, cut roughly
 into 2cm dice
125ml cold water
2 teaspoons lemon juice
1 free-range egg, beaten

Sauce

50g butter
½ medium onion, finely chopped
2 slender celery sticks, trimmed
 and finely sliced
3 tablespoons Pernod
40g plain flour
400ml whole milk
1 teaspoon Dijon mustard
4 tablespoons double cream
leaves from 2 sprigs of tarragon,
 finely chopped
a handful of curly-leaf parsley leaves,
 finely chopped
3 tablespoons baby capers,
 well rinsed
1 teaspoon flaked sea salt
ground white pepper

What with all the fishing I sneak off to do over the summer, I eat a fair amount of trout, but unlike many fishermen I have not tired of its taste. I do not kill every fish, as I do not see the point of a freezer crammed full of trout that have to be eaten. Luxuriating in a creamy sauce, hinting aniseed, beneath a crispy golden roof, this is one of my favourite recipes for both rainbow and brown trout.

To make the pastry, sift the flour and salt into a large bowl. Drop in the butter and toss around with a large metal spoon until it is lightly coated in the flour. Mix the water and lemon juice together and pour into the bowl. Use a table knife to cut across the mix, chopping the butter into the flour, until the dough comes together. When it forms a loose lump, tip it on to a board and quickly shape it into a fat slab with your hand.

Roll out the dough on a well-floured work surface to a rectangle around 40cm × 20cm. Fold one-third of the pastry into the middle, then fold the other end over that. Press the edges together firmly with the pin, then rotate the pastry a quarter turn. Roll into the same size of rectangle and start the process again. You are basically building up the layers that make this rough puff fluff. Continue five more times: rolling into a rectangle, folding, pressing and turning once more. Don't worry too much if a chunk of butter occasionally makes its way through in the early stages. Just keep the board and pin very well floured to prevent the pastry from sticking. Wrap the slab in clingfilm and chill for 1–2 hours (or overnight). If it is very firm when you come to use it, allow the pastry to warm through for a few minutes before rolling.

Preheat the oven to 200°C fan/220°C/Gas 7. To make the sauce, melt the butter in a medium-sized, nonstick saucepan over a low heat. In it gently fry the onion and celery for a couple of minutes before adding the Pernod. Continue cooking the vegetables for 8–10 minutes until soft but not coloured, stirring occasionally. The Pernod should evaporate, leaving only the butter and vegetables. Sprinkle the flour into the pan and cook for a minute before gradually adding the milk, while stirring constantly with a whisk (this will help eradicate any unwanted lumps as you go). When all the milk has been added, stir in the mustard. Cook the sauce gently for 10 minutes or so, stirring continually, until smooth and glossy. Remove from the heat and stir in the cream, tarragon, parsley and capers. Season. (It will need a little more salt than you may expect to bring out the flavours.) Cover the surface of the sauce with clingfilm to prevent a skin forming and leave to cool for at least 30 minutes. If it seems thick, do not worry, as when heated in the pie it will loosen as it absorbs the trout juices.

Line a small baking tin with a large sheet of foil and brush it with a little oil. Put the cleaned trout into the tin, head to tail if using two, and cover with a second piece of oiled foil. Scrunch the edges together to form a large, flat parcel. Bake the trout for 15 minutes, then leave to stand without opening for 15–20 minutes. It needs to be barely cooked, as it will enter the oven again under the pastry. Turn the oven down to 180°C fan/200°C/Gas 6.

» To assemble the pie, open the foil and unrobe the skin from the fish –
it should come away easily. Slide the fish off the bones in large pieces and
put it in a bowl. Flip the fish over and do exactly the same thing on the other
side. Discard the skin and bones, but tip 2–3 tablespoons of any residual
juices collected in the foil into the white sauce and stir in. Spoon a little of
the sauce into a 1.5-litre pie dish and top with a few pieces of fish; continue
layering the sauce and fish until both are used up.

Roll out the pastry on a floured work surface until around 2cm larger than
the pie dish. Brush the edge of the dish with beaten egg and carefully place
the pastry over the filling. Trim and knock up the edges with a sharp knife.
Make a cross-hatch pattern across the top and brush lightly with more beaten
egg. Put on a baking tray and bake in the preheated oven for 30–35 minutes
until the pastry is golden brown and the filling is hot. Check every now and
then to make sure the pastry doesn't burn before the filling is ready, and turn
down a few degrees if necessary.

Serve the pie hot with some runner beans dressed with a little butter, salt
and red wine vinegar. Then grab your rod again and head for the shadier
parts of the river.

Baked trout with squash & cider

Serves 1–2

6 thin 1cm-thick crescent slices
   of deseeded onion squash
½ onion, very finely sliced
40g butter, chilled, cut into
   small cubes
1 whole trout (about 500g), scaled,
   gutted and degilled
a small sprig of rosemary
2 slices of lemon
a grating of nutmeg
flaked sea salt and black pepper
50ml cider
a little finely chopped curly-leaf
   parsley, to serve (optional)

Another treatment for late-season trout, once the rod has done its work.

Preheat the oven to 200°C fan/220°C/Gas 7. Cut out two large pieces of foil
(it must extend at least 5cm from each end of the trout) and two slightly
smaller pieces of baking paper. Put one piece of foil on the work surface and
cover with a piece of baking paper. Lay half the squash slices and half the
onion slices on the baking paper, then scatter over half the butter. Lay the
trout on top, then insert the rosemary sprig and lemon slices into its body
cavity. Lay the rest of the squash, onion and butter over the fish. Grate over
a little nutmeg, grind over a lot of black pepper and sprinkle over a generous
pinch of salt. Bring the paper up the sides a little before pouring over the
cider. Place the other piece of baking paper and foil on top of the fish (the foil
on the outside) and roll up the sides, folding about three times all the way
around, but leaving some room for the bag to puff up.

Bake in the oven for 25–30 minutes. On unwrapping the parcel, a knife placed
in the thick part of the meat behind the top of the fish's head should only meet
with the faintest resistance when the knife tip is near the spine; otherwise,
cook further in increments of 5 minutes until done.

Slide the fish and the other ingredients on to the plate, and scatter with a little
parsley if you wish. It seems obvious that the right drink for this is more cider.

Plaice with tartare sauce

Serves 2

flaked sea salt and black pepper
1 whole plaice (about 800-900g),
    or megrim or flounder, gutted
    and degilled
35g butter, plus extra for greasing
lemon wedges, to serve

Tartare sauce

2 medium free-range egg yolks
1 small garlic clove, roughly chopped
1 heaped teaspoon Dijon mustard
½ teaspoon flaked sea salt
black pepper
½ teaspoon caster sugar
2–3 teaspoons tarragon vinegar
150ml sunflower oil
50ml extra virgin olive oil
1 small banana shallot,
    finely chopped
6 small gherkins, drained
    and chopped
4 tablespoons baby capers,
    well rinsed
1 tablespoon finely chopped tarragon
1–2 tablespoons finely chopped dill
2–3 tablespoons single cream

Plaice very much reminds me of the West Country, where you find it advertised on all the pub blackboards. It also reminds me of my grandmother, who never passed up an opportunity to eat one (if found advertised with breadcrumbs). Plaice are rather out of fashion these days, which in the case of some fisheries is probably a good thing. Compared to grandiose turbot, it is a modest fish with a very fine, distinctive yet hard-to-describe taste – one that I adore, and I love tartare sauce to go with it. I find a plaice beautiful to look at, with its humble brown body dotted about with techno-orange thumb prints. It makes me drift off in fishmongers, entranced by nature's immaculate design, until a voice says: 'Excuse me, sir – would you like to pay for that?'

Preheat the oven to 200°C fan/220°C/Gas 7.

To make the mayonnaise base for the tartare sauce, put the egg yolks, garlic, mustard, salt, two or three grinds of black pepper, sugar and vinegar into a food processor or blender and blitz until well combined. Slowly add the oil in a thin stream until the mayonnaise is thick and creamy. Scrape into a bowl. Add the shallot, gherkins, capers, tarragon and dill to the mayonnaise. Add just enough cream to loosen the mixture a little and create a soft, dropping sauce that slides slowly from the spoon as it is lifted from the bowl.

Butter a large baking tray or shallow ovenproof dish and sprinkle it with salt and black pepper. Place the fish on the tray, white-side down, dot the spotty side with the butter and season well. Bake in the centre of the oven for approximately 10 minutes, or until the fish is just cooked and lightly browned. The flesh behind the head should show only the faintest resistance when a knife tip is pushed almost to the bone. When cooking megrim or flounder, they may require slightly less cooking time.

Carefully remove the four fillets and cheeks from the fish with two table knives. The skirt has particularly delicious yet fiddly meat that I devote time to picking clean. Serve with greedy dollops of tartare sauce and lemon wedges. Any remaining sauce will store well in the fridge for a few days.

Note: The bones, fresh or cooked, make good stock.

Grilled whole turbot with coriander sauce

Serves 4

1 whole sustainable turbot
   (about 1kg), gutted and degilled
a splash of sunflower oil
2 dessertspoons flaked sea salt
a little smoked paprika (optional)

Coriander sauce

2 teaspoons coriander seeds
½ teaspoon flaked sea salt
35g coriander leaves,
   very finely chopped
4 tablespoons good
   extra virgin olive oil
juice of ½ medium lemon

With its thick skin and fine flesh, this grand flatty is superb for the barbecue and its fine flesh needs only the simplest of dressings, if any. There is said to be a subtle difference in taste between the meat from the white side, which has seen no sun, and the meat from the upper dark-skinned side, and I have heard Basque cooks describe these nuances with great intensity.

Get the barbecue going and in the meantime make the coriander sauce. Gently toast the coriander seeds over a medium–low heat in a frying pan, swirling them often so that they do not burn. When you smell their fragrance, or begin to hear them pop, tip them on to a board. Roughly grind the seeds with the salt using the flat bottom of a heavy glass (or else use a pestle and mortar) and put in a mixing bowl. Put the coriander leaves with the olive oil in a blender and blitz until very smooth. You may need to remove the lid and push the coriander down a few times. Tip into the mixing bowl and squeeze in the lemon juice. Stir well and leave to one side.

Just before you want to cook the turbot, lie it flat and wipe all moisture from each side until it is as dry as possible – a clean tea towel is best for this. Use scissors to snip off half the tail and cut the skirt fins from each side to limit the chances of the fish sticking to the grill. Rub the smallest dot of sunflower oil over each side of the fish before salting heavily; the salt will season as well as help raise it from the grill bars.

When the embers glow orange and white, lay the fish in the centre of the grill and cook for approximately 7–8 minutes, dark skin-side down. The grill should be set about 18cm from the charcoal. Do not prod unnecessarily. Turn the fish with the aid of a large metal spatula and cook on the white side for approximately 5–6 minutes. Be very careful to keep it in one piece, although the skin often sticks and rips a little – this is of no great matter. Lift the turbot on to a large platter and, if you like, dust the crispy skin with smoked paprika.

Artfully streak over some of the dressing and serve the rest alongside the fish. Serve the fish whole, for people to pull apart at the table, taking the flesh off the bone using two table knives.

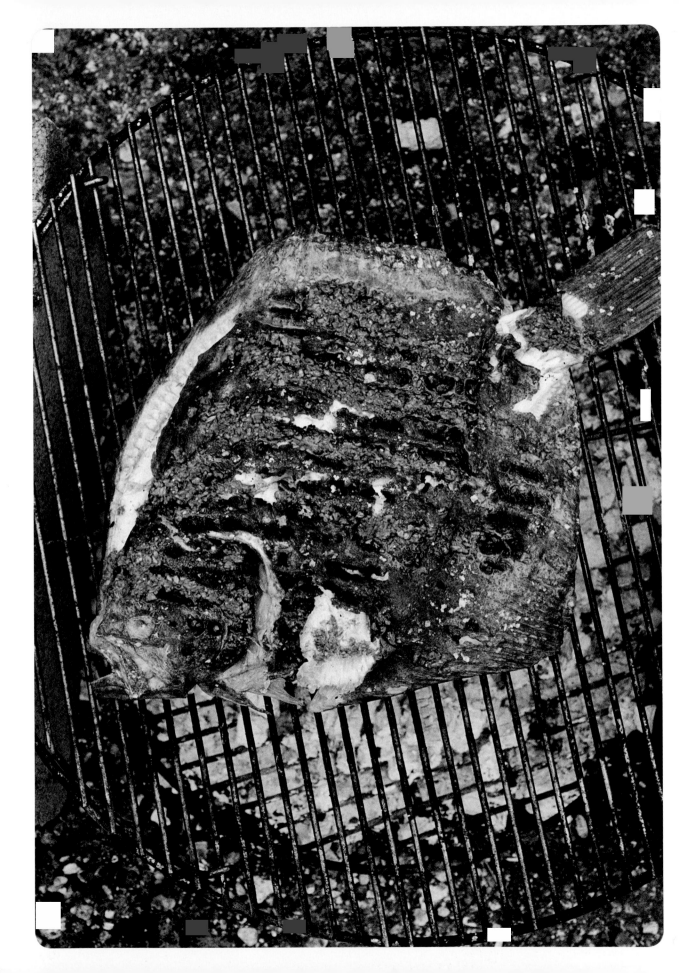

Grilled bream with rosemary, anchovies & lemon

Serves 2

1 whole black bream or guilt-head
   bream (about 700–800g),
   scaled, gutted and filleted
leaves from 1 good sprig of
   rosemary
½ teaspoon flaked sea salt
2 slices of lemon, cut wafer thin
4 brown anchovies in oil, drained
1 tablespoon olive oil, plus extra
   for frying

We are lucky to have the black bream in our English waters. Arriving in May, they are big contributors to my summer table. The season runs right through to the end of autumn, although their fat can become a little smelly at the latter end of the year (I don't know why). The idea of the lemon is a nice tip I picked up from a fellow cook and friend, Stevie Parle.

Preheat the grill to its highest setting. Pat the fish fillets with kitchen paper to ensure that the flesh is dry. Chop the rosemary leaves with the salt until very fine. Scatter a little over the fillets. Cut each slice of lemon into four pieces and lay these little citrus triangles anywhere on the fish skin, higgledy-piggledy but not overlapping. Place the anchovies, two per fillet, where the lemon isn't. Splash the oil over the top.

Take a frying pan big enough to hold both fillets and get it nice and hot over a high heat before adding a tiny smidgen of oil. Put the fish fillets in flesh-side down, where they should sizzle immediately. Put the fish under the grill, fairly close to the element, which will melt the anchovy and faintly char the lemon. Cook for 5 minutes. Because the fish is in a hot pan, it will not need turning over. Err towards under- rather than overcooking. You want that just-past-raw element and a faint translucency in the flesh.

Ideally, serve the fish on lentils dressed with a little red wine vinegar, olive oil and salt. Super-simple and very summery.

Sardines with garlic, coriander & fennel seeds, & sherry vinegar

Serves 2–3

4 tablespoons olive oil
½ teaspoon dried chile flakes
10 small sardines, scaled and gutted
flaked sea salt and black pepper
1 good teaspoon coriander seeds
1 good teaspoon fennel seeds
½ red onion, finely chopped
2 large garlic cloves, finely sliced
a good splash of sherry vinegar
2 tablespoons roughly chopped
   flat-leaf parsley
good bread, to serve

I had spent a considerable amount of the morning writing about food, simplicity and my ongoing quest to remove stages and sometimes ingredients from recipes, as I am increasingly fond of stripped-down cooking, then I went on a walk up Portobello Road in London, bought some particularly good-looking sardines and this is what happened when I got home.

Preheat the grill to its highest setting. Take a large, flameproof frying pan and splash half the oil around the bottom. Scatter over half the chile flakes and lay the sardines on top, head to tail. They should be snug but not stacked. Sprinkle liberally with salt, the rest of the chile and then a grinding of black pepper. Sprinkle over the seeds and red onion. Scatter one sliced garlic clove over the fish. Splash over the rest of the oil and put the sardines under the grill, keeping them quite close to the element. Cook for about 4½ minutes, or until the garlic chips start to brown and you can hear the fish sizzling away. After this time, turn them over and apply the rest of the garlic and a bit more salt and black pepper. Put under the grill for another 4 minutes. They will be done!

Take the pan from under the grill and splash the fish all over with sherry vinegar and scatter with the chopped parsley. Devour with good bread, making sure you wipe torn pieces through the juice and oil in the bottom of the pan.

Boquerónes, but with sardines

Serves 3–4 as a pre-dinner snack

6 small sardines, scaled, gutted and filleted
2½ generous teaspoons flaked sea salt
50ml white wine vinegar
juice of 1 lemon
8 tablespoons good olive oil
black pepper
2 large garlic cloves, finely sliced
2 tablespoons finely sliced flat-leaf parsley
good bread, to serve

Boquerónes are made with anchovies, but I've chosen to replace them with sardines, as many fishmongers do not keep fresh anchovies. Lifted from a plate with a toothpick and eaten in the sunshine, this delicious snack makes me feel like I'm on holiday. If the weather is bad, rub some sun cream under your nose purely for that vacation smell.

Lay the sardine fillets skin-side down in a shallow flat-based dish and scatter the salt evenly all over them. Pour over the vinegar and lemon juice. Turn the fillets over so that the skin is now facing up. Cover the sardines and leave them like this for 2 hours in the fridge.

Briefly rinse the fillets under a cold tap to wash away any excess saltiness. Pat dry with kitchen paper. Lay the fillets on another dish and splash over with a couple of tablespoons of their marinade. Cover with oil, a good grinding of black pepper, the garlic and parsley.

Leave the fillets for another couple of hours in the fridge, covered, to allow them to come into their own. Eat with really good bread and enjoy them with wine.

Anchoïade

Serves 6 as a pre-dinner snack

12 Kalamata olives, pitted
2 garlic cloves, peeled
6–8 good anchovies in oil or salt,
    drained, or rinsed and dried
½ teaspoon dried thyme or rosemary
dried chile flakes to taste (optional)
1 level teaspoon Dijon mustard
3 teaspoons red wine vinegar
4 dessertspoons extra virgin olive oil
15g butter (or 1 more dessertspoon
    olive oil)

To serve

good crusty sourdough baguette
radicchio leaves (optional)

Oh, the anchovy! I love them like a bat loves a moth, like a starfish loves a mussel, like a crow loves a lamb's eye and a blackbird loves a netted raspberry, like a … enough now! Here is one of my favourite ways to eat the anchovy, a pleasant companion on travels with knife and loaf.

Method one: by robot

Put all the ingredients in a small bowl and blitz with a stick blender until totally combined. (This can also be done in a blender but not a food processor, as the quantity of ingredients is too little for the blades to work effectively, unless the kit includes a smaller bowl.)

Method two: by hand

Chop the olives, garlic, anchovies, thyme or rosemary and chile flakes, if using, until finely – or, should I say, microscopically – minced. Whenever you feel you are there, you're probably not, so keep on chopping. When done, put the mixture in a bowl or non-porous mortar and gently pound everything together with the flat end of a rolling pin, or a pestle, until well combined. Stir in the mustard and vinegar, then vigorously beat in the oil and butter with a small whisk. (I like the oil and butter version, but you can always just add a bit more oil – it's up to you.)

Serve with a good crusty sourdough baguette, some radicchio leaves and small beakers of rough white wine.

Lapland fish soup

Serves 6

40g butter

1 teaspoon fennel seeds

3 bay leaves

3 celery sticks, finely sliced

1 onion, cut into medium dice

4 carrots, sliced a little thicker
than the celery

2 potatoes, cut to the size
of board-game dice

flaked sea salt and black pepper

150ml dry white wine

400g whole trout or salmon,
gutted, filleted and skinned

400g whole pollock, gutted,
filleted and skinned

200ml double cream

a handful of dill, finely chopped

I love this soup; it is so deliciously warming. I should know, as it was -43°C when I first ate it. Crilla, our guide, dug a hole in the snow and, using his flint strike, a knife and lichen pulled from the trees, soon had a decent fire going, crackling and popping with green pine needles. The soup was lowered on to the fire in a battered camping pot. Served up in mugs, it did as much for my hands as my tongue. In that clean, frozen air and snowy glare, it was a truly delicate and memorable soup. I foolishly gave the last of the cold remnants to my favourite dog, which sparked a brief but bloody fight with the others. When I first tasted this dish, it was made with char, a pretty trout native to Sweden, and grayling, an unlikely looking member of the same family. We ignore grayling in the UK kitchen, but if you fish or know someone who does, I recommend you try eating one. I have replaced the char with trout and the grayling with pollock. Pollock must be very, very fresh in order to deliver its potential.

Slowly melt the butter in a medium saucepan with the fennel seeds and bay leaves. Add all the vegetables, turn up the heat a little, then sweat them with the lid on, stirring occasionally, until they are soft but not coloured. This should take about 20 minutes. Season the vegetables well. Add the wine, replace the lid and simmer until the potatoes are just cooked (another 5–6 minutes or so).

Meanwhile, cut up the fish into good mouthful-sized chunks. In the pollock you may find a row of short pin bones between the fillet and the belly; cut on either side of this row and pull the strip out. Carefully drop the fish into the saucepan, then gently and briefly turn it through the vegetables. Add enough water to just cover the fish. When all the liquid comes up to a simmer, barely cook the fish (for no more than 4 minutes), as you really want it to be as tender as possible. Remember that in the time it takes to add the cream and then serve the soup it will still be cooking.

Pour in the cream and stir it through oh so delicately so as not to break up the fish. Taste the stock to check the seasoning. Scatter the dill over the soup. Need I say ... serve promptly.

Mackerel sweet-and-sour

Serves 2–4

2 very fresh whole medium mackerel,
   gutted, filleted and pin-boned
2 tablespoons cornflour
½ teaspoon fine sea salt
3 tablespoons sunflower oil
boiled or egg-fried white rice, to serve

Sweet-and-sour sauce

2 large spring onions
2 tablespoons sunflower oil
2 garlic cloves, finely chopped
5cm piece of root ginger, peeled
   and finely chopped
2 teaspoons dark soy sauce
1 tablespoon rice wine vinegar
1 tablespoon soft brown sugar
3 tablespoons tomato ketchup
1½ teaspoons nam pla
   (Thai fish sauce)
100ml cold water
200g pineapple (weight after
   being peeled and cored), cut
   into mouth-sized chunks
1 finger-length dried red chile,
   deseeded and chopped into 3
1 teaspoon cornflour
black pepper

With so many mackerel coming into my kitchen over the summer and autumn, I'm endlessly trying to think of new ways to enjoy them. I could write a book on mackerel recipes alone. I didn't think of sweet-and-sour until recently, and now I like it so much I have not tried anything else new for a while.

To make the sauce, slice the white part of the spring onions lengthways into quarters. Cut the quarters in half across the middle. Cut the green parts lengthways into strands and set aside. Heat the oil in a large frying pan or wok until very hot. Add the white part of the onions, the garlic and ginger. Stir-fry for 30 seconds. Reduce the heat and stir in the soy sauce, vinegar, sugar, tomato ketchup, fish sauce and the cold water. Cook for a few seconds, stirring, until the sauce is well combined, then add the pineapple and chile. Cook for 3–4 minutes until the pineapple is softened and the sauce is hot. Mix the cornflour with 1 tablespoon cold water and stir into the sauce. Cook until thickened and glossy and season with plenty of black pepper.

Cut each fish fillet into three pieces and toss with the cornflour and salt on a plate until evenly coated. Pour the oil into a small, nonstick frying pan or wok and put over a high heat. When the oil is hot, drop the floured fish pieces into the pan using tongs and regulate the heat so as not to burn them. Fry hard for about 2 minutes on each side until golden and crisp. Drain on kitchen paper. Do this in batches and keep the cooked fish in a warm oven.

Reheat the sweet-and-sour sauce until bubbling, then spoon it into warmed dishes and place the hot fish on top. Scatter the chopped green spring onion on top. Serve immediately with steamed or egg-fried rice.

Warm smoked mackerel with celeriac remoulade

Serves 6 as a pre-dinner snack

1 whole smoked mackerel
   (about 450g)

Remoulade

2 large free-range egg yolks
2 generous teaspoons good
   Dijon mustard
1 teaspoon wholegrain mustard
3–4 teaspoons white wine vinegar,
   or to taste
150ml sunflower oil
50ml good extra virgin olive oil
flaked sea salt
½ medium celeriac (about 500g)

To serve

a loaf of good rustic
   sourdough bread or Poilâne
a little cold unsalted butter
black pepper
lemon halves

This is the kind of thing I love to eat at home on one of those unexplainably relaxed and scruffy days, when small beakers of wine keep being poured; the kind of day you'd happily wear that pair of trousers that you'd never wear in public. This is simple to scrabble together, punchy in taste and has a wonderful combination of soft and crunchy textures. Perfect!

Smoked mackerel is nice,
but twice nicer when warmed,
and it is with this dish
that my verdict is formed!

Make the remoulade. Into a food processor drop the egg yolks. (Keep the whites if you plan to make meringue or the diet omelette of a neurotic luvvy.) Add the mustards and vinegar. Whizz until all are combined. Slowly add the sunflower oil in a thin stream. Soon the mayonnaise will thicken and become glossy. If at any point the mixture appears to be getting too rigid, let it down with the tiniest drop of warm water and then keep on as you were. Now add the olive oil slowly (and the same applies to adding warm water to adjust the thickness). The mayonnaise should have a creamy texture, just holding its own, and have a nice edge but not be overly tart – you can add more vinegar (or maybe a splash of lemon juice) if necessary, but remember you can't take it out. Add salt to your liking, making sure it is properly stirred in before adding more.

Cut away the thick skin from the celeriac to get to the pure white flesh, removing any of the faint swirly marbled appearance on the surface. On a mandolin, or with a very sharp knife, slice the celeriac to the thinness of a 1p coin. Lay the pieces on top of each other in batches, and with a large, sharp knife, slice the celeriac into as thin threads as possible. Do this as quickly as possible – if the celeriac is left to idle on the board, it will discolour.

Drop the celeriac into a mixing bowl and flop in enough mayonnaise to luxuriously cover the pieces once mixed well together (any additional mayonnaise is always a good thing to have in the fridge). Leave to stand for half an hour or so to let the celeriac relax its form.

Preheat the oven to 160°C fan/180°C/Gas 4. Slice the bread and have it ready to go down in the toaster. Place the fish on a baking tray and warm in the oven for about 6 minutes. If using a whole mackerel, leave the golden-brown skin on – people can remove it before eating and it looks pretty. Toast the bread as the fish heats.

Assemble the plate with the toast, a generous slice of cold butter, the remoulade and lastly the warmed mackerel. A black pepper grinder and some additional lemon halves for squeezing are good to have nearby.

Dorset breakfast

Serves 1

The fish

1 small, very fresh whole mackerel,
  head and tail left on but gutted
  and degilled
a little olive oil
flaked sea salt and black pepper

The eggs

15–20g butter
2 large free-range eggs
flaked sea salt and black pepper

The rest

15g butter
a good slice of Bramley apple
flaked sea salt
2 slices of black pudding,
  or more if small
toast

There is no such thing as a Dorset Breakfast, generally – but there is in my life. This is the sum parts of my friend Elaine's breakfast offerings and my love of mackerel fishing. The following combination might seem downright bizarre, but let me tell you it all works really well, although a certain amount of synchronisation is involved, as with all multi-part cooked breakfasts. This breakfast was banned in my sister's house in Dorset for a year, due to some West Bay mackerel being left in her fridge-freezer unannounced and it breaking down shortly afterwards when she was away for three weeks.

Preheat the grill to its highest setting. Lightly oil and salt the mackerel and grill it on a baking tray for about 4 minutes on each side, close enough to the element to nicely blister and brown.

Get going on the rest. Melt the butter in a large frying pan. Sprinkle the apple with a little salt and sugar, then fry in the butter with the black pudding, turning them over after 4 minutes or so (the apple should pick up some good colour and the black pudding should be crispy on both sides).

Get the eggs started by melting the butter in a small nonstick pan, then breaking in the eggs. Stir them continuously over a very low heat for 4–5 minutes; I like them really soft and slightly runny (and strictly no milk). Season with a pinch of salt and a good grinding of black pepper.

Of course, it's quite hard to write this recipe, as any cooked breakfast is a juggling act between the oven and various pans. Needless to say, all parts should cross the finish line at the same time. Damn, I forgot to mention the toast! Don't let the toast be the straggler that finishes last and lets a good breakfast go cold.

Arrange everything on the plate how you like it – egg on the toast or not, according to your neurosis. All combinations on the fork are good. I highly recommend a local newspaper and a cup of instant coffee with this, followed by a trip to the seaside.

Tuna tartare

Serves 2 (or 4 as a starter)

200g very fresh sustainable yellow
   fin tuna loin (preferably from just
   behind the head)
1/3 medium–small fennel bulb,
   trimmed
1/4 medium–small red onion
a small handful of coriander leaves
1/3 dried red chile
1/2 small garlic clove, peeled
2 dessertspoons pine nuts
1 very good medium orange
juice of 1/2 small lemon
3 dessertspoons extra virgin olive oil
flaked sea salt and black pepper

I find the sheer rawness of a fish tartare exciting and invigorating, and
I'm sure I can feel the various departments of my body taking the specific
nourishment they need. This is more of a Sicilian than a French approach,
made using pine nuts, orange and chile. It needs nothing but a fork to help
it towards the mouth (having said that, I do like a little pert salad with it).
Super-fresh and rigid mackerel is a good replacement for tuna. I specify
yellow fin tuna because blue fin tuna is nearly extinct and should definitely
not be eaten.

Lay the tuna on a board and cut it lengthways into thin slices (about 5mm
thick). Cut each slice into thin strips and then into very fine dice. Use a very
sharp knife, as a blunt one will mash the splendid fish. Place the tuna in a
good-sized mixing bowl. Minutely dice the fennel and onion and add to the
tuna. If there are any little feathered leaves on the fennel, chop them with the
coriander and then add these too. Chop the chile and garlic microscopically
fine and drop them in. Scatter in the whole pine nuts and the finely grated
zest from a quarter of the orange.

Squeeze the juice from half the orange and add the lemon juice and oil to the
bowl followed by a vigorous grinding of black pepper and a confident amount
of salt. Gently combine everything together, making sure it is thoroughly mixed.

Gently press the tartare into moulds, such as small teacups, and upend each
portion on a plate. Serve immediately. If you want, accompany with a little
salad dressed with balsamic vinegar, olive oil and salt, and a couple of good
cherry tomatoes.

Tuna tostada

Serves 6

1 large ripe Hass avocado, stoned,
  peeled and roughly diced
juice of 1 lime
a small handful of coriander leaves,
  chopped, plus extra leaves to serve
flaked sea salt
6 large or 12 small corn tortillas,
  for frying
sunflower oil, for frying
1 medium red onion, halved
  and very finely sliced
300g very fresh sustainable yellow fin
  tuna (in a block, not cut into steaks)
a little dried oregano

Chipotle mayonnaise

4 chipotle chiles (smoked jalapeños)
2 good teaspoons tomato purée
a generous pinch of ground cumin
1 teaspoon cider vinegar
4 generous dessertspoons basic
  shop-bought mayonnaise

I seem to write repeatedly about the restaurant Contra Mar in Mexico City and this is because it is my favourite place in the world to eat fish. On one trip, I went every day to try to eat the complete menu. This is one of my favourite dishes, recreated as well as I can remember it. You must eat in Contra Mar should you be visiting Mexico City, bearing in mind that the restaurant is only open for lunch and has no booking, so you can be sure of a queue.

First make the mayonnaise. Cut the stalk from the chipotle chiles, then open them up and remove the seeds. Pour over just enough boiled water to cover them and leave to rehydrate for at least an hour or two, or until swollen. Discard the water and use a blender to purée them finely with the vinegar, tomato purée, cumin and mayonnaise. (The cumin should only be the faintest suggestion and not overwhelming, and the mayonnaise will probably need letting down with a little water first, as it should be droppy and not too stiff.)

Mash the avocado with the lime juice and most of the coriander, then season well with salt and leave to one side. Trim the tortillas, cutting around a template so that they are about 8cm in diameter. (This seems a wasteful shame, but they are better served small and snack-like. You can used the trimmings to thicken Mexican soups, or deep-fry them and serve with guacamole. You might also get two rounds from one large tortilla.) Heat a pan filled with 5cm oil to 180°C (do not allow the oil to overheat). Fry the tortillas in it for about 40 seconds on each side until they are a rich gold, then drain on kitchen paper. Your fried tortilla is now a tostada. Carefully fry the onion slices in the oil for 6 minutes, stirring every now and again, until they are golden brown all over. Transfer them quickly to some kitchen paper to drain and crisp up.

Slice the tuna thinly (about 3mm) across the grain of the meat, as you would a fillet of beef. Take six plates and lay two tostadas on each one. Smear a good dessertspoon of the avocado mixture evenly over each tostada; it should not be a mean scraping. Lay three or four slices of tuna on top, slightly overlapping the pieces. Season the raw tuna with a good pinch of salt. Artfully dribble a couple of teaspoons of the chipotle mayonnaise over the fish. Sprinkle over some of the crispy onions followed by a tiny pinch of dried oregano. Finish with a few pert coriander leaves. When assembling this, remember that every bite should be the sum of all parts.

Eat immediately, outside, with a bottle of ice-cold beer.

Cod with mussels & celery

Serves 4

1kg live large mussels

2 level teaspoons coriander seeds

2 tablespoons olive oil

4 green celery sticks, sliced on a
   severe diagonal

3 fat garlic cloves, finely sliced

150ml good dry white wine

600g skinned sustainable line-caught
   cod fillet, pollock, or coley,
    the thickest you can find and
    in one piece

flaked sea salt and black pepper

a squeeze of lemon juice (optional)

chopped celery or flat-leaf parsley
   leaves, to garnish (optional)

toast, to serve

This is a gentle dish of wonderful colours. I find this kind of cooking has an uncomplicated and pleasing purity to it. I cannot stress enough that the fresher the cod, the better. I like to get a piece of fish that is very thick, cut by the fishmonger to my specification. Bigger is better, but if you get a smaller fillet, it will just need less time to cook.

Should you want to make the dish a little more substantial, serve the cod and soup over large, thin slices of French bread that have been well grilled and splashed with olive oil, and accompany with garlic mayonnaise.

Tip the mussels into the sink. Any mussel you find already open is not necessarily dead. Tap it on the edge of the sink. If it closes and remains tightly shut, it's a good 'un; if it stays open, then alas, it is dead. Discard. Pick up each remaining mussel, grab hold of the little green beard protruding from the side and pull it forward until it comes away. It may require a little tugging, as the mussel is loathe to let it go. Fair enough! Scrub the mussels well, scraping off any barnacles with the back of a knife, and drop into a colander. Give them a final rinse under the tap.

Drop the coriander seeds into a flameproof casserole and toast them very gently over a medium heat until their smell comes to the nose, then add the oil. Add the celery and fry it gently for 6 minutes until it begins to soften (don't allow it to colour). Throw in the garlic 2 minutes before the end.

Add the mussels to the pan, then pour over the white wine. Cover with the lid and cook for 2–3 minutes, stirring once, until all the mussels have only just been steamed open. It is important not to overcook them, as they will lose their juicy quivering succulence. Take the pan off the heat, remove the mussels with a slotted spoon and transfer to a bowl, leaving the liquor and celery in the pan. Set them aside for about 3 minutes, or until cool enough to handle.

Place the fish in the casserole and season well. Bring the liquid up to a gentle simmer before covering the cod with the lid. Cook over a medium heat for 15–18 minutes, or until the fish is only just cooked. You want the flakes to part but with the faintest resistance.

While the fish cooks, discard any mussels that haven't opened. Remove the mussel flesh from half the shells and set aside with the unpicked ones. This makes eating easier whilst retaining an element of set design. Pour any extra mussel liquor that collects in the bowl back into the casserole.

When the fish has cooked, return the picked mussel flesh and remaining mussels in shells to the pot, cover and heat through for 1 minute more until hot. Add a squeeze of lemon, if you like. Serve in deep, warmed plates garnished with plenty of chopped celery or parsley leaves, if liked, and accompanied with toast.

Endive salad with smoked cod roe dressing

Serves 4

Smoked cod roe dressing

80g smoked cod roe
1 teaspoon Dijon mustard
1 free-range egg yolk
juice of ½ large lemon
4 tablespoons light olive oil
1 garlic clove, crushed

Croûtons

50g good rustic bread
2 tablespoons extra virgin olive oil

Salad

2 carrots, peeled
4 Jerusalem artichokes, peeled
   just before using
1 head of endive
a large handful of watercress
10 large radishes, sliced lengthways
1 tablespoon extra virgin olive oil
lemon juice, to taste
dried chile flakes, to taste

This was the result of using up leftovers from a week of shooting recipes for this book. We were all cooked out and liverish, and I felt a little lazy when throwing everything together; but this is often the way good things are found.

Start by making the dressing and croûtons. Preheat the grill to its highest setting. Mash the cod roe with the mustard, egg yolk and lemon juice, then slowly whisk in the light olive oil. When the oil is incorporated, slowly add warm water in the same way until the consistency of the dressing is like pouring double cream. Stir in the crushed garlic. To make the croûtons, rip up the bread into about 1cm chunks, toss with the extra virgin olive oil and then place under the grill, or fry, turning occasionally until golden brown.

To make the salad, shave the carrots lengthways with a potato peeler into the salad bowl and do the same with the Jerusalem artichokes. Pull the leaves off the endive and roughly snap them up, then add to the salad with the watercress, followed by the sliced radishes. Splash the oil over and follow with a little lemon juice and chile flakes according to taste. The lemon juice should definitely be present but not overwhelming.

Toss the croûtons through the salad and spoon over the dressing to your preference. Eat immediately.

Salt pollock with peppers, oranges & chickpeas

Serves 4

450g pollock from the thick end
   of the fillet (the tail will not do)
2 tablespoons coarse rock salt
3 red peppers
2 large oranges
½ × 400g can chickpeas, drained
   and rinsed
2 garlic cloves, very finely chopped
⅓ medium red onion, finely sliced
2 handfuls of marjoram
5 tablespoons full-bodied olive oil
1 generous tablespoon sherry vinegar
crusty bread, to serve (optional)

The pollock must be prepared 24 hours in advance. Home-made salt pollock will give you a gentler result than the pale, bullet-stopping block of toughened salt cod found in Spanish or Portuguese shops (which in any case can be tricky to buy and a bother to soak).

The night before you want to eat, lay the pollock, skin-side down, in a soup plate and scatter the salt evenly over the flesh. Cover with clingfilm and place in the fridge. Leave for 24 hours.

The next day, heat some water to a gentle simmer in a saucepan big enough to welcome the pollock. In the meantime, put the peppers over a direct flame or close to the element of a preheated grill, turning them occasionally, until totally blackened and charred. Allow to cool.

Rinse the salt from the surface of the pollock and lay it in the water; it should be totally covered. Bring the water back to a gentle simmer and cook the fish for 8 minutes until it wants to separate with a little prompting and the middle of each flake is ever so sticky and translucent. Tip away the water and allow the fish to cool.

Cut the top and bottom from each of the oranges and stand them on a board. Cut the skin and pith off all the way round. Hold each orange over the serving bowl and use a small knife to cut out the segments from the membranes so that they fall in. If a lot of juice seeps from the fruit, drain it into a glass and drink it – the final dish must not be sodden with orange juice. Add the chickpeas and garlic to the bowl, followed by the red onion.

Remove the charred skin from each pepper, remembering that a black fleck here or there is not a problem. Remove the seeds and white membrane from inside. On no account wash off the skin or seeds, as a lot of the charred flavour and sweetness will be rinsed away. Tear the peppers into long, thin strips and put them into the serving bowl.

Gently lift the pollock from the pot, peel away the skin and separate the large flakes carefully, removing any bones. Lower the flakes into the serving dish. Pick the marjoram in tiny little tufts, only including the tenderest stalks. Scatter the marjoram into the bowl. Add the oil and vinegar, then, in no more than a few gentle turns with your hands, combine the ingredients with the same care you would use when handling a newborn, ensuring that the orange segments do not break up.

Serve with good rough, crusty bread, if liked.

Kedgeree

Serves 2–4

200ml whole milk

150ml cold water

2 bay leaves

400g undyed sustainable smoked
  haddock, smoked pollock
  or smoked coley (ideally use
  the wide end of the fillet to
  get bigger flakes)

60g butter

1 large onion, cut into small, neat dice

seeds from 8 green cardamom pods,
  crushed

1 teaspoon turmeric

1 heaped teaspoon mild curry powder

basmati rice, measured up to the 125g
  mark of a measuring jug

a pinch of saffron (optional)

4 free-range eggs

a handful of finely chopped curly-leaf
  parsley

flaked sea salt and black pepper

lemon wedges, to serve

For me, when the weekend allows more time and a leisurely pyjama-ed pace, this is a truly splendid, buttery, smoky, spiced, yellow breakfast from a time when breakfast was taken as seriously as it should be. Great with tea, but fabulous around eleven o'clock with a cold gin and tonic garnished with a slice of cucumber in place of lemon.

Take a saucepan with a tight-fitting lid and pour in the milk and water. Add one of the bay leaves and bring the liquid up to a gentle simmer. Gently lay the haddock in the saucepan, skin-side down, and once the simmering returns, poach it gently for 3–4 minutes with the lid on the pan. Turn off the heat and lift the fish out very gently. The delicate handling of the haddock should be compared to that of bathing an infant. The fillets should separate when broken by hand, but with each flake ever so slightly reluctant to separate from its fellows. This all sounds a bit over the top, but if the fish has lost its faint translucence and falls apart with ease, the dish is not going to be so good. Flake all the fish on to a plate, being careful to remove any bones and skin, and put to one side. Allow the milk to cool in a bowl, adding enough water to make it up to 300ml, if necessary. Wash the pan.

Melt the butter in the same saucepan over a medium heat and add the onion with the remaining bay leaf and the cardamom (discard the husks or keep them in sugar, like you would vanilla pods, as this is very pleasant when stirred into a punchy little post-lunch coffee). Fry the onion for 7–10 minutes or so, stirring regularly, until it is very soft and deep golden. Sprinkle in the turmeric and curry powder and cook for a further minute or two before carefully turning the mixture out on to the plate with the fish. Don't bother cleaning the pan.

Tip the rice into the pan, followed by 300ml of the fish cooking liquid and the saffron, if using. (Using milk to poach the haddock as well as water gives the dish an added richness.) Put a lid on the pan and bring the rice and stock up to a brisk but not out-of-control simmer. Cook the rice for 11 minutes without removing the lid again. Turn off the heat, lift off the lid and put a once-folded napkin or tea towel over the pan before returning the lid as snugly as possible. Left like this for 8 minutes, the cloth will absorb steam from the rice making it good and dry for fluffing.

While the rice is cooking, soft-boil the eggs. Heat another pan filled with just-boiled kettle water. Bring to the boil. Cook the eggs in the rolling water for 5 minutes so that they cross the finish line at the same time as the rice comes off the heat. Drain the eggs and briefly rinse under cold water as you peel them.

Remove the lid and napkin or tea towel from the rice and fluff gently with two forks. Place it over a medium–low heat. Tip in the onions and stir through thoroughly. Follow with the haddock and parsley, taking real care not to bash the fish flakes up too much. When all is nicely warmed and the seasoning has been checked, divide the kedgeree between plates and crown each with a soft egg cut in half and nicely seasoned. Garnish each plate with a lemon wedge. If accompanying with a G and T, Miller's gin or Sipsmith are my favourites.

» Note: Now, on the subject of peas, I like kedgeree both with them and without, but some people get really antsy, saying that peas have no place in the dish at all. Here is a quote from the great food writer Waverley Root on the subject of lobster belonging, or not, in bouillabaisse. For some, it applies when hijacked for kedgeree: 'A man who does not put lobster in bouillabaisse would starve his children. A man who does would poison wells.' Do what you like. If you do want peas, pop them in the boiling water before the eggs, then add to the rice.

Taramasalata

Serves 6

150g smoked cod roe
40g stale white bread, no crusts
½ red onion
1 good hard garlic clove, finely
    chopped
150–200ml light olive oil
60–70ml water
juice of ¾ lemon
hot pitta bread, to serve

Do away with that horrible pink stuff and try this instead.

Make an incision down one side of the skin of the roe, open it up and use a teaspoon to scrape out the eggs, then drop them into a food processor. Grate the stale bread (which should be nice and dry) into fine crumbs and add these to the roe. Coarsely grate the onion through the setting on your grater that you would do a kiddie's Cheddar for Bolognese, then scrape into a small sieve positioned over the processor bowl and use a spoon to press the juice through the sieve over the roe and the bread. Discard the pulp. Add the garlic to the mix.

Secure the lid of the processor and hit go. Now slowly dribble in the oil. The mixture will become quite thick. At this point, add the water and lemon juice according to your judgement, stopping the motor every now and again to taste the taramasalata so as to get the right consistency and acidity; you can put lemon in, but you can't take it out. The mixture should not be too loose, but only just hold its own and be very smooth and creamy.

Scrape the contents into a bowl. Eat, remembering in your eagerness not to ambush your delicate fingertips on the hot steam within the pitta bread. I like to have butter on the pitta as well as tarama.

Cockle chowder

Serves 4–6

35g butter
200g thick-sliced smoked ham, chopped into pieces the size of sugar lumps
1 small onion, finely chopped
1 long celery stick, finely sliced
leaves from 1 good sprig of thyme, finely chopped
1 garlic clove, finely chopped
a generous grating of nutmeg
2 small bay leaves
flaked sea salt and black pepper
900ml whole milk
kernels cut from 1 large corn cob
1 large baking potato, such as Maris Piper, peeled and diced to the size of a sugar lump
400g cooked plump picked cockles
150ml double cream
salted crackers, to serve

This is true comfort food and can be thrown together in a trice. Heartening and sweet, full of surf-and-turf goodies, this dish is my understanding of the phrase 'warms the cockles of your heart'. Use fresh-picked cockle meat and not the sour little duds bottled in vinegar. Fishmongers usually sell the picked kind, as do some supermarkets.

Melt the butter in a saucepan, then add the ham, onion and celery with the thyme, garlic, nutmeg, bay leaves and plenty of black pepper. Gently sauté for about 10 minutes, or until the onion is totally soft. The vegetables should not be coloured.

Pour in the milk, then add the corn and potato. Simmer until the potato is just tender, but on no account collapsing. At this point, throw in the dear little cockles. Continue to simmer the soup very gently for 2 minutes more – it must not be rapid or the cockles will toughen. Add the cream, stir in some salt and serve in deep bowls with salted crackers. This tastes even better when you are sitting on a wall under a grey sky.

Chickpea & brown shrimp fritters

Serves 2–4

200g chickpea flour
400ml cold water
1 small banana shallot,
   finely chopped
1 large free-range egg
125g cooked whole brown shrimps,
   unpeeled, or ready-prepared peeled
   brown shrimps from a packet
3 tablespoons flat-leaf parsley,
   finely chopped
2 teaspoons flaked sea salt
sunflower oil or light olive oil,
   for frying
lemon wedges, to serve

On a trip to Tarifa in southern Spain, my then girlfriend, now wife, and I found a small and cosy little harbour café with everyone inside drinking sherry and pecking at little plates with toothpicks. Speaking fluent Spanish, she quickly got talking to the waiter, who advised that we try the shrimp fritters. Good idea! We kept on ordering more and more until defeated. I just couldn't leave the last one uneaten on the plate. The air was warm, the beer was cold and the shrimp fritters memorable.

This is my own recipe, as the proprietor only skirted around the quantities. The trick is to make them as thin as you can. If at all possible, the shrimps must be unpeeled, as they will fry to crisp and crunchy. However, as whole brown shrimps are not that easy to find in the UK unless you are by the sea, use the packet peeled ones you would expect to find in potted shrimps.

Mix all the ingredients, apart from the oil and lemon wedges, together, adding enough water to make sure the mixture is the consistency of pancake batter or double cream. It should not be too thin; of its own accord, it must spread out in the pan but not right to the edge.

In a frying pan, heat 4 tablespoons of oil over a medium–high heat. Take a small ladleful of the mixture and pour it into the oil; it should immediately sizzle. (It is important that the fritters are very thin; too thick and they become cakey and unpleasant.) If needs be, gently swirl the underside of the ladle over the mixture to spread it out a bit. Cooking the fritters in small batches, let each one fry for 2–3 minutes or so before lifting it with a spatula, turning it over and frying it on the other side for the same time. If it doesn't appear to be done, then cook for a little longer, maybe turning once more. The fritters should be richly coloured and brown with very crispy edges. You will need to add more oil every so often, as they soak it up when they cook.

Drain the fritters on kitchen paper. It is imperative that they are eaten hot. Serve with lemon wedges and, if desired, cold lager.

Razor clams with chorizo, hazelnuts & tomato

Serves 1, 2 or 4

8 live large razor clams

50ml water

2 medium vine tomatoes, quartered,
deseeded and cut into medium dice

50g chorizo, skinned and cut into
small dice

30g hazelnuts, roughly chopped

3 medium garlic cloves, finely sliced

a handful of flat-leaf parsley,
roughly chopped

finely grated zest of ½ unwaxed
lemon

2 tablespoons olive oil

flaked sea salt and black pepper

a little sherry vinegar

I closely guarded my razor shell collection as a boy, keeping my findings in a little wooden box, occasionally poring over them like a miser over gold coins. I had no idea that this currency was the scabbard of a creature I would grow up to eat with a passion.

Seeing razor clams bundled like Cuban cigars in an elastic band, pale feet lolling out like the tongues of tired horses, I feel sad, as I'm sure they also have the gentlest of temperaments. The problem is they are delicious and some of the sweetest of all shellfish. In this particular recipe, I have done a Spanish number on them, as chorizo works excellently with their meat.

Preheat the a grill to its highest setting. Put a saucepan big enough to fit all the clams over a medium heat. When hot, drop in the clams with the water and cover the pan with a lid. Steam the razors for 2 minutes, or until they have just opened. Remove them from the pan and allow them to cool on a plate. Meanwhile, mix together the tomatoes, chorizo, hazelnuts, garlic and parsley in one bowl and the lemon zest and oil in another.

Open each clam, keeping the shell intact. Pull out the body in one piece, if possible. You will notice a little grey bag in the centre of the body. Carefully cut this out with a small, sharp knife, checking there is no grit left behind, and discard. (This surgery can be done keeping the clam whole, but if it comes in two, no matter.)

Lay each clam back in its full shell and lay them on a small baking tray. Evenly scatter over the tomato, chorizo and hazelnut mixture, then grind over some black pepper and follow with a few pinches of salt. Dribble over the oil, then slide the tray under the grill so that it lies about 12cm under the element. Cook the clams for 4 minutes, or until the hazelnuts and chorizo are a little coloured. Remove from the grill and transfer to a plate. Dress with a little sherry vinegar and any juices left on the baking tray. Eat promptly, then wish you had made more.

Lobster salad

Serves 2

700g live lobster
flaked sea salt and black pepper
1 large ruby grapefruit
1 medium ripe vine tomato,
  chopped into small dice
½ small red onion, finely sliced
2 tablespoons olive oil
juice of ½ lime
1 medium ripe Hass avocado,
  stoned, peeled and cut to the size
  of board-game dice

I love lobster drenched in garlic butter and pay my respects to the grand old Thermidor, but sometimes I want a fresher way, with little tampering. Here's something different that reminds me of the crawfish I have eaten on beaches under the shade of fluttering palms or a crudely rigged-up tarpaulin. Pairing crustacea with grapefruit is nothing new, but the combination is fantastic.

Drop the lobster into a large pan of salted boiling water. Bring it back to the boil, then immediately turn off the heat. Leave the lobster in the pot for 18 minutes before removing and allowing to cool. To remove the meat from the claws, snap them off and put them in a clean kitchen towel. Lightly bash them with a rolling pin, then break them open and extract the meat. Take the tail in your hands and squeeze both sides together until you hear a snapping sound, then peel it as you would a prawn. (Alternatively, you can put it on a work surface, curved-side up, and split it open with a knife.) Remove the meat. Don't be alarmed by any green creamy stuff that goes on to the tail from the head – it is perfectly edible but unsightly in this recipe; wipe it away from the meat, but do not rinse it away, as this will also wash away flavour. Slice the lobster meat into mouthfuls. The head and shells may be frozen and kept for stock.

Cut both ends from the grapefruit, then stand it on a board and cut off all the remaining skin and pith. Holding the fruit in one hand, cut out the flesh from between the membranes. Put the segments in the serving bowl. Add the tomato, onion, oil and lime juice followed by the lobster meat. Season well. The salt is particularly important – a little more than you may normally use will really bring out the taste of the tomato and avocado, which you add last of all. Very carefully turn all the ingredients together, but not too much, as the avocado starts to smear everything. Serve immediately; the salad can become too wet if left to stand for too long.

Grilled squid with haricot beans & chard

Serves 2

45g dried haricot beans,
    soaked in water overnight

1 large ripe vine tomato,
    cut roughly into medium dice

½ small red onion, halved and
    finely sliced

2 tablespoons olive oil,
    plus extra for frying

flaked sea salt and black pepper

juice of ½ lemon

a large chard leaf, green part only,
    cut into ribbons

2 medium squid, cleaned,
    tentacles and fins reserved

12 mint leaves

There are two ways to cook squid; either long and slow (*see* page 155) or nice and quickly. Anything in between results in chewy fish. Provided the beans are pre-boiled, this is a lunch that can be put together very quickly. The fishmonger's habit is to scrape the purple skin from the squid's flesh. This is a shame, as when cooked it provides a great taste and a dramatic colour; ask them not to.

Drain the pre-soaked beans and then boil in fresh water for 1–1¼ hours, making sure they're always covered in water, until tender to the bite. Drain them and allow them to cool a little. Just before cooking the squid, tip the beans into a bowl and combine them with the tomato, onion, oil, 1 teaspoon salt and the lemon juice, then turn the chard ribbons through the beans.

Open up the squid cones, purple skin-side facing the board. Holding a knife at a 45-degree angle, criss-cross the flesh with diagonal shallow incisions about 5mm apart to make a diamond grid. Rub a generous amount of oil into the scored flesh and then do the same to the tentacles and fins.

Put a large frying pan (big enough to take all the squid in one layer) on a very high heat and get the pan hot, hot, hot. Salt the squid generously. Take the cones and lay them scored-side down; they should sizzle immediately. If you do not hear this noise, the pan isn't hot enough. Put in the rest of the squid and leave all to fry hard. After 30 seconds the main body of the squid should start to curl up like a carpet rolled from both ends. This might need a little prompting, which you can do with your fingers by bending in each end to get it going. You want the meat to pick up a lot of colour and get that wonderful sweet toffee-ish residue so particular to this fine cephalopod. Turn the legs and fins around every now and again. After 5 minutes your squid should be ready, leaving you with two pipes of squid and well-browned extremities.

Finally, add the mint leaves to the salad (don't add them any earlier, as they wilt easily) along with a grinding of black pepper. Toss together and divide between two plates. Position your squid in the middle, legs draped over the body. Spoon some of the salty, tart tomato dressing from the bottom of the salad bowl over the squid. Eat immediately.

Squid with tomatoes & brandy

Serves 4–6

50g butter

2 medium onions,
   very finely chopped

leaves from 3 sprigs of thyme,
   chopped

2 bay leaves

flaked sea salt and black pepper

5 good ripe vine tomatoes

6 garlic cloves, finely chopped

1 large (about 1kg) or 2 small
   (about 500g each) squid
   or cuttlefish, tentacles and fins
   reserved, cleaned

2½ tablespoons light olive oil
   or sunflower oil

100ml water

1 dessertspoon tomato purée

125ml brandy

4 tablespoons double cream

a good handful of finely chopped
   curly-leaf parsley

buttered long-grain rice, to serve
   (optional)

This is rich and eye-rollingly delicious. It is important to use really large squid (be careful to remove any harpoons or sailors when preparing it). Prepared with littl'uns, the dish lacks the robust flavour and chunkiness that suit it. After cooking, there will be a little more washing up than normal, but it is really worth it and some dishes just demand that. To make it go further, canned cannellini, flageolet or haricot beans are fab with this, added 5 minutes before the end of cooking.

In a flameproof casserole, melt the butter and add the onions, thyme and bay leaves with a good grinding of black pepper. Fry gently for about 15 minutes, stirring occasionally, until golden and totally soft. While the onions fry, cut out the stems of the tomatoes and criss-cross the bottoms. Place in a deep bowl and steep in just-boiled water until covered. Leave them here for no more than a minute before draining away the water. Pull the skin from the tomatoes, then discard. Tear each tomato open and pull out the seeds over a bowl so as to reserve them with the juices. Put the flesh into a blender and purée. At this point, stir the garlic into the onion, then add the tomato flesh. Hold a sieve over the pan and pour in the seeds, pressing as much juice through with a spoon as you can – you have got the maximum out of your tomatoes. Stir all together well and allow to cook for a couple of minutes or so, then turn off the heat.

Cut the squid or cuttlefish in half lengthways down the cone and open both pieces out. Thoroughly dry off any wetness from the seafood with kitchen paper. It must be as dry as possible, as it will fry and colour better. Chop each half into 2cm-wide ribbons. Cut up the tentacles and fins to a similar size. Put all the flesh in a bowl with the oil and mix well so that it is evenly coated.

Put a large frying pan on a high heat. When the pan is intensely hot, throw in a third of the squid or cuttlefish with a really generous pinch of salt. Fry hard, stirring occasionally, until very well coloured. Repeat in batches twice more (including more of the salt and oil). Add each batch to the onions when completed. Be careful to include what I can only describe as the sticky 'squid toffee' that will gather in the bottom of the pan. (If it could be turned into crisps, I would eat it regularly.) This is very tasty and will lend a lot to the stew – whatever cannot be scraped up with a spoon can be lifted at the end by diluting with a splash of water.

Return the casserole to the heat and add the water and tomato purée. Stir well and bring to a simmer. Add 100ml of the brandy and put the lid on. Simmer gently for 40 minutes (if using cuttlefish, cook it for a little longer; remembering you may need to add more water) and then another 20 with the lid slightly off, allowing the juices to reduce a little. The seafood should be perfectly tender. Stir in the remaining brandy and the cream and serve scattered all over with the parsley. Add more salt if necessary.

This goes well next to some buttered long-grain rice pressed into a cup and upended on to the warm plate in a perfect mound. Nice!

Spaghetti vongole

Serves 2

1kg live palourde clams,
    well scrubbed

flaked sea salt and black pepper

3 tablespoons olive oil

3 medium garlic cloves, finely sliced

100ml dry white wine

150g dried spaghetti

35g butter, chilled, cut into
    small cubes

leaves from a large handful of young
    flat-leaf parsley, finely chopped

This is my favourite spaghetti dish, enjoyed even more at an outside table with hectic Italian waiters dashing around under the sun. Sometimes I order this dish only to find tomato in it, which I do not care for. There are two versions of this dish, so check first.

Although clams can be bought all year round, post February they are thin and wasted, but start fattening up over summer for the coming cold. Come October, they are good to go again.

A problem with palourde clams is that occasionally there is an innocent-looking saboteur in the bag: a dead one with both shells glued together with silt. Sometimes, as I stare sadly into my muddy grey sauce, I think 'that just couldn't be helped', but there are measures that can be taken. Tip the fresh clams in a large colander and agitate them under cold fast-running water for a minute or so. Apart from washing away any exterior sand, the shaking will hopefully break open potentially offending clams and reveal their dark designs.

Tap each clam on the side of the sink and discard any that don't shut tightly – they are dead. Bring a large saucepan of lightly salted water to the boil. Heat the oil in another largish pan that owns a lid and fry the garlic gently for 30 seconds or so until softened but not coloured. Increase the heat, then add the clams and wine and cover tightly. Cook for just 3–4 minutes, shaking the pan every now and then. The clams should have only just opened. Take great care not to overcook them.

Remove the pan from the heat. Lift the clams out with a slotted spoon and put them into a bowl. Return the pan to the hob and simmer until the liquid is reduced by half, then turn off the heat. Remove half the clams from their shells and leave the others untouched. This provides less work when eating, but keeps a little of the theatre. Discard any clams that haven't opened.

Add the spaghetti to the boiling water and cook for around 8–10 minutes until only just tender, stirring occasionally to keep the strands separate. Just before draining the pasta, bring the clam liquor up to a simmer and drop in the cold butter cubes two at a time, whisking constantly until the sauce thickens.

Drain the spaghetti in a colander and tip it into the sauce. Add all the clams, with a good grinding of black pepper and the chopped parsley. Toss everything together well and serve pronto. Some may like a squeeze of fresh lemon juice, but not I.

Paella

Serves 6

4 tablespoons olive oil
4 chicken thighs, each chopped into
   3 through the bone to give 12 pieces of
   chicken (ask your butcher to do this)
2 teaspoons flaked sea salt
1 large onion, cut into medium dice
2 bay leaves
1 large red pepper, cored, deseeded
   and sliced
225g young runner beans, topped, tailed
   and de-strung, cut into diagonal slices
4 garlic cloves, very finely chopped
1 large ripe tomato, very finely chopped
1 level teaspoon saffron threads
1 teaspoon pimentón
   (smoked Spanish paprika)
black pepper
1¼ litres cold water,
   or fish or chicken stock
300g paella rice (medium-grain rice)
500g live mussels, cleaned, beards
   removed
500g live clams, well scrubbed
250g uncooked shell-on
   Mediterranean prawns
1 medium squid, cleaned and cut into
   5mm rings, the tentacles cut down the
   middle
lemon wedges, for squeezing

No wonder the Spanish are so proud when they have dishes like this! In the UK, it is all too easy to find paella with bizarrely yellow, porridge-like or dried-out rice, sporting a couple of wretched prawns with a withered mussel or two. To be fair, Spanish tourist traps can produce something equally miserable. But when good, paella is fabulous and is uncomplicated to make, although it does require concentration and timing. When it's cooked over a barbecue, the extra ingredient of wood smoke adds an even more delightful element. Although many paellas are made with both chicken and fish stock, water does the trick well, provided enough goodies are in the rice to create a fabulous stock. Other versions of the dish I've tried from mountain regions contain rabbit and snails, but this feast of shellfish, chicken and succulent rice is the story I'm going to tell.

Heat the oil in a paella pan at least 40cm in diameter, or large frying pan, over a medium–high heat. Season the chicken thighs very generously with the salt and fry until well browned on all sides, turning occasionally. Add the onion and bay leaves and stir in well. Cook for 4–5 minutes until softened and lightly browned. Add the red pepper and runner beans and cook for a couple of minutes before adding the garlic. Toss everything together for a minute more, then add the tomato and continue cooking for another 2 minutes or so.

Scatter the saffron and pimentón into the pan, season with black pepper and stir. Pour over the water and bring up to a fairly rapid simmer. Leave to cook for 15 minutes, stirring occasionally.

Stir in the rice, making sure the majority of it goes into the stock rather than being left stranded on jutting pieces of veg and chicken, like stranded sailors on a rock. Simmer for a further 8 minutes, or until the rice is beginning to get tender.

Meanwhile, pick through the mussels and clams, discarding any that are broken or that fail to close when tapped on the side of the sink.

Scatter the mussels and clams over the paella and then shuffle them into the rice with a little help of a spoon if needs be. Do the same with the prawns and continue to simmer for a further 12 minutes. Once everything is in, don't stir the pan, as a tasty, toffee-ish, light crustiness wants to form on the bottom. However, a small sampling here and there will help you regulate the heat, as it should not taste burnt. Add the squid about 5 minutes before the end of cooking and stir it lightly into the top of the rice.

When the liquid has been absorbed, the prawns are pink, the shellfish are presenting their goodies, the squid is cooked and the rice is tender yet firm, it is done. Pick out any molluscs that haven't opened. Serve immediately with wedges of lemon to squeeze over.

King scallops, two ways

**Serves 2 as a starter,
4 as a pre-starter**

*Way 1: Raw, with ponzu sauce
and ginger*

3cm piece of *kombu*
75ml *mirin*
75ml Japanese soy sauce
(please use a new bottle)
juice of ½ medium lemon
1 tablespoon sesame seeds
4 large king scallops, cleaned, corals
discarded and deep half-shells
reserved
1 small thumb-sized piece of very
fresh root ginger, peeled, finely
sliced and pieces shredded
lengthways into thin hairs
1 spring onion, finely sliced

**Serves 2 as a starter,
4 as a pre-starter**

*Way 2: Cooked, with a sharp
lemon dressing*

1 medium lemon (this should be cut
in half lengthways)
1 tablespoon baby capers, well rinsed
½ small celery stick, de-strung and
very finely chopped
½ small red onion, very finely
chopped
2 tablespoons extra virgin olive oil
flaked sea salt
4 large king scallops, cleaned, corals
and deep half-shells reserved
sunflower oil, for frying

Here are two quick and easy recipes for scallops – one for those who like the scallop raw and one for those who prefer it cooked. I like both ways very much and would urge anyone who has not eaten scallops raw to do so. In the Japanese-style recipe (Way 1), the sweetness of the scallops coupled with the tangy dressing leaves you with a sharp afterglow and a feeling of purity. The Japanese ingredients, such as *kombu* (dried kelp) and *mirin* (Japanese sweet cooking sake), are now available in good supermarkets, health food shops and online. I have made the ponzu sauce in the smallest amount possible. The extra will keep well in the fridge and is excellent in a light lunch, poured over cooked and cooled broccoli, or on grilled mackerel. These two recipes are only worth making with fresh scallops in the shell, which are stratospherically superior to those already hoiked from their home and drowned in a tub of their own juice (poor things!). Ask your fishmonger to prepare the scallops for you if you don't fancy doing it. When cleaning the scallops, it is essential to remove the belt-like membrane from around the flesh, which becomes chewy when cooked and is equally annoying eaten raw. The shells make handy ashtrays for parties, or otherwise a rather fetching bikini top.

Way 1: Under a running tap, rinse away any obvious white salty residue from the *kombu* and put it to one side. Heat the *mirin* in a small saucepan and, when it comes to the boil, turn down the heat and simmer it briskly, evaporating the alcohol, until you are left with a couple of tablespoons worth. Combine the *mirin* and soy sauce in a bowl with the *kombu*, which will give a wonderful marine depth. Add the lemon juice and chill the sauce in the fridge for 1 hour.

Meanwhile, toast the sesame seeds gently in a small frying pan over a medium heat until their smell comes to the nose and they darken a shade in colour. Allow them to cool on a plate.

Slice each scallop into three rounds and arrange them slightly overlapping in the half-shell. Pour 1 dessertspoon of sauce over each scallop, then scatter over a little ginger, the sesame seeds and some spring onion. Eat immediately.

Way 2: Cut the top and bottom from the lemon. Stand it upright on a chopping board and cut away the skin and as much pith as possible. Hold the lemon in one hand and cut segments out of half of it, then chop the segments into about six small pieces each. Mix with the capers, celery, onion and olive oil in a bowl, then season generously with salt. Leave to stand for 20 minutes.

Get a small, nonstick frying pan blisteringly hot. Dry the scallops on some kitchen paper. Pour a little sunflower oil on a plate and turn the scallops and their corals in it. Sprinkle the flat sides of the scallops and one side of the corals with salt. Place each scallop, flat-side down, in the hot pan with the corals. Fry the white meat for 1½ minutes on each side without disturbing it, so that it picks up a rich brown colour and a wonderful sweetness. The corals will need turning and removing from the pan sooner than the white meat – after about ½–1 minute on each side. Remove the scallop whites from the pan and slice them though the middle diagonally. Put them in the shell with the corals and spoon over a little of the lemon dressing. Eat immediately.

Sopas de mariscos (Shellfish soup)

Serves 4

700g uncooked shell-on prawns

2 tablespoons sunflower oil

2 cloves

1.2 litres water

4 black peppercorns

1 bay leaf

2 tablespoons finely chopped
   coriander stalks

1 medium red onion, finely chopped

½ teaspoon ground cumin

½ teaspoon dried oregano

5 medium juicy ripe tomatoes

3 medium chipotle chiles
   (smoked jalapeños), deseeded
   and finely chopped

3 small garlic cloves, finely chopped

1 green pepper, cored, deseeded
   and thinly sliced

2 teaspoons flaked sea salt

2 limes

1 avocado

coriander leaves, to garnish

Definitely one of my favourite fish soups with its refreshing zip of lime juice, this tasty tomato and prawn broth is just one of many variations that I sipped in seaside hangouts along the Mexican coast when the midday sun stopped my fishing. It is just as good when made with other shellfish such as clams or crab instead of prawns, so use what you will. Chipotle chiles (smoked jalapeños) are now relatively easy to find in large supermarkets.

Snap the heads from the prawns and reserve them in a bowl. Pull the shells from the raw grey meat and put them with the heads. Cut an incision down the curve of the back and hoik out the waste sac. (Alternatively, splay out the shell-on tail and gently twist the spiky middle piece. Pull it away tenderly and the undesirables should follow, still connected.) Once peeled and cleaned, mince the prawn meat roughly and refrigerate until needed.

Heat half the oil in a good-sized saucepan and chuck in the heads and shells with the cloves. Get them frying vigorously – they want some rich colouring. Squash and press the heads with the base of a mug or flat-ended rolling pin; the creamy innards from the inside are very tasty and will lend a lot to the stock. Once the heads have been bashed, fry all the shells for a further 3 minutes or so before pouring in the water. Bring the stock to a gentle simmer, then turn down the heat. Add the peppercorns and bay leaf and let the surface no more than wobble for 45 minutes, skimming off any scum that rises to the surface.

While the stock cooks, in another large pan, fry the coriander stalks and onions with the cumin and oregano in the remaining oil for 6 minutes, or until tender and translucent. Meanwhile, cut the cores from the tomatoes and criss-cross the bottoms with a knife. Put them in a bowl and steep them in just-boiled water. After 1 minute, drain and peel the tomatoes. Scoop out the seeds into the stock and use a blender to purée all the flesh with the chipotles and garlic. Turn up the heat under the onions a little and pour in the fresh tomato purée. It should bubble instantly. Simmer it like this for 5 minutes or so.

Taste your stock and season it appropriately with the salt until the full shrimp flavour comes out. It will probably take a little more salt than you think, but add it a bit at a time. Put a large sieve over the saucepan containing the onions and pour in the stock. Take a mug and give the heads and shells one last press to get as much flavour from them as you can. Discard the shells.

Stir everything in the saucepan together and taste the soup once more. Season again if necessary. Gently simmer for 15 minutes or so. Drop in the prawn flesh and cook for a further 3 minutes, or until just pink and cooked through.

Turn off the heat and squeeze in the juice of one lime followed by more if you see fit. It should give a wonderful sharpness to the soup, but not overpower it. Cut four paper-thin slices from the remaining lime. Stone and peel the avocado, then cut it into large chunks. Put the soup into bowls and drop in three or four pieces of avocado and a slice of lime. Garnish with coriander leaves.

Dad's prawn curry

Serves 4

a good pinch of saffron threads

1 tablespoon hot water

35g butter

1 medium onion, finely chopped

2 small bay leaves

seeds from 10 green cardamom pods,
    crushed, husks reserved

a grating of nutmeg

flaked sea salt

1 small hard garlic clove,
    finely chopped

2 good teaspoons mild curry powder

75ml vermouth

150ml coconut milk

a small handful of flaked almonds

600g cooked peeled large
    Atlantic prawns

75–100ml double cream

buttered rice, to serve

My father was British Ambassador in Laos during the sixties and this is a curry influenced by the cooking of French-colonised Asia that he passed on. He used to make it with packets of standard-issue peeled Atlantic prawns when it was just us three mice and the cat was away. My brother and I would literally count the prawns on our plates to make sure we had the same amount. One prawn difference guaranteed unrest, a subsequent clip over the ear and a ruined evening. Dad was the only person we did not object to having more – as long my brother and I had the same.

I like Bolst's brand of curry powder, in its fetching little tins, which are very handy for fishing weights or picture hooks and the like.

Place the saffron in a teacup, pour over the hot water and leave to one side.

Melt the butter in a heavy-based frying pan over a medium heat. Cook the onion with the bay leaves, cardamom seeds and husks, nutmeg and a large pinch of salt for 6 minutes or so, stirring occasionally, or until the onion softens and turns golden. Add the garlic and curry powder, stirring constantly for a minute longer so as not to let the garlic burn. Pour in the vermouth and, just before it has all evaporated, tip in the coconut milk and the saffron with its water.

Turn off the heat. Toast the almonds in another pan with no oil over a medium heat, stirring occasionally. When golden, transfer to a small bowl. Put the prawns into the curry sauce and, returning it to the heat, bring it to a gentle simmer (do not boil it!). Cook for a couple of minutes before swirling in the cream. Season carefully and scatter with the toasted almonds.

Make sure it is evenly divided and eat with buttered rice.

Crab gratin

Serves 4

25g butter, plus extra for greasing
1 small onion, finely chopped
1 teaspoon finely chopped
   thyme leaves
2 fat garlic cloves, finely chopped
1 teaspoon flaked sea salt,
   plus extra for seasoning
1 teaspoon Dijon mustard
2 teaspoons tomato purée
50ml Dry Martini
2 teaspoons plain flour, sifted
200ml whole milk
150g good soft brown crab meat
200g white crab meat

Topping

40g fresh white breadcrumbs
40g Gruyère cheese, grated
1 tablespoon finely chopped
   curly-leaf parsley
2 dessertspoons olive oil
½ teaspoon coarsely ground
   black pepper
flaked sea salt

White! This is the most common answer when people are asked which of the very different meats of the crab they prefer. Certainly, the intense sweetness of the white is delightful, especially when coupled with a quivering dollopette of mayonnaise. But what of the dark stuff? It can seem like the preference of scavengers who still eat whelks and tripe, and appear among the more unfortunate types in a Dickens story. Well, personally, I love whelks and tripe, and humble brown meat – it is the essence of crab. For those who don't like it, the brown crab is the main point of this recipe, so please move along. For those who savour this rich, intense, creamy velvet, I present you with a bubbling, crunchy-topped and delightful way to spend the first part of your lunch or dinner.

Melt the butter in a saucepan and in it sweat the onion with the thyme for 7–8 minutes over a medium heat, adding the garlic for the last couple of minutes. Cook until rich golden and beginning to brown. Add the salt, mustard and tomato purée. Pour in and cook out the Martini for a few minutes until it has evaporated completely. Stir in the flour and cook for 30 seconds before slowly pouring in the milk bit by bit, stirring all the time. Very gently simmer the mixture for 5 minutes or so. The mixture may be too thick initially, but it will thin out nicely.

Flop in the brown crab meat (if there are any big, dense bits, mash them out a bit with a spoon). Stir the sauce over the heat for a couple of minutes or so more before taking it off the hob and folding in the white crab meat. Lightly grease a medium-sized gratin dish and transfer the mixture. Preheat the grill to just below its highest setting.

For the topping, mix together the breadcrumbs, Gruyère, parsley, oil and black pepper in a bowl, season with salt, then scatter the gratin over the top and place under the grill for 10–15 minutes, sufficiently far away from the element (about 10cm should do) so that the creamy crab is hot by the time the gratin is golden and crispy. Enjoy with a really good glass of white Burgundy.

Veg & foraged foods

Potato gnocchi with wild garlic & Parmesan cheese

Serves 2

Gnocchi

250g floury potatoes, such as
  King Edward or Maris Piper,
  skins left on, quartered
3 teaspoons finely grated Parmesan
  cheese, plus extra to serve
flaked sea salt and black pepper
100g '00' flour, plus extra for dusting
1 large free-range egg yolk

Wild garlic sauce

a couple of ice cubes
100g wild garlic leaves
4 tablespoons olive oil
flaked sea salt
2 teaspoons lemon juice, or to taste

When the smell of wild garlic invades the woods and lanes, I'll be out ramming the stuff into plastic bags. It is delicious in many forms, whether cooked like spinach, tossed in salads, included in soups or lightly battered and deep-fried. I was taught to make gnocchi by a shy and charming Italian chef, with his confident brother, the maître d', translating. (Oddly, the brother turned out to be as animated about the town of Teddington as he was about food.) Once the potato is cooled, forming the gnocchi is surprisingly quick and easy. If all goes well, they can be ready to eat 15 minutes later. Gnocchi are better made to be cooked straight away, using freshly cooked potatoes and not last night's boilers.

Heat a saucepan of water and boil the potatoes until soft throughout but not collapsing. Drain them thoroughly and allow to cool completely.

For the sauce, heat a large saucepan one-third full of water, bringing it to a simmer. Fill a bowl with water and put to one side with a couple of ice cubes clicking around within. Drop the garlic leaves into the simmering water for 30 seconds, submerging any leaves that stick up. With a slotted spoon, scoop out the leaves. Plunge them into the ice bath to immediately stop them cooking so that they keep their colour. Lift the leaves out, ball them up in your hands and wring as much water out as possible, then chop incredibly finely. (It is worth noting that once the leaves have cooked they will lose a lot of their pungent garlicyness, so if this will be missed, then chop two or three raw leaves in with the cooked ones to return a little punch.) Put the garlic leaves in a small bowl with the oil and enough salt to know they are seasoned. Squeeze in some lemon juice – just enough to give it an edge – and put to one side. Refill the pan to halfway and bring to the boil.

Pass the boiled potatoes, skins off, through a ricer or use a grater on the setting you would do children's Cheddar on. Mix the Parmesan with a pinch of salt and the flour. Put the flour mix in a mound on a flat work surface and make a little crater in the centre. Surround the outside of the mound with little piles of the potato. Break the yolk into the crater. Pinch the flour together with the potato, as you would if making crumble topping. When it is roughly combined, head for the egg and keep on lightly fingering it into the mixture. Over a minute or so, pinch all together until only just combined. Gather up the loose ball, just lightly pressing it together and slightly rolling it to pick up any stray pieces. Do not knead the dough or it will be overworked, making the eating heavy. Cut the ball into four. Dust the work surface lightly with flour, then roll each piece into a long sausage as thin as a chipolata. With a knife, cut pieces of dough from the sausage to the width of a sugar lump. Pick each piece up and press in the sides with thumb and forefingers. Dust them lightly with flour.

Gather up the gnocchi and drop them in the rolling water. Cook them for 2–3 minutes. They should all rise to the surface, then they need another 30 seconds. Drain in a colander and divide among the plates. Dress with spoonfuls of the wild garlic sauce and grate over some Parmesan followed by a grinding of black pepper.

Buttered eggs with brown shrimps & dill on asparagus

Serves 2

35g butter

50g cooked peeled brown shrimps

4 medium free-range eggs

flaked sea salt and black pepper

12 young asparagus spears, trimmed
  of any woody stalk

2 teaspoons finely chopped dill

a little lemon juice

fried bread, to serve (optional)

Asparagus with eggs is a great pairing that's even better with brown shrimps –
and a little dill.

Bring a large pan of water to the boil. Meanwhile, melt the butter gently
in a medium–small saucepan and throw in the shrimps. Take the pan
off the heat and break in the eggs. Season well. Drop the asparagus into
the boiling water.

While the asparagus cooks, start scrambling the eggs, stirring them
continuously over a very low heat for approximately 4–5 minutes.
Add the dill just before you stop cooking the eggs. You may need to remove
them from the heat, still stirring a little, before they reach their desired
consistency, as they can jump from desirable to undesirable very quickly;
it is essential that they are runny but not glassy. Drain the asparagus once
tender and sprinkle with a few drops of lemon juice followed by some salt.

Serve the eggs on top of the asparagus and eat immediately. This can be
wonderful with a little fried bread, but that may make the synchronised
cooking a little harder.

Watercress & Gruyère soufflé

Serves 2–4

3 large bunches of watercress
a few ice cubes
80g butter, plus extra for greasing
80g plain flour, plus extra for dusting
600ml whole milk
150g good Gruyère cheese,
   finely grated
6 large free-range eggs, separated
flaked sea salt and black pepper
lightly dressed green salad, to serve
   (optional)

Soufflés are a fine thing yet often associated with complications. They are, however, easy to make but, having said that, they behave as I do in a church service: after the vicar has whispered 'all stand', I spring up, but after only seconds, my rigid posture more resembles a sulking teenager. Get guests to the table quickly; a little neurotic fussing is acceptable.

Preheat the oven to 200°C fan/220°C/Gas 7. Butter the inside of a soufflé dish and dust with 1 teaspoon of flour. Turn the flour around the dish and tip out the excess. Cut a strip of baking paper and tie it around the outside of the soufflé dish with kitchen string, leaving 5cm rising above the rim to make a paper collar.

Place the watercress on a board and trim off only the truly tough stalks. Pick out any flora that don't look like watercress and remove any unwelcome fauna. Bring a saucepan of water to the boil and fill a big bowl with cold water with some ice cubes clicking about within. Drop the watercress in the pan, and when the water returns to the boil, cook it for 30 seconds, then immediately lift it out and put it straight into the icy bath. When properly cooled, drain it thoroughly and gently wring out any remaining water with your hands. Purée the watercress in a blender or in a bowl with a stick blender. Leave it to one side.

Melt the butter in a medium, nonstick saucepan and stir in the flour. Cook for a few seconds, then gradually add the milk, stirring constantly with a whisk to eradicate lumps. It will all clag up initially, but persevere with the milk and all will loosen again by the time the milk is incorporated. Remove from the heat and add 65g of the grated cheese. Stir well until melted, then add the egg yolks two at a time, whisking well between each addition. Stir in the cooled watercress purée and check the seasoning one last time.

Whisk the egg whites in a large bowl until stiff. Fold roughly a quarter of the egg white into the cheese sauce to slacken the mixture. Tip the contents of the pan back into the bowl with the remaining egg white and fold in gently. Pour the mixture into the prepared dish and sprinkle with the reserved cheese. Put on an oven tray and bake in the centre of the oven for 22–25 minutes, or until the soufflé is well risen and golden brown. It should be a little runny inside. Command your guests to sit down just before it is ready. A lightly dressed green salad goes very well with it.

Boiled new potatoes with Stinking Bishop & spring onions

Serves 2

500g new potatoes, the smaller the better, well scrubbed
flaked sea salt and black pepper
3 small spring onions
200g Stinking Bishop (or use Wigmore or Époisses)

The pleasure of this dish is doubled by its ludicrous simplicity. No surprise that it comes from the modest and beautiful thinking behind Fergus Henderson's kitchen at St John restaurant in London. Stinking Bishop, a cheese with a rind washed in perry, or pear cider, is my favourite British cheese, made by Charles Martell in Gloucestershire. It really does what it says on the label. If storing it in the fridge, make sure it is in an airtight container because it has a knack of penetrating everything else with its honk.

Cook the potatoes in a large pan of gently simmering salted water for 10–15 minutes, or until tender. Five minutes before the potatoes are done, clean, trim and finely slice the spring onions. Drain the potatoes well and immediately cut them in half lengthways, if necessary, wearing rubber gloves to protect your hands from the heat. Pile them into a large serving bowl and season well.

Scoop the Stinking Bishop out of its rind and drop spoonfuls of it on to the hot potatoes. Scatter the spring onions on top followed by a good grind of black pepper. It is essential the cheese be applied while the potatoes are piping hot and eaten forthwith. Excellent, I think you will agree.

New potatoes in green sauce

Serves 2–4

500g new potatoes
flaked sea salt and black pepper

Green sauce

4 tablespoons finely chopped
  curly-leaf parsley
1 heaped tablespoon
  finely chopped mint leaves
1 heaped tablespoon
  finely chopped basil leaves
1 heaped tablespoon
  finely chopped tarragon
1 small hard garlic clove with no
  green shoot, very finely chopped
1 medium banana shallot,
  very finely chopped
6–7 brown anchovies in oil,
  drained and finely chopped
1 generous teaspoon Dijon mustard
3 teaspoons red wine vinegar
  or lemon juice
6 tablespoons good extra virgin
  olive oil

This is a fantastic accompaniment to barbecued or steamed fish, goes very well with all meat, and is simply a very pleasant little lunch in its own right.

To make the sauce, mix the herbs, garlic, shallot and anchovies together in a bowl. Stir in the mustard, vinegar or lemon juice and oil and leave, covered, for half an hour or so at room temperature to become what it's meant to be.

Put the potatoes in cold water with a teaspoon of salt and bring them up to a gentle simmer. Cook them for 14 minutes until tender. It is essential that they are not overcooked, as they must be sliced without falling apart. Cut the potatoes to the width of 5mm while hot (rubber gloves may help to combat finger pain and an occasional wetting of the knife under a hot tap will make the cutting easier).

Combine the sliced potatoes gently with the green sauce, a grinding of black pepper and more salt, if needed, then serve. Alternatively, allow the potatoes to cool and serve the dish at room temperature.

Fried new potatoes with rosemary, paprika & fried egg

Serves 1

250g new potatoes or leftover
   boiled potatoes

2 dessertspoons olive oil

2 small hard garlic cloves with
   no green shoots, finely chopped

1 teaspoon chopped rosemary leaves

flaked sea salt and black pepper

1 free-range egg

a little smoked paprika

I heard a story of some British truckers ordering egg and chips from a garage café in Spain. One of them was heard shouting at the waiter: '*Quintos* egg and chips, mate!' Then he slapped his watch face with two thick fingers and followed it up with: 'And snappy!' Here is different version of egg and chips that is quick to prepare should you have some leftover newies. The smoked paprika steps in as a wonderful sort of rich 'bacon' powder.

If using fresh new potatoes, boil them until only just done (approximately 8–10 minutes). Slice the potatoes about 5mm thick, leaving the skins on.

Pour half the oil into a pan that is large enough to give the potatoes space rather than being piled on top of each other. Fry the potatoes over a medium heat for 10 minutes until golden brown and crispy, manoeuvring them with a spoon so as to keep as many slices lying as flat as possible. Take care to regulate the heat, should you fear the oil might burn or see smoke rising from it. Transfer them to a bowl lined with kitchen paper to drain the grease, then remove the paper and toss the garlic, rosemary and ½ teaspoon of salt.

Put the pan back over the heat and add the remaining oil. Fry the egg for a couple of minutes, spooning a bit of hot oil over it. The yolk should be runny and the base a little crispy and browned.

Shovel the egg on top of the potatoes and season it with a little salt and black pepper and a good dusting of smoked paprika. Serve it snappy and eat with a good strong cup of coffee.

Carrot & orange salad

Serves 2

2 medium carrots, coarsely grated

50g raisins

2 good medium tart juicy oranges

½ teaspoon cumin seeds

2 tablespoons good olive oil

black pepper

½ teaspoon flaked sea salt

I don't always want toast and cereal, eggs and bacon for breakfast. There are so many other wonderful foods that can provide a fresher start to the day. This is a suggestion from my wife; a dish she used to eat when on Kibbutz in Israel with her family.

Put the carrots in a bowl, then add the raisins. Cut both ends from the oranges and cut the pith and skin away with a knife. Taking the fruit in your hand, cut each segment from the membranes into the carrot and add it to the bowl. Dry-fry the cumin seeds over a medium–low heat in a small frying pan for 4 minutes, or until their toasted smell comes to the nose. Add them to the salad.

Toss everything with the oil and season with an enthusiastic grinding of black pepper and the salt. Invigorating!

Panzanella

Serves 4

6 large ripe vine tomatoes

½ small red onion, finely diced

2 fat garlic cloves, finely sliced

2 tablespoon baby capers, well rinsed

6 anchovies in olive oil, drained
   and finely chopped

juice of ½ small lemon

¾ cucumber, peeled, halved
   lengthways, deseeded and cut
   into 1cm-thick slices

200g stale dense white rustic loaf,
   torn into largish mouthfuls

6 tablespoons extra virgin olive oil

2 teaspoons red wine vinegar

about 1½ teaspoons flaked sea salt

a handful of young curly-leaf parsley
   leaves, roughly torn

a small handful of mint leaves,
   ripped up

Refreshing on hot days – and delightfully simple to make when feeling sluggish in the heat – this is a salad perfect for outside eating near a bottle of very cold white, with condensation running down the side.

Cut the green stalk out of each tomato, then score the base with a small cross and place in a large bowl. Submerge them in just-boiled water and leave to stand for 30 seconds before lifting out. Slip the skins off the tomatoes, then cut them into quarters. Scoop out the seeds into a sieve over the bowl you intend to put the salad in and press the juice through into the bowl. Discard the seeds. Cut the tomato flesh into irregular pieces and put them into the bowl with the tomato juice. Scatter over the onion, garlic, capers, anchovies and lemon juice. Add the cucumber and toss well.

When ready to serve, stir the bread and 5 tablespoons of the oil into the salad. Season with the vinegar and more salt than you might normally use, adding and tasting bit by bit. Allow the salad to sit in a cool place for 10 minutes before serving. Scatter with the parsley and mint and add the remaining tablespoon of oil, if necessary. Serve immediately.

Minestrone

Serves 6

Chicken stock

2 tablespoons olive oil

2 chicken carcasses, chopped
  into 6 pieces

1 small onion, skin left on,
  roughly chopped

3 large new-season garlic cloves,
  inner skins left on, roughly
  chopped, or 2 normal garlic cloves,
  peeled and roughly chopped

a sprig of thyme

a small handful of parsley stalks

4 black peppercorns

2 teaspoons flaked sea salt

1 good teaspoon tomato purée

1.2 litres water

The vegetables

2 medium ripe tomatoes

500g broad beans in their pods, shelled

1 tablespoon olive oil

3 spring onions, finely sliced

75g young leeks, trimmed, cleaned
  and finely sliced

300g courgettes, finely diced

½ teaspoon flaked sea salt

2 new-season garlic cloves,
  finely sliced, or 1 normal garlic
  clove, finely sliced

4 medium chard leaves,
  finely shredded

8 medium asparagus spears, trimmed
  of any woody stalk, finely sliced,
  head left whole

To finish

juice of ½ small lemon

3 tablespoons extra virgin olive oil

½ teaspoon dried chile flakes

flaked sea salt

12 large basil leaves

Parmesan cheese

Minestrone means a lot of different things to a lot of different mothers in a lot of different kitchens in a lot of different towns from a lot of different regions and this one does not include pasta. No doubt some grandmothers will turn in their graves.

To make the stock, heat the olive oil in a large pan over a medium–high heat and add all the stock ingredients except the tomato purée and water. Fry everything hard, stirring from time to time, until the chicken carcasses and some of the veg are browned. Add the tomato purée 1 minute before the vegetables are ready. Add the water and bring the stock up to the gentlest heat so that it barely simmers but rather murmurs. On no account boil it or the fat will emulsify with the water and make a greasy broth. Leave it to cook for no more than 1½ hours, skimming when necessary. After this time, you will be hard pushed to get any more flavour from the bones and they will start to collapse and subsequently make the broth misty; ideally, you want clear stock.

Strain the stock from the wreckage through a fine sieve and leave it to settle. Skim as much fat as possible from it again after it has cooled a little. (Making the stock the day before has its benefits, as you can pick the cold fat – like ice from a pond – from the top after it has been chilled overnight; reheat it before moving on to the next step.)

Around 30 minutes before removing the stock from the heat, cut the cores from the tomatoes and cut a criss-cross in the bottoms with a knife. Steep them in just-boiled water and leave for 30 seconds. Take them out (reserve the hot water to boil the beans, instead of throwing it away). When cool enough to handle, peel away the skins. Cut the tomatoes in quarters and discard the seeds. Slice the quarters into thin slivers and keep to one side in a bowl. Heat the tomato water in a small pan and in it boil the broad beans for 3 minutes. Drain and plunge them instantly in cold water to stop them cooking. Peel the joyfully green beans from their skins and put them to one side.

Put the cleaned stock pan over a medium heat and pour in the olive oil. Gently fry the spring onion, leeks and courgettes, seasoned with the salt, for about 5 minutes, adding the garlic for the last couple of minutes, until all are tender but not coloured. Pour in the stock, leaving any sediment behind. Bring the stock up to the gentlest simmer once more, then add the tomatoes, chard and asparagus and cook them for another 3 minutes or so until the chard has properly softened. Add the broad beans and simmer for a final 2 minutes.

While the vegetables cook, combine the lemon juice and extra virgin olive oil with the chile flakes and a little salt. Stack up the basil leaves, roll them up and then slice this small herby sausage from end to end into thin slivers. Add the basil to the oil and lemon juice just before serving, so that it does not turn khaki as a result of sitting around.

When the soup has cooked, ladle it into shallow bowls and then spoon over a little of the basil oil. Grate over as much Parmesan as you see fit, then eat.

Young broad beans cooked in their shells

Serves 6–8

2 medium onions, halved and
    finely sliced
150ml light olive oil
1kg young broad beans in their pods
    ('no thicker than a lady's finger'),
    rinsed, de-strung and stalks
    removed
2 tablespoons lemon juice
a generous pinch of caster sugar
flaked sea salt
200ml just-boiled water
2 tablespoons chopped dill
2 garlic cloves, very finely chopped
300ml Greek-style yoghurt
warmed flatbread, to serve

This recipe is here in order to pay homage to one of my favourite food authors, Jeremy Round, sadly deceased.

His book the *The Independent Cook* (published by Pan Books) is one of the finest publications about seasonal food ever. Not only is it an enjoyably funny read, but it is also very informative for anyone who wishes to learn about the rhythms of Mother Nature, both at home and abroad. Needless to say, it is stuffed with very original and tasty recipes too. Alas, the book is no longer in print, but second-hand copies can usually be found on Amazon.

This recipe is a classic example of a dish that does not look all that appetising, but is delicious nonetheless. Prettiness on a plate is a plus, but the bottom line is the taste, so ignore the grey hue of the beans once they are fully cooked. You will need young beans from early on in the season – May.

I would like to add a small extract from Jeremy Round's original recipe for reassurance: 'After living in Turkey for a while, you begin to get used to, and soon positively yearn for, such long-overcooked vegetables.'

In a large heavy-based saucepan, sauté the onions in the oil over a medium–low heat until softened but not coloured – 6 minutes or so. Turn the heat down to low and add the beans, lemon juice, sugar and 1 teaspoon of salt. Cover and stew for 15 minutes or so, stirring occasionally. Add the water and a third of the dill. Adjust the heat so that the liquid comes up to a low simmer and replace the lid. Cook the beans for about 1–1½ hours, or until completely tender. Allow them to cool. In a small bowl, stir the garlic into the yoghurt with an extra pinch of salt.

When the beans have returned to room temperature, stir in the remaining dill and serve with the yoghurt and some warmed flatbread, such as pitta.

Spanish salad

Serves 4

½ iceberg lettuce, roughly chopped
2 hard-boiled free-range eggs,
    peeled and thickly sliced
2 medium ripe tomatoes, sliced
    or cut into 6 segments
1 large carrot, grated
½ red onion, sliced into thin rings
a handful of black olives, pitted
½ small can sweetcorn, drained
2 bottled artichoke hearts, quartered,
    or some canned white asparagus,
    drained and halved
1 standard-sized can eco-friendly
    tuna, drained
table salt and dust-like ground
    black pepper
white wine vinegar, to taste
olive oil, to taste

I adore Spanish cooking, but this classic offers about the only chance to get something salad-like in this vast country of meat, potatoes, olive oil and tiny fried pre-pubescent fishes. It's a chuck-it-all-in special and, although it can vary, there are certain things I think it should contain.

Chuck the iceberg into a large bowl and scatter the eggs and all the vegetables over the top, keeping back the tuna so that it can be plonked right in the middle. Season, then dress with vinegar and oil (ideally, these will be in one of those naff condiment carriers that might also contain damp salt and dust-like black pepper). Eat and wait for the arrival of your fried sardines.

Courgette soup with chard bruschetta

Serves 6

3 tablespoons olive oil

1 medium onion, finely chopped

7–9 medium courgettes (about 1kg),
    cut into 1.5cm slices

3 garlic cloves

a good grating of nutmeg

black pepper

a small sprig of rosemary

30g Parmesan rind, if you have
    some handy

550ml whole milk

1 teaspoon flaked sea salt

Chard bruschetta

flaked sea salt

4–5 big Swiss chard leaves

extra virgin olive oil, for splashing

a squeeze of lemon juice

6 thin slices of rustic bread
    or ciabatta

1 good large garlic clove, peeled

To serve

Parmesan cheese

a little extra virgin olive oil

So often I get asked what to do with the glut of courgettes that fill a grower's arms, apron or basket. Here is a recipe based on a soup that I ate in Italy. It was so good I ordered it again that night (I ate it in the same restaurant for dinner after a long circular walk that conveniently brought me back to its front door).

To make the soup, pour the olive oil into a large, heavy pan and in it soften the onion over a medium heat for 8 minutes or so, stirring occasionally. Add the courgettes with the garlic, nutmeg, a good grinding of black pepper, rosemary and Parmesan rind (this will give depth to the soup in the absence of stock). Mix everything together before covering with a lid and leaving to cook for a further 20–25 minutes, stirring occasionally. After this time the courgettes should be very soft while retaining a pleasant green colour. Pick out the rosemary stalk, which will have dropped its leaves.

While the courgettes sweat it out, start making the bruschetta. Put a pan of salted water on to boil. Rip up the chard leaves and boil them for 5 minutes or so until tender. Drain the chard thoroughly and chop it very finely while it is still hot. Put it in a bowl with a generous splash of extra virgin olive oil, some salt and a light squeeze of lemon juice – just enough to give it a little edge. Leave the chard to one side. Preheat the grill to its highest setting.

To finish the soup, add the milk to the courgettes and gently simmer for 10 minutes or so without the lid. Do not let the soup boil. Take out the Parmesan rind and purée the soup in a food processor or with a stick blender until very smooth. Return it to the pan and place it over a very low heat to keep it hot. Season with the salt – probably a little more than you would normally use. Add a little more milk if you feel the soup is too thick.

To finish the bruschetta, splash the slices of bread with more olive oil and toast them on a baking tray under the grill until they take on a rich golden colour. They do not want to be shatter-dry, but instead a little chewy in the middle. When cooked, rub them with the garlic.

Ladle the soup into bowls. Load some chard on to the bruschetta, then place them on to the soup. Grate Parmesan over the bruschetta and slash the soup with one last pass of extra virgin olive oil. Eat with a glass of good white wine.

Artichoke with poached egg & Hollandaise sauce

Serves 2

2 large globe artichokes, stem cut
   away from the crown
2 large portobello mushrooms, peeled
a knob of butter
flaked sea salt and black pepper
a squeeze of lemon juice
a splash of olive oil
2 free-range eggs
thin slices of ham, to serve (optional)

Hollandaise sauce

75ml tarragon vinegar
juice of ½ lemon
225g unsalted butter, cut into
   small cubes
3 large free-range egg yolks
flaked sea salt and black pepper

This is a dish I used to cook under head-chef Martin Haddon at the Halycon Hotel. It is about as luxurious as a vegetable gets and I think it deserves a fine plate, a white tablecloth (not like the one in the picture!) and an outrageously good bottle of white wine. Not great for the waist, but great for the soul. It requires effort, but it's worth it.

Heat a large pan of water, big enough to sit both artichokes snugly whilst being totally submerged. When it comes up to the boil, tuck them in, put a side plate on top, put a lid on and leave to simmer for 30 minutes. To test, pull one of the midway leaves and it should come away relatively easily.

While the artichokes cook, put the mushrooms with their stalks in a food processor with a knob of butter and turn them into a black pulp. Flop this into a frying pan and place it over a very low heat, stirring occasionally. The object is to cook away all the water, leaving a dry mix (this should take about the same time as the artichokes). Season well and leave to one side.

While the mushrooms and artichokes go about their business, make the Hollandaise sauce. Put the vinegar and lemon juice in a saucepan and bring to the boil. Leave to bubble furiously until it has reduced to around 2 tablespoons, then transfer to a largish bowl and leave to cool for a few minutes. Put the butter in another saucepan and heat gently until melted. As it bubbles, skim away the little white islands of milk solids that rise to the top. Don't cook it over too high a heat or it will burn. Carefully pour the hot clarified butter into a warmed jug, discarding the white, milky sediment left behind.

Half-fill a saucepan with water and bring it to a simmer. Beat the egg yolks into the vinegar reduction and perch the bowl on top of the pan without touching the water. Beat with an electric whisk, or furiously with a hand one, until pale and thickened. Gradually add the melted butter to the egg yolks in a dribbly stream, whisking constantly for 2–3 minutes more until the sauce is thick and glossy. Remove the pan from the heat to prevent the sauce from overheating, and season well. Cover the surface with a sheet of clingfilm to stop a skin forming and leave to one side.

Remove the cooked artichokes from the pan and place them in cold water to cool. Drain and peel away the petals, nibbling on their fleshy lobes as you go. When most of the leaves have been removed, you will come across a peaked cap of leaves with a pink tinge to the top. Squeeze the point and pull; they should all come away in one go. Underneath you will find a furry disc in the middle of the artichoke heart; this is called the choke, for obvious reasons. Scrape this out with a spoon, taking care to remove it all as otherwise it'll ruin the eating experience. Turn the heart upside down, and if you notice any fibrous veins along the underside, cut these away. In order to stop the hearts turning dull blue as they oxidise, put them in a little bowl and tumble them in a good squeeze of lemon juice and a splash of oil.

» Put a small pan of water on to boil. When it is boiling healthily, give the water a spin with a spoon and crack in both your eggs. Turn the heat down to low and poach the eggs for 2 minutes, making sure that the white is cooked but the yolk is runny. Remove them from the water with a slotted spoon and leave on a clean tea towel to cool, but leave the water there with the heat turned off.

Preheat the grill to its highest setting. Lay both the artichoke hearts on a small baking tray, cupped-side up. Flash them under the grill for a couple of minutes or so until hot. Meanwhile, warm the mushroom mixture if it has cooled completely. Take the artichokes from under the grill and divide the mushroom mix between them, making a little indentation for the egg in the middle. Pop both the poached eggs back into the hot water for 20 seconds or so, then lift them out again, making sure all the water has dripped off them, and place them in the centre of the mushrooms. Season well, then blanket the eggs and mushrooms with a generous amount of the Hollandaise sauce. Put this splendid arrangement under the grill and brown the Hollandaise for about 30 seconds or so. You have to be very careful not to scramble it. Eat immediately. Accompanying this with thin slices of cured ham can be nice.

Gem lettuce with anchovies & peppers

Serves 6

4 red peppers
1 good hard garlic clove,
   very finely chopped
2 tablespoons sherry vinegar
3 tablespoons good olive oil
flaked sea salt and black pepper
4 Baby Gem lettuces
juice of ½ lemon
24 really good brown anchovies in oil
   or salt, drained, or rinsed and dried

San Sebastian is a particularly excellent town for eating in. With so many delicacies to try, I advise saving time by tucking your napkin into your collar on the drive to the restaurant from the airport. Order sweet spider-crab tarts, giant grilled ceps and salt cod from the pinxto bars, get involved with the cured meats, worship at the temple of the anchovy and smile at the cider. Maybe the hake throats in egg are not for everyone.

When filming in one of San Sebastian's private men's dining clubs, I was brought into the kitchen to help while interviewing one of its moustachioed members. I have to say I was a bit disgruntled to have my potato peeling criticised and later furious at not being invited to the club supper after helping to prepare it. I stood there like a lemon, hanging around to clean away plates while they rudely gesticulated with their cutlery and shouted at each other about boar hunting with their mouths full. A taste of the ox stew was obviously out of the question, but they sent me a side plate of this salad. I wish I could say it was disgusting, but it was annoyingly good. Bear in mind that this recipe is to be eaten as soon as you've prepared it, as it does not take kindly to having to wait for anybody.

Put the peppers directly over the naked flame of your gas rings or under a grill preheated to its highest setting. Turn them every now and then until their skins are totally charred – and by that I mean black. Leave them to cool for 20 minutes or so. Open the peppers over a sieve on top of a bowl so as to reserve the sweet juices without the meddlesome seeds. Thoroughly remove

» the skin from the peppers. On no account do this under running water, as you will wash away the lovely charred taste while adding water where it is not wanted. Carefully remove all the seeds. Tear the peppers lengthways to the same width as the anchovies and add them to the juice in the bowl. Add the garlic to the peppers, and then the vinegar and oil. Season with salt, while remembering that although the peppers should be well seasoned in their own right, the anchovies will provide an extra saltiness. Leave to one side.

Trim away any damaged leaves or unsightly brown bits from the lettuce leaves or stalk end. Cut the gems lengthways into six, taking trouble to keep each piece intact. Place the pieces in a large bowl, squeeze over the lemon juice and grind over a little black pepper. Mix kindly, so that all the lettuce takes on a lemon edge but doesn't break up. Arrange the lettuce pieces over a large, flat plate and drape an anchovy over each and the appropriate amount of prepared peppers.

A good glass of cold crisp Albariño will complement this salad beautifully; quite the reverse of my treatment at the hands of a few rude Basques.

Pimientos de Padrón

Serves 4 as a pre-dinner nibble

250g *pimientos de Padrón*
2 dessertspoons light olive oil
coarse sea salt

One of the staple dishes of Spanish tapas, these little green peppers have a mild and pleasant flavour, but every now and then the odd one can exact a terrible ferocity. Platefuls do not last long, so buy lots when you find them in Spanish delis, as they are addictive and cook quicker than popcorn.

Wash the peppers and drain them in a colander, then pat them dry with kitchen paper. Heat the oil in a frying pan over a medium heat and tip in the peppers. They should sizzle immediately.

Fry the peppers for approximately 5 minutes until well blistered and browned. Serve on a plate lined with kitchen paper, with the peppers scattered generously with chunky sea salt.

Frijoles de la olla (Stewed black beans from the pot)

Serves 8

50g pork lard
2 medium onions, cut into
     medium dice
3 garlic cloves, peeled
stems from a good bunch of coriander
1½ teaspoons dried oregano
2 teaspoons dried epazote or 3 leaves
     of fresh epazote (optional)
500g dried black beans
2–3 litres water
flaked sea salt

To serve

Wensleydale cheese
diced ripe avocado dressed with lime
     juice and salt

As proper Mexican food becomes increasingly popular in this country, black beans are now quite easy to find. Simply stewed in this way, the beans can be eaten alongside tender pork or barbecued fish, included in the famous breakfast *Huevos Rancheros* (*see* page 254), or smeared in tacos. I often have a big batch of cooked beans in the fridge to be reheated as an easy office lunch or poured into a thermos and taken winter fishing.
Creamy, deliciously earthy and deep, this really is Mexico in a bowl.
Although the lard can be replaced with groundnut or sunflower oil, without that piggy backdrop this dish is not quite as enjoyable. Traditionally, the beans are often cooked with a pungent herb called epazote, a raggedy-looking weed resembling something between a nettle and hemp. It is said to help prevent negative symptoms of eating beans, but unfortunately I have not found this to be true. It does, however, lend a wonderful taste to the beans and grows well in this country even if it is hard to purchase. If you require it fresh, contact Peppers by Post (www.peppersbypost.biz; 01308 897766), or for dried epazote, contact Cool Chile Co. (www.coolchile.co.uk; 0870 902 1145).

In a large pot, melt the lard and then throw in the onions, garlic, coriander, oregano and epazote, if using. Stir together and when the onion has softened tip in the beans. Cover with 2 litres of water and bring them up to a gentle simmer, then cook with the lid off for approximately 2½ hours. For the last 40 minutes or so, stir the beans vigorously every now and then, as this will make them very creamy, as well as stopping them stick to the bottom of the pot (which they have a propensity to do). Add more water if at any stage you feel the beans are becoming a little thick while still undercooked.

The beans are ready when they are totally soft to the bite and their liquidity is marginally thicker than pouring double cream. Season the beans very generously with salt in order to fully bring out their flavour.

Enjoy simply in a bowl with a little Wensleydale cheese and some diced ripe avocado treated with a little lime juice and salt. Alternatively, serve alongside the *Carne Con Chile* (*see* page 51). Warmed corn tortillas are a good mopper-upper for beans.

Cucumber & cumin salad

Serves 2–4

1 large cucumber, peeled
   and very finely sliced
2 teaspoons flaked sea salt
2 teaspoons cumin seeds
½ small red onion, halved
   and finely sliced
juice of ½ lemon
2 tablespoons extra virgin olive oil

Every time I make this, the sight of the cucumber in the colander reminds me of wet clothes lying inside a washing machine. This is a good addition to the outdoor summer table or picnic: gentle, clean and simple when eaten with grilled flatbread and sheep's milk yoghurt.

Put the cucumber in a colander and tumble it thoroughly with the salt. Leave to stand over the sink for around 2 hours. The salt will draw out the water, which drains away, leaving the cucumber floppy but still crunchy – an intriguing textural experience.

Put the cumin seeds in a dry frying pan and toast over a medium heat for 2–3 minutes, or until their smell comes to the nose, swirling them about the pan regularly so that they don't burn. Remove from the heat and tip into a serving bowl (this stops them cooking).

Lift the cucumber from the colander and wring it out in your hands like a flannel, to squeeze out the remaining water. (Should you happen to be making a Bloody Mary at the same time, squeeze it into the jug.) Put the cucumber into the serving bowl with the cumin and toss together with the red onion, lemon juice and oil. Leave to stand for about 10 minutes before enjoying.

Sweetcorn soup

Serves 3–4

4 corn cobs, husks removed
4 tablespoons sunflower oil
1 onion, finely chopped
1 scant teaspoon dried oregano
½ teaspoon ground cumin
1 garlic clove, finely chopped
500ml fresh chicken stock
　(*see* page 240)
200ml cold water
flaked sea salt
40g Wensleydale cheese,
　crumbled into small pieces

Salsa

2 large ripe tomatoes
leaves from a small bunch of
　coriander (about 20g), finely
　chopped, stalks reserved for
　the soup, finely chopped
½ small red onion,
　very finely chopped
1 large chipotle chile (smoked
　jalapeño), finely chopped
juice of ½ large juicy lime
1 teaspoon flaked sea salt

I worship the fresh, tender sweetcorn of late summer and during its fleeting season will happily eat cobs for breakfast as well as lunch and dinner. The Mayans believed that mankind was fashioned from maize kernels and I'm happy to go along with this. It seems only right, then, that this recipe takes a Mexican approach. It is a soup to give an aching jaw some rest from continual gnawing at cobs. Chipotle chilies (smoked jalapeños) are pretty easy to find, but if you can't, use a good pinch of smoked paprika instead.

Make the salsa just before starting the soup so that all the ingredients have time to work as one. Cut the core from each tomato and cut a criss-cross in the bottom. Steep them in just-boiled water for 30 seconds or so. When they are cool enough to handle, peel and quarter them, then remove the seeds. Roughly but finely chop them up and put the flesh in a bowl. Add the chopped coriander leaves, red onion and chile to the tomatoes along with the lime juice and salt. Mix well and leave to sit.

Stand each corn cob upright on a board and cut down each side as close to the core as possible, to remove the kernels. Heat a large saucepan and add 3 tablespoons of the oil. As soon as the oil is hot, scatter the kernels into the pan and cook over a high heat for 5–6 minutes, stirring regularly, until well browned and sticky on the outside – almost burnt. Transfer the corn to a bowl with the toffee-like residue scraped from the bottom of the pan. Return the pan to the heat and add the remaining oil. Fry the onion over a medium–low heat with the coriander stalks, oregano and cumin until the onion is well softened but not coloured. Add the garlic near the end so that it cooks without burning. Return the corn to the pan and pour over the chicken stock and add the water. Bring the soup to a simmer, season well and cook for about 15 minutes until the sweetcorn is very tender, stirring occasionally.

Remove from the heat and blitz the soup with a stick blender until it is as smooth as possible, then, ideally, pass through a fine sieve into a clean pan and return to the heat (you don't have to sieve the soup, but it's much better without the kernel skins). Check the seasoning and add a little extra water if necessary until the soup has the consistency of single cream.

Ladle the soup into warmed bowls and scatter over the Wensleydale cheese. Spoon some of the salsa into the middle of each bowl, putting any remaining salsa in a small bowl for those who want it, and serve immediately.

Cauliflower with curry leaves & tomatoes

Serves 4

1 medium cauliflower

2 tablespoons ghee or butter

1 dessertspoon black mustard seeds

1 small red onion, finely chopped

20 curry leaves (ideally fresh)

1–2 hot green bird's-eye chiles,
    deseeded and finely sliced

2 teaspoons turmeric

1 small thumb-sized piece of root
    ginger, peeled and finely chopped

2 garlic cloves, very finely chopped

1–1½ teaspoons flaked sea salt

2 vine tomatoes, quartered,
    deseeded and roughly sliced

a handful of coriander leaves, roughly
    chopped, to garnish (optional)

Indian takeaways can take so long to arrive, so here's something to cook while you wait (and provide a pleasurable alternative to sag aloo). It's also great as a quick lunch. Curry leaves are available from good Oriental stores and are best fresh. This dish is great served with yoghurt and naan bread.

Break the cauliflower into florets of about 2–5cm long and chop up the stalk likewise if necessary. Keep any respectable leaves. Drop the cauliflower and leaves into plenty of boiling water and par-boil for 4 minutes, or until tender but retaining a little firmness. Do not overcook. Drain the cauliflower, immediately cool in cold water, then drain again.

Melt the ghee or butter in a wok (or large frying pan) over a medium heat and tip in the black mustard seeds. When they start to pop, add the onion and curry leaves and fry briskly until the onion just starts to colour. Add the chiles, turmeric, ginger and garlic. Cook for a further minute, stirring often to prevent burning, before adding the cauliflower and salt. Finally, drop in the tomato and keep tossing everything over the heat until the tomato has only just softened. Check the seasoning one last time, garnish with coriander, if you like, and serve immediately.

Caesar salad

Serves 4

2 large free-range egg yolks

juice of 1 fat juicy lime

2 small garlic cloves, finely grated

12 salted brown anchovies in oil, drained and finely mashed

75ml light olive oil, plus extra for brushing the bread

a generous splash of Worcestershire sauce

8 slices of bread from a small baguette, each about 5mm thick

2 pert medium Romaine lettuces, broken into whole leaves, washed and dried

30g Parmesan cheese, finely grated

There is much debate about the true creator of the Caesar Salad, but frankly I'm not too interested in getting so heated over a salad. I like anchovy in mine; purists say Worcestershire sauce. Fine! I like and add both. I do, however, feel that any Caesar boasting crispy bacon, chargrilled chicken and board-game dice croûtons will pretty much guarantee you a truly dismal experience, as 9½ out of 10 of such UK Caesar salads are shockers. I hope, however, that you find this one enjoyable.

Preheat the grill to its highest setting. In a bowl, whisk the eggs yolks together with the lime juice, garlic and anchovies. Slowly start adding the oil in a thin dribble whilst continuing to vigorously whisk everything together so that the mixture combines into a glossy emulsion. Finish the seasoning with the Worcestershire sauce.

Brush the baguette slices on both sides with a little oil. Place them under the grill on both sides until golden and crisp.

Take each lettuce leaf by the stalk and use a pastry brush to paint the dressing on both sides. Drop them in a salad bowl as you go and, when done, scatter over the Parmesan and drop over the croûtons. Mix briefly at the table and eat.

Stuffed tomatoes

Serves 6

100g short-grain rice

450ml cold water

½ teaspoon saffron threads

½ cinnamon stick

6 large beef tomatoes

4 tablespoons olive oil, plus extra
    for drizzling

1 large white onion, finely chopped

½ teaspoon ground cumin

½ teaspoon caraway seeds

1 heaped teaspoon dried oregano

3 garlic cloves, finely chopped

1 small glass dry white wine
    (about 125ml)

75g Kalamata olives, pitted and
    chopped

4 tablespoons finely chopped flat-leaf
    or curly-leaf parsley

finely grated zest of 1 unwaxed lemon

50g pine nuts

25g sultanas

flaked sea salt and black pepper

It's not vegetarian food I have a problem with, it's the English concept of vegetarianism. A huge percentage of the world's great dishes exclude meat or fish whilst remaining delicious. There is no reason to suffer bad risotto or endless butternut squash. Here is something Greek. Try to buy the tasty long pine nuts you find imported from Italy and Turkey rather than certain stubby Chinese ones that leave a bitter taste on the back of the tongue, sometimes lasting days.

Pour the rice into a saucepan and cover with the water. Drop the saffron and the cinnamon stick into the pan. Bring the rice up to a healthy simmer and cover. Cook for 15–20 minutes until the rice is tender. Drain the rice, remove the cinnamon stick, spread the rice on a large dinner plate and leave to cool.

Preheat the oven to 190°C fan/210°C/Gas 6½.

While the rice cooks, cut a lid from the top of each tomato, preferably keeping the stalk attached, and reserve. With a teaspoon, scoop the little pockets of seeds out of the tomatoes into a sieve over a bowl and push down to get the juice from the seeds. Discard the seeds and the hard part of the core. Chop the flesh from the core and add to the juice.

Pour the oil into a good-sized saucepan. Over a medium heat, fry the onion, cumin, caraway seeds and oregano until the onion is golden, adding the garlic for the last 2 minutes so as not to burn it. Pour in 150ml of the tomato pulp and the wine and simmer briskly to cook away any obvious watery element. Turn off the heat and stir in the chopped olives, parsley and lemon zest.

Into a small frying pan, tip the pine nuts and dry-fry them over a medium heat, swirling them continuously so that they don't burn. After about 5 minutes they should be a rich golden colour. Tip them into the onions and add the sultanas.

Turn the rice into the onion mix and stir everything together, adding a good grinding of black pepper and seasoning well with salt (a lot of food is under-seasoned). Stuff the tomatoes so that they look generous with the filling bursting out of the top a little. Place the lids on top. Line an oven dish with baking paper and place the tomatoes in two little rows within. Pass over with one final drizzle of oil and a little salt for the outside of the tomatoes.

Bake the tomatoes for 35–40 minutes. The skins should be brown and in certain places starting to blacken. The tomatoes should be totally soft, but not completely collapsed. This is definitely something for eating *al fresco*, maybe with a glass of really cold retsina (although it can make certain people a little bit loopy – ahem!).

Aubergines with dill & vinegar

Serves 2–4

2 large aubergines, washed and green
stem removed
flaked sea salt and black pepper
1 tablespoon coriander seeds
2 spilling tablespoons white wine
vinegar
2 large garlic cloves, finely sliced
lengthways
1 large vine tomato
6 tablespoons light olive oil
a sprig of mint (ideally spearmint)
a large sprig of dill

The aubergine excels on a grill over wood smoke. Please make sure each slice
is cooked through, as when not, it is a particularly unpleasant vegetable to eat.

Slice the aubergines lengthways, about 6mm thick. Toss in a large bowl with
1 level tablespoon of salt and lay out on a clean tea towel. Leave for half an
hour or so. Meanwhile, get the barbecue going.

Toast the coriander seeds in a pan over a low heat until their fragrance comes
to the nose, swirling them regularly to prevent them from burning. Put the
seeds in a small bowl and only slightly crush them with the end of a rolling
pin. Pour over the vinegar. Add the sliced garlic and leave to one side.

Mix the aubergines with 4 tablespoons of the oil in a bowl and rub all over well.
The oil must be evenly dispersed. Be careful, as the thirsty aubergine will soak
it up quickly. Cook on the barbecue for 7½–9 minutes, turning once. The flesh
should be very well coloured and the tip of the knife should slide through easily.

While the aubergine cooks, cut out the stem from the tomato then quarter
it and remove the seeds. Chop the quarters into squares a little smaller than
board-game dice and put to one side.

Remove the aubergines to a plate, grind over a little black pepper and scatter
over the tomato with a little extra salt. Pour over the remaining oil, then
scatter over the coriander seeds and garlic before splashing over the vinegar.
Tear over the herb leaves and serve immediately while warm.

Beetroot ravioli

Serves 4–6

Filling

225g beetroot, skins left on, washed
    and trimmed
125g ricotta cheese
20g Parmesan cheese, grated
a grating of nutmeg
½ teaspoon flaked sea salt, plus extra
    for salting the water
black pepper

Pasta

300g '00' flour
100g fine semolina, plus extra
    for dusting
3 medium free-range eggs
about 6 free-range egg yolks

To finish

50g butter
12 sage leaves
Parmesan cheese, for grating

Making ravioli is not a big deal; it's fun. Don't worry if you muck up a few – just rescue the stuffing and have another go. You cannot help but feel a sense of achievement when you stare down lovingly at your work. This is my favourite filling, for the showy colour as well as the taste of fresh beetroot. You can add juice to the pasta dough for drama but, once cooked, the colour will fade, so despite the picture, I have left it out of the recipe.

Submerge all the beetroot, with their skins on, in cold water and bring to the boil (removing the skins before cooking will result in a lot of flavour and colour being lost). Boil them, lid on, for approximately 30–40 minutes, depending on whether you are cooking one large beetroot or a couple of smaller ones. You may need to top up the water. The beetroots are done when a knife slides into them easily. Take them out of the hot water and allow to cool.

Put the ricotta in a clean J Cloth and gently squeeze out most of the water – it does not need to be strangled dry. Put it in a bowl with the Parmesan, nutmeg, salt and a good grinding of black pepper. When the beetroot is cool, grate it finely into a sieve so that any excess water drains away, then mix it with the rest of the ravioli filling. Taste and alter the seasoning if necessary. Cover the filling and put it in the fridge to firm up a bit.

To make the pasta, put the flour and semolina into the food processor followed by the whole eggs. Hit go, blending the ingredients together. Drop in four of the additional egg yolks, one by one, as you might not need them all. When the crumb-like mixture starts to ball, it is ready. It should be nice and pliable, with a faintly tacky feel; a little too sticky is better than too dry. Add the remaining yolks if you need to. Remove the dough from the processor and gently knead it for a minute or so on the work surface. Form it into a ball, wrap it in clingfilm and put it in the fridge for an hour.

Set up your pasta machine on the side of the table. Make sure you have a good length of work surface free to lay the pasta along and scatter this lightly with semolina. Unwrap the pasta and cut it into three pieces. Starting with the rollers on their most open setting, wind a piece of the pasta through the machine. If the pasta sticks to the rollers, dust the pasta with a little flour. Fold the pasta in half lengthways, put the setting down two notches and wind the pasta through again, folded-end first, as this will force air bubbles out of the open end. Fold the pasta in half and reduce the setting again. (The point of the folding is to get a good width on the pasta as well as length; the pasta should be as wide as the rollers by the time you finish.) Continue the rolling with an ever-decreasing opening on the rollers until the pasta goes through the finest setting. If the pasta rips on the narrower settings, check the rollers to make sure they have not got any dried old pasta on them – or rust, for that matter. You are now ready to make the first batch of ravioli.

Lay out the pasta sheet on the work surface. Again, there should be a scattering of semolina under the pasta – it would be a shame for it to stick when it came to lifting and closing the ravioli. Starting two-fingers' width in from one end of the pasta, put a teaspoon of the filling just below an imaginary

» horizontal central line. Place the ravioli filling at two-fingers'-width intervals all the way along, remembering to leave the same two-finger gap at the other end too.

Put some water into a little bowl; this is your glue. Paint along the entire length of the pasta edge closest to you. Then paint down both sides of each filling ball, starting just above the central line. Very carefully fold the top edge of the pasta over to meet the bottom edge. Gently pull the side of your hand down between the fillings to stick the folded sheet together, then use a knife to cut down the centre of the gaps. Pick up each ravioli piece and press the open sides together, starting from one side and pinching your way around the square to close it and chase the air out of the final corner; sealing the edges willy-nilly will only trap air inside, resulting in burst ravioli. They must be firmly sealed; try hard not to trap the filling in the edges, as this will also result in blow-outs when cooking. Repeat this process with the other pieces of dough until all the ravioli are made.

Lay the ravioli on a tray covered in a good amount of semolina to prevent them from sticking. If preparing them in advance, they must not be stacked and only put clingfilm over them if the tray sides keep it off the surface of the pasta dough.

Bring a large pan of salted water to the boil. Meanwhile, melt the butter in a frying pan. When it is foaming, add the sage leaves and gently fry them on both sides until crisp but not browned (about 2 minutes). By this time, the butter will have gone a nutty brown; this is perfect – it should not be black. While the sage cooks, turn the boiling water down to a healthy simmer (the pasta should not be bumping around like a sheet in a strong gale), drop the ravioli into the water and cook for 4–6 minutes. If you want to test one, cut off a corner of the pasta and nibble it; it should not be soft like canned spaghetti – soft, certainly, but retaining the faintest bite.

Divide the ravioli between bowls and spoon over the sage butter, finishing this plate of joy with a grating of Parmesan.

Beetroot, tomato & lovage salad

Serves 2

2 small–medium beetroot (similar in size to the tomatoes), skins left on, washed and trimmed
2 large ripe tomatoes
½ small red onion, finely sliced
a good splash of red wine vinegar
2 tablespoons good olive oil
flaked sea salt and black pepper
5 lovage leaves, finely sliced

This is a wonderful salad, clean and sparky, and very good with poached or grilled lamb.

Put the beetroot in a saucepan of cold water. Bring to the boil, turn down the heat and simmer for 30–40 minutes until tender. Cool, then slip off the skins.

Roughly slice the beetroots and transfer them to a salad bowl. Roughly chop the tomatoes and add them to the beetroot. Scatter the onion on top and splash with a good amount of vinegar – the salad shouldn't be too sharp. Add the oil and plenty of salt and pepper. Scatter the lovage on top.

Toss the salad just before serving so as not to make the whole affair beetroot-pink too early on.

Roasted squash with sage & Pecorino

Serves 4–6

1 large butternut squash

olive oil, for roasting

flaked sea salt

a scattering of dried chile flakes

1 medium red onion, halved
   and finely sliced

20 large sage leaves

30g pine nuts

1 tablespoon good balsamic vinegar

Pecorino or Parmesan cheese,
   for shaving

This is a great addition to an informal spread. Eaten as a vegetarian dish, it is a fine thing. You can add some mozzarella at the end, along with the Pecorino or Parmesan cheese.

Preheat the oven to 200°C fan/220°C/Gas 7. Cut the squash in half lengthways and scoop out the seeds. Cut the flesh into sickle-shaped pieces around 2cm thick. Flip some oil all over the bottom of a baking tray that is big enough to take all the pieces without them having to be stacked and throw a little salt on to the oil. Lay the squash segments down in one layer. Scatter more salt and some dried chile flakes over the top, and splash with more oil. Roast for about 40 minutes.

While the squash is cooking, toss the onion slices in a little oil to coat them and season with salt. Halfway through the squash's cooking time, lift one of the segments; the flesh that is touching the tray should be taking on some good dark colouring and browning on the edges of the flesh. Cook them for longer if this has not been achieved. At this point, turn them over, then scatter the onions over the top; the idea is that they will crisp and brown.

Toss the sage leaves in a little oil. About 6 minutes before the squash slices are ready, scatter the leaves over the top to dry and crisp. Toast the pine nuts if you prefer them this way.

When the cooking time is up, take the tray out and arrange the segments on a nice plate with the sage and onion scattered all over. Splash over the balsamic vinegar and scatter over the pine nuts. Take a piece of Pecorino or Parmesan and, using a potato peeler, cut shavings from the cheese to float down and finish the dish.

Gourd with cheese

Serves 1

1 blue hubbard, red kuri or onion
    squash, a little larger than a
    cricket ball
20g butter
flaked sea salt
1 small goats' cheese, such as Crottin
    or Capricorn, rind removed
a small grating of nutmeg
black pepper

Genius packaging and eating from Mother Nature and, dare I say it, great
for the office microwave lunch – far better, surely, than a damp sandwich.

Preheat the oven to 170° fan/190°C/Gas 5. Cut the top from your gourd,
just deep enough so that you can get a teaspoon inside it. Hollow out the
pith and seeds. Rub the butter around the inside and season with a little
salt. Poke in the cheese and grate and grind over the nutmeg and a good
grinding of black pepper.

Pop the lid on the gourd, then place it on a tray and roast it for about
30 minutes, or until the skin and flesh feel soft to the touch. Remove the
little darling to a plate, lift the lid and tuck in with a spoon, being careful
not to burn your lips.

Walnut & spinach bourani

Serves 2

a handful of walnuts
2 tablespoons olive oil, plus extra
    for drizzling
1 small onion, finely chopped
1 garlic clove, finely chopped
½ teaspoon ground cumin
200g spinach, tough stalks removed,
    finely shredded
2 tablespoons Greek-style yoghurt
flaked sea salt
a little lemon juice
warmed flatbread, to serve (optional)

I eat this now and then in one of the cafés on the Uxbridge Road, London,
where Muslim men sit all day drinking strong coffee, talking intensely and
waving their arms as if arguing with each other when in fact they are just
chatting. This is very easy to put together quickly.

Break the walnuts up a bit and rub them between your hands to flake off as
much of their skin as you can. Heat the oil in a frying pan and fry the onion
gently with the walnuts, stirring occasionally, until the onion is totally soft.
Add the garlic and cumin and cook for a further 2 minutes.

Drop the spinach into the pan, where it will crackle and pop as it collapses.
Keep feeding the pan with spinach as it wilts until it is all in there. Cook until
all the green water has evaporated. Remove from the heat.

Flop the yoghurt into the pan and warm it through. Do not boil it, as strange
things happen to yoghurt when it is scalded. Season the spinach generously
with salt and a twist of lemon juice. Turn it out into a little bowl and drizzle
once more with a little oil.

This is great when eaten with warmed flatbread. Follow with a stiff little
coffee and head back to work.

Sausage-stuffed marrow with white sauce

Serves 6

50g butter
2 onions, finely chopped
1 tablespoon malt vinegar
150g good smoked streaky bacon
1 teaspoon dried thyme
450g prime sausagemeat
black pepper
flaked sea salt (optional)
160g Bramley apples (weight
    after being peeled and cored)
12 sage leaves (or 9 whoppers),
    finely chopped
1 fat marrow (about 1.4kg or the size
    of a dachshund's body)
good white crusty loaf, to serve

White sauce

25g butter
1 teaspoon English mustard powder
1 heaped tablespoon plain flour
250–300ml whole milk
100g Cheshire cheese, grated
a grating of nutmeg
flaked sea salt (optional)

This is good, hearty farmhouse stuff and, I hope, an easier alternative to the more traditional whole stuffed marrow. I am increasingly aware of people's dislike for marrow but, in certain cases, do not believe these protesters truly remember how one tastes. Please have another go, as it's only fair on this excellent vegetable.

To make the stuffing, melt 30g of the butter in a large frying pan and add the onions. When they begin to turn golden, add the vinegar and cook it out until it has totally evaporated. Mince the bacon in a blender while the onions cook and add it after the vinegar stage with the thyme. Keep everything gently frying together for a further 5 minutes or so. Add the sausagemeat to the mix, breaking it up. Cook everything together over a medium heat until the sausage is cooked and lightly coloured (about 10 minutes). Add a good blast of black pepper and check if it needs salt. Transfer the stuffing to a large bowl and allow it to cool. Superficially wipe the pan clean with a little kitchen paper.

Chop up the apple into little chunks. Melt the remaining butter in the frying pan and, when hot, fry the apple hard, tossing frequently, until quite coloured but not totally soft (about 6 minutes or so). Throw in the sage and fry for a further minute before adding the contents of the pan to the stuffing. Combine everything together thoroughly. Preheat the oven to 170°C fan/190°C/Gas 5.

Now make the white sauce. Melt the butter in a small, heavy-based saucepan before adding the mustard powder and flour. Stir gently for 30 seconds or so. Start adding the milk bit by bit. I would advise using a whisk, as it will help keep out the lumps. It will all clag up at first, but loosen as you add the rest of the milk, bit by bit, while stirring vigorously. Let the white sauce bubble away ever so slightly for 10 minutes, stirring occasionally, before adding the cheese. Cook until totally melted. Add the nutmeg. Check the seasoning, adding salt if necessary, and turn off the heat.

Cut the marrow into six circular sections, each about 5cm wide, keeping the ends for another dish. Take each wheel, hollow out the pith and seeds and chuck them out. Then cut six square pieces of baking paper, each large enough to put a piece of marrow on. Lay the paper pieces on a baking tray with the marrow on top of each, leaving a gap between each one. Fill each marrow piece generously with the stuffing; it should be quite compact. Slide the tray into the oven and bake until the marrow is tender but not mushy (about 25 minutes), testing it by sliding a knife into the skin.

Turn off the oven and switch on the grill at its highest setting. Remove the marrow and spoon the cheese sauce over the top of each piece so that it goes to the edges. Pop back under the grill, but not too close to the element, and cook for 2 minutes until well browned. Serve with a good white crusty loaf and a bottle of tangy cider.

Ceps & apples in puff pastry

Serves 2

40g dried porcini mushrooms

5 Cox's apples, peeled

60g butter

a splash of sunflower oil

flaked sea salt and black pepper

2 splashy tablespoons brandy

2 medium shallots, halved
    and finely sliced

1 bay leaf

2 garlic cloves, finely chopped

Puff pastry

225g plain flour, plus extra for dusting

a good pinch of fine sea salt

185g butter, chilled, cut roughly
    into 2cm dice

125ml cold water

2 teaspoons lemon juice

1 free-range egg, beaten

I was trying to think of an alternative to potatoes that could be eaten with beef and here is my autumn inspiration. The crispy pastry is very good for chasing gravy around the plate.

To make the pastry, sift the flour and salt into a large bowl. Drop in the butter and toss with a large metal spoon until it is lightly coated in the flour. Mix the water and lemon juice together and pour into the bowl. Use a table knife to cut across the mix about 30 times, chopping the butter into the flour until the dough comes together. When it forms a loose lump, tip it on to a board and shape it into a fat slab. Wrap in baking paper and chill in the fridge for an hour.

Roll out the dough on a well-floured work surface to make a rectangle 40cm × 20cm. Fold one-third of the pastry into the rectangle, then fold the other end over that. Press the edges firmly with the rolling pin, then rotate the pastry a quarter turn. Roll into the same-sized rectangle and start the process again. You are building up the fluffy layers that make this rough puff pastry. Continue five more times: rolling into a rectangle, folding, pressing. Don't worry if a chunk of butter makes its way through in the early stages. Just keep the board and pin very well floured to prevent the pastry from sticking. After the last repetition, wrap the slab in clingfilm and chill for 1–2 hours (or overnight). If it is very firm, allow the pastry to warm before rolling.

Put the mushrooms in a bowl and steep in enough hot water to cover. Allow them to rehydrate for at least an hour. Preheat the oven 170°C fan/190°C/Gas 5. Cut the apples along the sides, which should leave you with four pieces per core. Melt half the butter in a pan with the oil. Season the apples with salt and fry them for 10–12 minutes, turning them regularly until well browned all over. They should be soft all the way through, but not collapsing. Tip in the brandy and angle the frying pan towards the flame – it should set alight to the pan (or wave a lit match over the fumes from the pan). Toss the apples until the flame goes out. Put the apples to one side.

Melt the rest of the butter in the pan and sauté the shallots with the drained mushrooms, having squeezed out but retained the liquor. Add a good grinding of black pepper and the bay leaf. When the shallots are very soft and the mushrooms are beginning to take on some colour, toss the garlic through for a minute or so. Pour in the mushroom liquor and reduce it almost completely. The mix should not be at all watery, but moist. Fold the apples back through the mushroom mixture. Allow the mixture to cool completely.

Roll out the pastry to one-and-a-half times the size of a sheet of A4 paper and transfer it to a wide baking tray lined with baking paper. With the long side facing you, position your filling along the lower half, leaving a 1.5cm border all the way around. Paint around the outer edges of the pastry with the beaten egg. Fold the top edge of the pastry over to meet the bottom edge. Very lightly press any air out from inside the pastry, going from one end to the other. Crimp the edges with a fork. Glaze the top of the parcel with the beaten egg and make three small incisions through to the filling. Bake for 30 minutes until deep golden, risen and crispy. Eat as is or serve next to a large rib of beef with rich gravy.

Mushrooms baked with hazelnuts & Pecorino

Makes 4

4 large portobello or field mushrooms, wiped clean

50g blanched hazelnuts

25g semi-fresh white bread (ideally focaccia or a white sourdough)

4 tablespoons finely chopped young curly-leaf parsley

3 small garlic cloves, finely chopped

50g Pecorino cheese, finely grated

finely grated zest of ½ medium unwaxed lemon

2 tablespoons olive oil, plus extra for the mushrooms

flaked sea salt and black pepper

This recipe says autumn to me and would be well camouflaged if placed on a forest floor. I have used portobello mushrooms, but should you be lucky enough to stumble upon some field mushrooms or a giant parasol, then they would work well too.

Preheat the oven to 200°C fan/220°C/Gas 7, with a roasting tray for the mushrooms inside it. Cut the mushroom stalks down to the same level as the gills and rub the caps with a little oil, then set aside (these can be used at another time for stock).

Scatter the hazelnuts over a baking tray and toast them in the oven for about 4 minutes, or until they turn golden and emit a toasted smell (don't forget them – I have incinerated at least £200-worth over the years). Leave to cool for a few minutes. Tear up the bread, put it in a food processor and blitz to medium–fine crumbs, then add the nuts and whizz them to medium–fine as well (were you to put the nuts in at the same time as the bread, they would be chopped too small). Transfer to a bowl. Mix in the parsley, garlic, Pecorino, lemon zest and the oil. Season with salt and plenty of ground black pepper.

Divide the mixture between the four mushrooms, lightly pressing it into the dark side of each cap but keeping it fairly loose. Remove the baking tray from the oven. Place the loaded mushrooms on the tray, with the stuffing facing up. Return quickly to the oven and bake for 12–18 minutes, or until the mushrooms are tender and the topping is rich gold. Serve hot with a little salad – shaved fennel with treviso leaves, dressed in a little lemon juice and good olive oil, would suit perfectly.

Pasta with wild mushrooms

Serves 2

150g dried egg tagliatelle
50g butter, chilled
a good splash of olive oil
150g wild mushrooms, trimmed,
  wiped clean and sliced if big
1 large garlic clove, finely chopped
a squeeze of lemon juice
flaked sea salt and black pepper
1 tablespoon finely chopped
  curly-leaf parsley
a grating of Parmesan cheese

There are two ways to enjoy your mushrooms quickly – either on toast or in pasta. Here is the latter. Desirable mushrooms for this dish would be girolles, yellow legs, ceps, blewitts, trompettes or fairy ring.

Put a large pan of water on to boil and a large frying pan on a high heat. Work swiftly so that the two parts of the dish come together at the same time. Drop the pasta into the water and cook until ready (*al dente* is fine, but quite often this seems an excuse for wildly undercooked pasta).

Meanwhile, melt half the butter with the oil in the frying pan and fry the mushrooms vigorously until they start to colour. Any obvious watery element should have been cooked away from them. Drop in the garlic and toss it through. Follow with just enough lemon to give the mushrooms an edge (but not too tart). Taste and season the mushrooms.

Drain the pasta, and just before the last of the cooking water drains out of the colander, take it to the frying pan and immediately add it to the mushrooms. Drop in the remaining butter, tossing the pasta all the time. The cold butter and water spun together will make a lovely emulsion, similar to cream. Divide the pasta between two plates, add a good grind of black pepper, a sprinkling of the parsley and a grating of Parmesan. Eat informally, leaning against the kitchen worktop whilst gazing at the rest of your fine haul of fungi.

Fried ceps with chives

Serves 2

200g ceps, bad bits cut out where
   necessary and wiped clean
light olive oil, for frying
flaked sea salt
1 good large garlic clove with
   no green shoot, peeled
a small bunch of chives
extra virgin olive oil, for drizzling
lemon juice, to taste
Parmesan cheese shavings, to serve
   (optional)

The year 2010 saw a bumper crop of ceps. I'm talking of the Penny Buns, as they are known in this country, that look like bread rolls lying in the moss and grass. This mushroom, for me, is something truly special in both its look and exquisite taste. I can only compare gazing into a large basket of ceps with the same love I had for my shoebox-full of *Star Wars* figurines as a boy, each one a coveted marvel. From the hunting to the cleaning to the cooking and the eating, I'm mesmerised by this awesome fungi. They are a true treat and sometimes I like to eat them as simply as possible.

Put a large frying pan over a medium heat. If the ceps have remained intact, cut them all the way through the stalk and cap into 5mm slices so that each one is a cross-section of the whole. Brush the cep slices generously on one side with light olive oil. When the pan is good and hot, lay the ceps, oil-side down, in the pan, where they should sizzle immediately. Scatter generously with salt. Leave plenty of room in the pan, as stacked or overlapping they will not brown properly. Sizzle them for approximately 2 minutes, resisting the urge to poke them around. Try not to burn the oil, occasionally adjusting the heat if necessary. While the mushrooms fry, paint the raw side with more oil using a pastry brush. When deep, golden nut-brown, turn them over and cook the other side.

While the fungi fry, finely chop the garlic and then the chives. Lift the ceps to a plate and scatter over the chives and garlic. Drizzle with a splash of extra virgin olive oil and then squeeze over a little lemon juice followed by any additional salt should they need it. A few shavings of Parmesan can be a lovely addition to this dish.

Alpine salad

Serves 6

3 medium free-range eggs

a little sunflower oil

12 rashers of smoked streaky bacon,
  finely sliced

2 slices of walnut or multigrain bread

150g lamb's lettuce

flaked sea salt and black pepper

Yoghurt dressing

100ml good full-fat yoghurt

1 small garlic clove, crushed

1 generous teaspoon Dijon or
  German mustard

a capful of white wine vinegar

1½ teaspoons caster sugar

2 tablespoons double cream

1 tablespoon sunflower oil

a squeeze of lemon juice

flaked sea salt and black pepper

In the Winter Alps, it is rare to see any greenery among the avalanche of bread, cheese, eggs, cream, white wine and sausage. This recipe is an exception and comes from my snowy cousin, Liz Moore, who lives in Switzerland.

Boil the eggs for 8 minutes and cool them immediately in cold water. They should not be runny but have a lovely moistness to the yolk. Getting it started with a little splash of oil, fry the bacon until very crispy, turning once. Drain on kitchen paper, reserving the fat in the pan. When cool, roughly crumble.

Cut the bread into little cubes and fry it in the bacon fat until golden. If all the oil is absorbed, splash in some more oil. The croûtons should be crispy whilst retaining a little squidge in the middle. Allow to cool on kitchen paper.

Beat together all the ingredients for the dressing until well combined. Put the lamb's lettuce into a large salad bowl and liberally splash over some of the dressing. Peel then roughly chop the eggs and scatter them over the leaves, followed by the crumbled bacon and croûtons, a couple of grinds of black pepper and some salt. Serve immediately; then have your sausage and potato course.

Coleslaw

Serves 6–8

150g cored and finely sliced
  red cabbage
150g cored and finely sliced
  white cabbage
2 large carrots
1 small red onion, finely sliced

Dressing

2 large free-range egg yolks
1 good teaspoon English
  mustard powder
1 teaspoon Dijon mustard
flaked sea salt and ground
  white pepper
25ml white wine vinegar
150ml sunflower oil
2 tablespoons good full-fat yoghurt

Limp – but with a crunch – and tumbled with thick mayonnaise, this is one of the few ways I really enjoy white cabbage. Good coleslaw is a far cry from the fast-food side order in a stumpy styrofoam cup. It's the kind of thing I veer towards on a Sunday or Monday night. A heavily buttered potato is the best vehicle: a cart piled high with loose hay.

To make the dressing, put the egg yolks, mustard powder, Dijon mustard, a good pinch of salt, a pinch of white pepper and the vinegar into a food processor. Secure the lid and hit go. Slowly dribble in the oil. If you're worried that it's becoming too thick while adding the oil, introduce the tiniest splash of warm water to let it down before continuing with the oil. You want your mayonnaise to be droppy, not drippy, thickish and glossy. Finally, add the yoghurt and whizz only briefly. Check for seasoning and add a little more salt or vinegar if necessary.

Put the sliced cabbages in a large mixing bowl. Peel the carrots, discarding the skin, then keep on peeling in big strips with the potato peeler. Cut the lengths in half, finally shred them as you did the cabbage and add to the bowl. Put the onion in a sieve and rinse away its attitude. Allow to drip-dry thoroughly before mixing in with the carrots and cabbage.

Flop the mayonnaise on top of the veg (I prefer mine a little more mayonnaisey than most, so judge how much to put in yourself, but you do want all the strips to be well covered). It's best to leave the coleslaw to mature for half an hour. Fabulous with crispy roast pork belly or in turkey sandwiches.

Endive in cream sauce with breadcrumbs

Serves 4

100ml white wine
450ml fresh chicken stock
   (*see* page 240)
3 large heads of endive, trimmed,
   root intact, quartered lengthways,
40g butter
40g plain flour
100ml double cream
2 teaspoons Dijon mustard
flaked sea salt and black pepper
25g Parmesan cheese
4 rashers of smoked streaky bacon,
   sliced into wide matchsticks
a dash of sunflower oil
40g fresh white breadcrumbs
¼ teaspoon dried thyme

I seldom see enough endive, except when it dutifully does its tired Christmas act alongside the pear and Stilton. But rarely does it come to the table cooked and that is a shame, as it is a most wonderful vegetable once introduced to heat.

Preheat the oven to 190°C fan/210°C/Gas 6½. In a wide-based pan, bring the white wine and chicken stock to a simmer. Poach the endive in this liquor until tender (about 10 minutes, providing the broth is simmering gently), turning halfway through the cooking time. Remove the endive with a slotted spoon, reserving the stock, and drain them very thoroughly in a colander.

Melt the butter in a saucepan over a medium heat. Sift in the flour, cooking the roux gently for a minute or so (do not brown the flour). Start adding the stock, ladle by ladle, until it is all used up, whisking all the time. Cook gently for another 5 minutes before stirring in the cream and finally the mustard. Continue cooking for a further 5 minutes. Season to taste. The consistency of the sauce should be that of good-quality pouring double cream.

Neatly lay the endive, cut-side up, in rows in a large gratin dish. Cover with the sauce and grate over the Parmesan before baking for 15 minutes.

Fry the bacon with the oil (to get it going) for 6–7 minutes until crispy but not burnt. Drain on kitchen paper. Throw the breadcrumbs and thyme into the bacon fat and fry until the breadcrumbs are golden and just beginning to be crunchy. Return the bacon to the pan and turn off the heat.

When the endive is ready, scatter over the breadcrumbs and bacon. Serve as is, alongside chicken or fish such as pollock or flounder.

Raw kale salad

Serves 4

1 tablespoon fennel seeds
200g tender curly kale
3 tablespoons rapeseed oil or olive oil
1½ tablespoons good cider vinegar
flaked sea salt
¾ tablespoon dark muscavado sugar

This struck me as a very interesting combination during a wonderful drunken post-dinner food chat. I couldn't wait to get home and try it and now eat my version regularly throughout the last months of the year. The kale should be young and tender-stalked, and bought from a proper greengrocer. Found bagged in supermarkets, it is often chopped straight through, stalks and all, sometimes making it ungiving and chewy. By spring, most kale gets pretty tough and would be better cooked.

Place a small frying pan over a medium heat and tip in the fennel seeds. Dry-fry them, swirling occasionally, until their toasted smell comes to the nose and they have darkened in colour. It is essential that they do not burn – moving them about is imperative.

Test the kale stalks; if they are tender and giving, you can include them in the salad, but if not, strip off the leaves and discard the stalks. Chop up the kale and put it in a bowl. Pour in the oil and vinegar and toss the leaves until well dressed. Season with salt and try again. Scatter over the fennel seeds and the muscavado sugar. Eat immediately.

Baked potatoes with garlic & cream

Serves 2

2 medium baking potatoes
flaked sea salt and black pepper
1 good hard garlic bulb
40g butter
50ml double cream

Potatoes, cream and garlic are on this earth to know each other. This is a loose affair, very easy, simple and totally pleasing. Good cold-weather food.

Preheat oven to 200°C fan/220°C/Gas 7. Run a skewer through the middle of both potatoes and put them on a small baking tray, then scatter 1 teaspoon of salt over them. Bake for 45 minutes–1 hour until totally crisp and cooked through. Around 25 minutes before the potatoes are ready, put the garlic bulb into the oven, where it will cook until coloured brown and sticky.

Remove the potatoes and garlic from the oven. Remove the skewers and split each of the spuds in half. Distress the insides with a fork and pack the butter into the flesh. Divide the garlic cloves, left in their skin, between both. Drizzle over the cream, bombard with black pepper and add a final flick of salt to really bring out the potato and garlic joy. Removing the garlic from the skins with a knife and fork is fiddly; if you so choose, squeeze out the contents into the spud before eating. I just drop the roasted cloves straight into my split spud. Punchy garlic, buttery potato, cream and salt equals joy.

Good roast potatoes

Serves 3–4

750g medium–large King Edward
    potatoes (about 4), or another
    floury variety
2 heaped teaspoons flaked sea salt
2½ generous dessertspoons goose fat
1½ good dessertspoons plain flour
1 teaspoon dried rosemary
1 good hard garlic bulb (optional)
black pepper

A good roast crispy armoured potato can be as memorable as the meat it lies beside. The trick is to cut the potatoes up small (a medium-large one into six), and maybe give them a head start in the oven if they have to share it with a roast. The meat creates so much moisture in the oven, so you can't get the potatoes properly crispy. You can also whack up the heat for a final blast while the meat rests after cooking. Best of all, cook them separately from the roast if you have a double oven. Waxy varieties of spud do not make good roasters; go for a floury variety such as King Edward.

Preheat the oven to 200°C fan/220°C/Gas 7. Peel and cut each potato in half lengthways, then each half into two or three, depending on size. Put the potatoes in a saucepan of cold water with half the salt and bring them up to the boil – but not a furious one. Cook for 5–6 minutes. Do not over-boil the potatoes or they will fall apart at the next step. Two minutes before the cooking time is up, spoon the fat into a roasting tray and put it in the oven.

Drain the potatoes straight into a colander and scatter over half the flour. Toss the potatoes in the flour to distress their edges. Scatter over the rest of the flour and the rosemary and do the same again. They should be evenly covered. Take the hot fat from the oven and tip in the potatoes. Jostle them a bit to make sure they each have a little room around them and are not on top of each other. This is very important, especially if you are doubling the measurements of this recipe. Immediately place the potatoes in the oven and cook them for 35–40 minutes, turning twice. If using the garlic, break the bulb into separate cloves and throw them over the potatoes 15–20 minutes before they are ready.

Scatter the remaining salt and a good blast of black pepper all over the potatoes and serve them crisp as baby armadillos after a forest fire.

Pommes boulangères

Serves 6–8

2 tablespoons olive oil

3 white onions, peeled (reserve
    and trimmings skins for stock)
    and finely sliced

leaves from 5 sprigs of thyme
    (reserve stalks for stock)

1 tablespoon white wine vinegar

125g butter

1.5kg waxy potatoes

flaked sea salt and black pepper

Stock

1 fresh chicken carcass
    (or leftovers from a roast)

a good splash of oil or a little butter

750ml cold water

flaked sea salt

It is said that this recipe gets its name from the idea that local wives would take their dish of potatoes to cook in the dying heat of the village baker's oven after work. Personally, I think this was more the sole privilege of the baker's wife, thus avoiding a catalogue of problems I will not go into.

I once made *pommes boulangères* with the trimmings from a fresh foie gras. All I can say is '*Mon Dieu!*'

First make the stock (unless you have some around – you just need a small quantity). If using the carcass from a roasted chicken, ideally use one that has not been stuffed with lemon, as this makes for a faintly bitter and unpleasant stock. Chop up the chicken carcass and fry the pieces in the oil or butter in your stockpot until nicely coloured and golden. Put the stripped stalks from the thyme and skins and trimmings from the onions you will use for the potatoes in the pot with the water. Bring up to the gentlest simmer and cook it like this, with the lid off, for an hour. When the time is up, skim off any fat that has risen to the top and add enough salt to make the stock very tasty in its own right.

Preheat the oven to 190°C fan/210°C/Gas 6½. Heat the oil in a pan, add the onions and thyme leaves and cook gently until the onions are totally soft but not coloured. This should take about 20 minutes. Just before turning off the heat, splash the onions with the vinegar and keep cooking until it has totally evaporated. Grease a baking dish with 25g of the butter.

Peel the potatoes and slice them lengthways to the thickness of a £1 coin. Place a layer of potatoes, slightly overlapping, across the bottom of the greased dish. Take a third of the onions and drape them evenly over the potatoes. Dot here and there with a third of the remaining butter and sprinkle over generously with salt and a proper bombardment of black pepper. Now add another layer of potatoes, more onions and more butter. Do this until everything has been used up.

Pour 500ml of the chicken stock over the potatoes. Cover the dish with foil and bake it for 40 minutes. After this time, remove the foil and leave the dish in the oven for a further 20 minutes until the top takes on some rich golden colouring. Remove from the oven and eat with something like a good steak and an honest bottle of red wine. Leftovers can simply be heated up in the oven and covered in Parmesan or hard sheep's milk cheese, which makes for a respectable little lunch needing no accompanying meat.

Roast parsnips & Stichelton

Serves 2

3 medium parsnips, peeled and
    quartered lengthways
1 tablespoon plain flour, seasoned
    with 1 teaspoon flaked sea salt
3 tablespoons duck or goose fat,
    or sunflower oil
Stichelton (or Stilton), as desired

I love this kind of thing when I can't be bothered to cook dinner but want something to snack on by the fire. No fuss, maximum pleasure. Stichelton is a truly fabulous cheese, similar to Stilton although slightly sweeter and with fewer blue veins, and made with unpasteurised milk.

Preheat the oven to 200°C fan/220°C/Gas 7. Par-boil the parsnips in rolling water until just tender, but with a little crunch inside (about 4 minutes). Toss them in the seasoned flour so that they are lightly coated.

While the parsnips boil, pour the fat or oil into a small oven tray and get it nice and smoking hot in the oven (it seems a lot, but you are almost frying the parsnips). Throw the parsnips into the hot fat and slam them in the oven to roast hard for 25 minutes, or until deep golden orange with browned bits, nice and crispy on the outside and totally squidgy within. They should be turned once or twice during cooking.

Drain the parsnips thoroughly of fat on kitchen paper. Put the Stichelton on a plate. Eat with the parsnips as you wish. Downright wintery.

Swede, apple & plum pickle

Makes 2kg

1 teaspoon black pepper

1 thumb-sized piece of root ginger, peeled and finely chopped

½ teaspoon ground cloves

1 bay leaf

500g demerara sugar

60g raisins

1 teaspoon flaked sea salt

500ml malt vinegar

2 onions, cut into medium dice

1 large swede (about 1kg), peeled and cut to the size of travel dice

1 large Bramley apple, peeled, cored and chopped twice as large as the swede pieces

8 large purple plums, stoned and cut into eighths

3 teaspoons ground arrowroot

Cheese and pickle sandwiches are a staple in the Warner home – it's my favourite filling of all – so here's a pickle recipe.

Put the pepper, ginger, cloves, bay leaf, sugar, raisins, salt and all but 2 tablespoons of the vinegar into a pan with the onions and boil gently until the onions have softened (about 20 minutes or so). Drop in the swede, apple and plums and simmer gently for 30 minutes more, no longer.

Meanwhile, to sterilise the jars, preheat the oven to 160°fan/180°C/Gas 4. Wash the preserving jars and lids really well (removing the rubber seals if they have them). Put them on a baking tray in the oven for 10 minutes.

Mix the arrowroot together with the reserved 2 tablespoons of vinegar in a small bowl to make a thin paste. Stir this into the pickle. Cook for 5 minutes more, stirring.

Divide the mixture between the sterilised jars and screw on the lids while it is still warm to create a vacuum. Allow the pickle to mature for at least a month before opening. Once open, keep in the fridge.

Raw Brussels sprouts with ricotta

Serves 2

10 cooked and peeled chestnuts
(vacuum-packed ones are fine)
1 tablespoon dark runny honey
12 medium Brussels sprouts,
trimmed and very finely sliced
juice of 1 lemon
3 tablespoons good olive oil
flaked sea salt and black pepper
3–6 slices of Coppa ham (optional)
125g good soft ricotta or goats'
cheese, broken up

Oh the controversy over the Brussels sprout! When overcooked the fart is perhaps preferable to the taste and the dim colour is reminiscent of those early '80s bathroom suites. However, cooked well it should be praised. Boiled with salt, black pepper, butter and a good hit of red wine vinegar, sprouts are my brassica of choice throughout the cold months. Eaten raw, they are a different thing again and invigorating in their mineral delivery.

Break each of the chestnuts into two or three smaller pieces. Just cover them with water in a small pan. Add the honey, then put on a gentle simmer to soften them a little (6 minutes or so). Allow them to cool in their liquid.

Drop the sprouts into a bowl and squeeze over the lemon juice followed by most of the oil, then season well with salt and a heavy bombardment of black pepper. If using, lay the ham flat over the bottom of two plates and let the greens fall on top. Add the chestnuts followed by the cheese here and there. Pass over one last time with the oil.

Guacamole

Serves 8–10

3 medium ripe Hass avocados,
    halved and stoned
2 medium very ripe vine tomatoes,
    roughly but not coarsely chopped
1 small red onion, finely chopped
a small bunch of coriander, leaves
    and stalks very finely chopped
½ jalapeño chile, very finely
    chopped, with seeds, or to taste
2 fat limes
1 dessertspoon sunflower oil
more flaked sea salt than you think
    you need
good corn tortilla chips, to serve

A lot of odd things are done in the name of guacamole. I've had some disturbingly crunchy ones, so, for a start, it is essential that the avocado flesh is creamy and ripe and, I hope, green not brown. Have a good feel before buying. I would always recommend the Hass over other larger, smoother-skinned varieties, which can be milky and tasteless. Olive oil, paprika and garlic – aïe! – there is no place for these things. Having said that, the addition of mayonnaise is okay, as this seems particular to the Guadalajara area of Mexico. Make more than you need; as the saying goes, guacamole '*desapareceran como ranitas abajo la garganta de un caiman*' ('disappears like frogs down the throat of a crocodile').

Scoop the avocado from its skin into a bowl and mash it well with a fork. Personally, I like a little texture but no big lumps. Add the chopped tomato and onion, then the coriander. Add the appropriate amount of chile, according to your tolerance (you can put it in, but you can't take it out). Squeeze in the juice from the limes, remembering that you don't necessarily need all of it. There should be a definite sharpness, but not a twisted sourness. Pour in the oil with an initial pinch of salt and stir. Be a little adventurous with the salt, adding it bit by bit and tasting as you go. The avocado will take more salt than you think.

Allow the guacamole to rest for 15 minutes and check the seasoning once more. Eat with some good corn tortilla chips and some seriously cold lager.

Note: I would not advise the following if cooking for others, but if you're annoyed to find you bought some really mean little dry limes, squeeze each half clamped between your teeth, as your jaws will get the most out of them.

Stubby beans

Serves 6–8

500g dried pinto beans, or haricot
    or borlotti beans
2 smoked ham hocks (about 1kg)
40g lard
2 onions, chopped
leaves from 8 sprigs of thyme
4 garlic cloves, finely chopped
1 teaspoon English mustard powder
½ teaspoon ground cloves
2 × 400g cans chopped tomatoes
50g dark muscovado sugar
10g flaked sea salt
black pepper
buttered Savoy or spring cabbage,
    to serve (optional)

It is only right that you eat these while tilting back in your chair with your boots on the table. Please hold the tin or enamel plate just beneath your unshaven chin (yes, ladies too) and spoon the beans crudely into your nearby mouth. Grunt occasionally and be sure to make a clattering scrapey sound with the spoon on the plate as you slurp the end of your serving over the rim. On the whole, I find Boston beans too thick and molasses-heavy. These are more like baked beans. The 'stubby' rather ungraciously refers to the end, or stub, of the pig – the smoky ham hock. I recommend *Blazing Saddles* as the perfect post-dinner film.

Put the beans in a large bowl, cover with plenty of water and leave overnight, or for 12 hours.

On the day you plan to cook the beans, put the hocks in a snug saucepan and cover with water. Bring them up to a cheery simmer and put a lid on the pot. Poach them like this for 1 hour.

Melt the lard in a large, flameproof casserole and in it fry the onions and thyme leaves for 7 minutes or so. When the onions have softened but not coloured, stir in the garlic, mustard powder and cloves, then cook for a minute or so more. Flop in the cans of tomatoes and sugar and stir together. Add the drained beans to the casserole, followed by the ham hocks, plus 1 litre of their stock (or 500ml of their stock and 500ml water, if the stock is very salty). Reserve any remaining ham stock for other things.

Bring the beans up to a gentle simmer and cover them with a lid. Have a peek after 5 minutes to see if they are cooking too fast as a result of the closed lid raising the temperature. Adjust it accordingly. Cook for 1 hour.

Now remove the lid. The beans will appear to be quite soupy, which is why you will now cook them for a further 30 minutes with the lid off in order to thicken the brew slightly. When you have done so, try the beans. They should be soft but, on the whole, intact. If they are still a little bitey, add a splash more water and cook for 20 minutes or so more, but I think this step is unlikely to be needed.

Add the salt and a heavy bombardment of black pepper and stir in well before lifting out the hocks. Turn off the heat. When the hocks have cooled a little, pull off their cape of fat. Try to work with the hocks while they are still warm, as they will be easier to deal with. Pull the meat from the bones and string it roughly between your fingers before throwing it in the pot. When all the ham has been added, stir it through the beans. When ready to serve, heat the beans and test the seasoning, then alter to your liking. This is delicious served with buttered Savoy or spring cabbage. 'Curm 'n' geddit!'

Note: If you wish, you can slice the ham fat thinly, pop it in a hot oven to crisp up and eat it with the beans or as a snack.

Green split peas

Serves 4

40g butter
1 onion, finely chopped
125g green split peas
2 litres cold water
flaked sea salt and black pepper
a grating of nutmeg
malt vinegar, to taste

I eat literally tonnes of these a year. They are a great accompaniment to white fish, ducks, pigeon, lamb and venison. When meat is not in the house, they are a wonderful substitute, and properly fill you up, especially with a fried egg on top, when you are really pinching the pennies. They are a thoroughly good friend. Split peas might take a while to cook, but I'm sure you have other things to be getting on with. Having said that, I will never learn and frequently scurry into the kitchen to check on them only to mutter 'Hurry up, hurry up!' Don't rush the cooking time, as they need to be totally soft.
While writing this I have oddly found myself humming the hymn that goes 'I was cold, I was hungry, were you there, were you there?' I guess I genuinely really do love green split peas.

Melt the butter in a saucepan. Add the onion and soften it over a medium–low heat for 7 minutes, without colouring, stirring occasionally. Add the peas and then the water. Bring all up to a jolly simmer. Cook the peas for 2–3 hours, or until totally soft, topping up the water if they are getting too thick. They should be the consistency of loose porridge, migrating slightly across the plate when spooned on to it. Season generously with salt and pepper and less so with nutmeg, remembering it should be a hint not a dominator. Stir in a little vinegar to give the peas only the faintest edge of sharpness.

Note: If you have leftovers, keep the cooked peas in the fridge until stiff, mould them into a deep fishcake-shape, flour it, then drop it in batter before deep-frying. Eat with malt vinegar. Oh yes!

Celeriac & apple purée

Serves 4

1kg celeriac
250g potatoes
350g Bramley apples
200ml double cream
3 garlic cloves, peeled
a small sprig of rosemary
3 tablespoons olive oil
flaked sea salt and black pepper
a good knob of butter

Celeriac is the root of a celery plant, but whereas some celery varieties are grown for the stalk, the celeriac ones are grown for the root. Some might not know what to do with this bearded cannonball, but it is no different to setting about a swede and, once the obstinate skin has been cut away, the flesh is there to offer up its extraordinary taste. I find it genuinely hard to describe raw celeriac; let's just say that celeriac has its own special tang. When cooked, it takes on a different and surprising truffle-like taste. It is one of my top three favourite vegetables (I would not like to put them in any order, as they all have feelings). Excellent with fish, such as turbot, bass or cod, celeriac also goes brilliantly well with all meats, especially game. Were you to simply purée celeriac on its own, it would be fabulous, but with the tart and sweet apple it becomes even better.

Cut away the skin of the celeriac using a sharp, sturdy knife, as a thin-bladed bendy one will not do the job well. The skin is thick and tough, so you'll be cutting off almost 5mm around the root. Chop the flesh into smallish pieces (about 5cm) and put them immediately into a large saucepan of cold water to prevent them oxidising and going brown. (If you find a large hole in the middle of the celeriac, this is quite normal; be assured it was not the lair of a giant grub.) Peel the potatoes, chop them into similar-sized pieces to the celeriac and throw them into the saucepan.

Put the saucepan on the heat, bring it up to the boil, then turn down the heat to a cheery simmer to cook for 20–30 minutes. Around 10 minutes before that time is up, peel and core the apple, chopping it to the same size as everything else, and throw it into the pot. Do not make the pieces too small, as they will turn to mush and drain away through the colander. While the vegetables boil, put the double cream in a small pan and add the garlic and whole rosemary stem. Put the pan on the heat and bring the cream up to a simmer, then turn off the heat.

The vegetables and apple are ready when a knife slides through the flesh of both the celeriac and potato with no resistance and the apple is totally soft. Drain well through a colander, then tip into a food processor. Pour over the cream and garlic, having removed the stem of rosemary, and then add the oil. Add a good amount of salt – it will take more than you think to bring out the taste. Blitz until velvety smooth and check the seasoning again. Alternatively, make the purée with a stick blender in the pot you used for boiling the vegetables. When spooned on to a plate, the purée should migrate slightly out to the side and not sit there stiffly like mash.

Serve with a good grind of black pepper over the top and a knob of butter melting in the middle. You can make the purée in advance and bring it back to heat as and when needed.

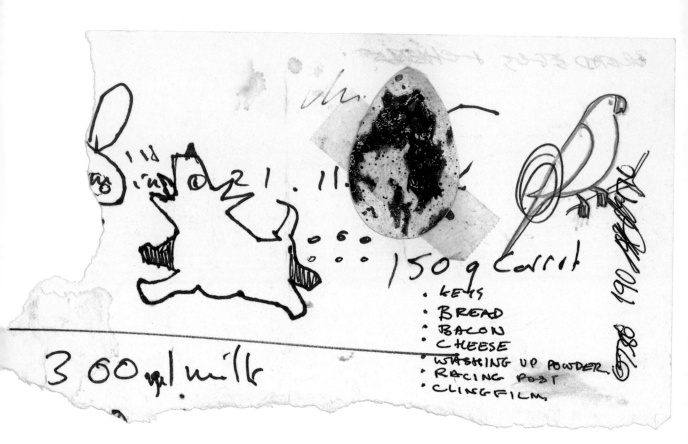

21.11.

150 g Carrot

- KEYS
- BREAD
- BACON
- CHEESE
- WASHING UP POWDER
- RACING POST
- CLINGFILM

300 ml milk

Bread, eggs & cheese

Huevos rancheros

Serves 2

1 tablespoon sunflower oil,
  plus extra for frying
1 small red onion, finely chopped
2 tablespoons finely chopped
  coriander stalks
¼ teaspoon ground cumin
400g can chopped tomatoes
100ml water
½ jalapeño chile, deseeded and
  finely chopped
juice of ½ medium lime
flaked sea salt and black pepper
6 tablespoons *Frijoles de la Olla*
  (refried black beans – *see* page 199)
4 corn tortillas
4 free-range eggs
20g Wensleydale cheese, crumbled

From the minute I wake, I am not a creature of habit. With such an overwhelming choice of global breakfasts with which to start the day, I rarely reach for the cereal box (although I do like Grape Nuts). This may be a little too much for a weekday start, as avocado on toast with oil would be a lighter option, but it is certainly a winner at the weekend. Warm corn tortillas, runny eggs, spicy tomatoes and velvety beans – *muy bueno*! If suffering from a hangover, this is good cure when coupled with an additional steadier of cold beer mixed with fresh lime juice. The beans need to be made in advance, as they take 3 hours to cook.

In a nonstick saucepan, heat the oil, then fry the onion and coriander stalks with the cumin over a medium heat, stirring occasionally. When softened but not coloured, flop in the chopped tomatoes and add the water and chopped chile. Simmer gently for 12 minutes or so until any obviously watery element to the tomatoes has gone (but the sauce should not be thick and reduced). Add the lime juice. Personally, I would now purée the sauce with a stick blender to really combine all the flavours, but this is not essential. Season with salt. Keep the sauce over a very low heat. In another pan, warm the refried black beans.

Heat a dash more oil in a large frying pan and add the tortillas. They will overlap, but fiddle them around with your fingers as they cook, so that they all get flipped over and each enjoys moments of direct heat and becomes totally floppy. Take them past this point so that areas of each become a little crisp. This will take 5 minutes or so. Transfer the tortillas to two plates.

Add more oil to the pan and fry the eggs. When done to your liking, shovel the eggs on top of the tortillas, lightly season the yolks, then splash over a few generous spoons of the sauce. Put a generous spoonful of the beans to one side and scatter them with the cheese. Eat immediately with a coffee or that cold beer.

Eggs Florentine, my mother's way

Serves 2

a capful of red or white wine vinegar

4 free-range eggs

350g chard, with not too much white stalk

1 tablespoon olive oil

flaked sea salt and black pepper

a grating of nutmeg

Cheese sauce

40g butter, plus extra for greasing

40g plain flour

450ml whole milk

50g Parmesan cheese, grated, plus extra for serving

flaked sea salt and black pepper

a grating of nutmeg

This is comfort food – and not that thing on a muffin with Hollandaise sauce that reminds me of going out for a mediocre brunch with dark glasses and a hangover, and not bothering to find somewhere nice to eat. Rather, it is the version that makes me think of Mum cooking and Sunday evenings eating in front of the Muppet Show, way back when. I've slightly re-jigged her version, as I am making it with chard instead of spinach. Also, I'm not truly satisfied with breaking an egg into the middle of the dish to cook under the sauce. It makes timing hard to get right, with a lot of inning and outing from the oven and burnt lips in between. I think pre-poaching the eggs is better for getting a runny yolk and firm white.

Fill a large saucepan with water and heat to a good simmer. Add the vinegar and let it come to a simmer again. Stir the water and, in quick succession, crack each of the eggs into the vortex, keeping the whites separate with a spoon, if necessary. You may want to do this in two batches. Cook the eggs for 2–3 minutes while they ghost around. Fill a bowl with cold water and, when the eggs are done, transfer them with a slotted spoon to the cold bath.

To make the cheese sauce, melt the butter in a saucepan over a medium–low heat and, when foaming, add the flour and incorporate with a whisk. After 30 seconds, start dribbling in the milk, which will automatically clag up. Don't worry, just keep on stirring and adding the milk. The sauce will loosen and behave. When all the milk is added, bring the sauce to a gentle bubble. Stir in the grated Parmesan and season with salt, black pepper and a little grated nutmeg. Cook gently for a further 5 minutes, stirring occasionally, then turn off the heat. Set aside.

Preheat the grill to its highest setting. Strip the chard leaves from the stalks and tear them up roughly. Slice a little of the stalk up, but don't use it all (keep the rest for soups or frying with breadcrumbs, garlic, bacon and lemon zest). Heat the oil in a saucepan. Rinse the chopped chard – the water droplets will help it to cook without burning. Fry it until it collapses. If it starts to singe, splash in a few more drops of water. When done (5 minutes or so), take off the heat and press out as much water as possible with the back of a spoon. This is important, as you don't want water leaking into the sauce. Toss with a little salt and a grinding of black pepper.

Warm the cheese sauce, if tepid, and grease two gratin dishes or ovenproof soup plates. Divide the chard in half and make it into a nest around the bottom of each dish. Use a slotted spoon to remove each egg from the water and briefly put the spoon on a kitchen cloth to absorb the drips. Place two eggs in the middle of each chard nest. Divide the sauce over the eggs, making sure it covers the chard too, so that it does not burn under the grill. Grate extra Parmesan over the top of each dish and add a final grinding of black pepper. Grill for 6 minutes, or until the top is browned and bubbling. Eat immediately, but be careful not to burn your lips.

Pickled eggs

Makes enough for a 2.25-litre preserving jar

20 large free-range eggs, preferably
  2 weeks' old as they are easier to peel
500ml malt vinegar
500ml cider vinegar
100g caster sugar
6 bay leaves
20 black peppercorns
10 juniper berries

Pickled eggs are becoming increasingly rare and are most likely to be found in establishments that themselves are sadly becoming extinct. To enjoy a pickled egg, especially one pickled in malt vinegar, is a ritual I will not rush. Whether you place one within a packet nest of salted crisps or harpoon it upon a cocktail stick then dust with cheap grey pepper, it's an excellent accompaniment to a dark, flowery ale. There is also some innate joy in ignoring others' disdain or relishing that 'secret society' feeling in front of those who, although they toy with the idea, still cannot tuck in. Long may this endangered egg sink in vinegar and may my great grandchildren learn to savour them too!

Although the backdrop of the pub is an important contributor to this joy, I do occasionally make a stash of pickled eggs for home, as they are good companions for cheese and ham sandwiches, and are great for taking on fishing trips.

To sterilise the jar, preheat the oven to 160°fan/180°C/Gas 4. Wash the jar and lid really well and put them on a baking tray in the oven for 10 minutes. Before boiling the eggs, make sure that they are at room temperature so that when introduced to the rolling water they do not crack. Allow the water to bubble again and then boil the eggs for 8 minutes. Tip the hot water from the pan and then cover the eggs with cold water and leave to cool.

Heat the vinegars together in a separate pan with the sugar and aromatics (bay leaves, peppercorns and juniper berries). Stir briefly until all the sugar has dissolved. Bring the pickling liquor to a simmer before taking off the heat and allowing to cool completely.

Peel all the eggs and place them in the sterilised jar. Pour over the pickle and secure the lid. Do not even consider biting the white for at least three weeks. When opened, finish the jar within a month.

Eggs mayonnaise

Serves 1

2 large free-range eggs, at room
temperature
4 good large anchovies in oil or
salt, drained, or rinsed and dried
(optional)
black pepper
a sprig of retro curly-leaf parsley,
to garnish

Mayonnaise

1½ teaspoons Dijon mustard
2 free-range egg yolks
2 teaspoons white wine vinegar
150ml sunflower oil
50ml extra virgin olive oil
flaked sea salt

Old fashioned, maybe, but a dish with a simplicity I delight in. This is the
perfect lunch to eat slowly with just a fork and accompanying newspapers,
delivering a joy, a deep satisfaction and a feeling of 'just enough'. The
anchovies are optional, but highly recommended.

Lower the eggs into rapidly boiling water and cook them for 6 minutes.
Drain and cool immediately in cold water to prevent them developing
a blue ring around the yolk. Leave to one side.

For the mayonnaise, in a food processor, or in a bowl with a stick blender,
combine the mustard, egg yolks and vinegar before slowly adding the oils in
a very thin stream. The mayonnaise should thicken and become glossy, but
if it over-stiffens before the oil is finished, let it down with a small splash of
warm water – but remember it needs to be thick enough to pipe on to the
eggs. The consistency you want is semi-stiff peaks; a dollop should just hold
its own. Season the mayonnaise generously with salt and extra vinegar if it
needs sharpening. Although this is unlikely, should your mayonnaise split,
on no account throw it away. Put one more yolk in the cleaned food processor
with a dash more mustard and dribble of vinegar. Add the split mixture to
it slowly with a little extra olive oil and a new mayonnaise will arrive.

Peel the boiled eggs, then cut them in half lengthways and arrange them on
the plate, flat-side down. Drape an anchovy along each egg half (and by all
means cross it with another if you want more). Artfully pipe the mayonnaise
on to each egg if you would like to imagine yourself lunching in a Paris bistro.
Otherwise spoon a big dollop on top. Decorate with a small sprig of parsley.
Pour wine, open papers and eat eggs slowly, mouthfuls separated by articles.

Eggs in aspic

Serves 6

6 free-range eggs
5 sheets (10g) of leaf gelatine
600ml fresh chicken stock
   (*see* page 240)
100ml medium-sweet sherry
flaked sea salt
a squeeze of lemon juice
leaves from 4 sprigs of tarragon

To serve

black pepper
hot white toast with butter

If you like jelly, or the happy bit between the cold pastry and the pressed meat of a pork pie, and you like runny eggs as well, then this is for you. If you don't, please turn over the page. This delight is only as good as the stock you use, so I would not advise using the shop-bought variety; on the whole, I find these insipid in taste and with the appearance of water that's leaked through the ceiling and into a bucket. Instructions on various brands of gelatine recommend a number of leaves that sets jelly too firmly for my liking. Generally, I put in one less sheet than told. The glasses or teacups you use for this recipe must be deep enough to sit the eggs upright and still be covered by stock.

If the eggs are in the fridge, bring them up to room temperature to help prevent them cracking when boiled. Lower them gently into rolling (but not ferociously boiling) water. Cook for exactly 4½ minutes before draining and plunging them into a large bowl of cold water to stop them cooking onwards.

Soak the gelatine in a little warm water for 5 minutes so that it goes wibbly. Heat the stock in a saucepan and simmer for at least 2 minutes, then pour in the sherry and turn off the heat. Take the gelatine out of the liquid, gently squeeze it and stir it into the stock until it is completely dissolved. Add salt – unless your stock is salty enough; it is essential to get the stock seasoning spot on. Add a little lemon juice, just to give a definite edge to the stock but not to invade it, and allow to cool. Peel the eggs.

Put six glasses or cups on a small tray and into the bottom of each glass or teacup pour a 2cm depth of stock and scatter with two or three tarragon leaves. Put in the fridge for 45 minutes, or until the aspic has just set. Press the pointy end of each egg into the stock so that it stands upright (you can cut a slither off the bottom of each egg to assist in this if you wish to), then pour in another 2cm of liquid and add a few more tarragon leaves. Chill for another 45 minutes. Continue until the eggs are covered in jelly. If the stock in the pan begins to set between stages, just warm it gently to loosen it, then let it cool and continue.

Chill the jellied eggs for a few hours before serving, but take them out of the fridge just beforehand so that they are not fridge-cold. Serve with a little black pepper on top, hot white toast, butter and perhaps a little glass of cold sherry.

Piperade

Serves 2

a slug of olive oil
½ small onion, finely chopped
1 red or green pepper, cored,
    deseeded and finely sliced
1 large ripe tomato, skinned
    and roughly chopped
1 garlic clove, crushed
flaked sea salt and black pepper
30g butter
4 large free-range eggs
good rustic sourdough bread,
    to serve

This is a Basque dish that I visit frequently when I want an alternative to straight scrambled eggs. When cooked by stocky Basques, it is normally made with olive oil. I like to keep the eggs a little softer and creamier than they do, so also add a little butter.

Heat the oil in a saucepan and in it cook the onion with the red or green pepper over a medium heat, stirring occasionally, until they both have properly softened and are starting to colour.

Meanwhile, cut out the stalk from the tomato and make a small cross in the base with a sharp knife. Put the tomato in a bowl and cover with just-boiled water. Leave for about 60 seconds or until the skin splits. Drain and peel. Cut the tomato into quarters, scoop out the seeds and reserve. Chop the tomato flesh roughly and add to the pan with the onions and peppers. With your hands, squeeze any juice from the tomato seeds through a sieve into the pan as well. Add the garlic.

Cook the water out of the tomato and onion mixture, stirring it often, at a brisk simmer for 5 minutes or so. (This is important, as if there is too much residual juice, it will later turn the eggs to the consistency of those you might find in a bad hotel breakfast.) Season generously.

Take the pan from the heat and drop in the butter followed by the eggs. Stir all together so that the eggs break, then return the pan to a low heat and cook, stirring constantly, for 2–3 minutes, or until the eggs are only just thickened and are creamy yet runny and with no glassy bits. Eat immediately with some good rustic sourdough and a little extra salt, should the dish need any.

Black toast, boiled egg & black tea

1 slice of white bread, for toast
1 free-range egg
1 average tea bag
sugar

I wasn't a sickly child, but if I ever did suffer from an upset stomach, I was popped into bed and given the following. My arms were tucked by my sides so tightly under the blankets that it took quite a while to struggle them free and try to eat this cure that my parents swore by. I can't remember if it really worked, but here you are.

Burn the toast to the point where you would normally scrape it with a knife, but don't scrape it as the carbon is part of the medicine. This is essential. Totally hard-boil the egg. Brew the tea for far too long. Only the faintest amount of sugar is allowed. Put everything on a tray, take it to the invalid and remove, uneaten, 1 hour later.

Pizza bianco

Serves 4–6

2 large waxy potatoes, peeled
flaked sea salt and black pepper
olive oil, for drizzling
2½ × 150g balls of mozzarella cheese
40g Parmesan cheese, grated
as much truffle as you see fit, shaved
  very finely, or truffle oil (optional)

Dough

250ml warm water
7g sachet easy-blend yeast
1 teaspoon caster sugar
300g strong white flour, plus extra
  for dusting
1 heaped teaspoon flaked sea salt
olive oil, for oiling and brushing

My taste in pizzas leans towards those with tomato and without cheese, or vice versa. This particular pizza blew my mind not least because it was covered in tissue-thin flakes of pungent white truffle. With no truffle at all, it is still fantastic and born for cold weather. Contrary to suspicions, it is not dry or cloying to the mouth, as the dough is crispy and the potato moist when applied in a thin layer, while all relax in the melted warm arms of lady mozzarella. I have here included the British summer truffle (misleading in its name, as it can be unearthed throughout half the year, from July to December) that can relatively easily be ordered online. It's not as raunchy, funky and intense as its pale cousin, but does a good job nonetheless. Alternatively, a little drizzle of that truffle oil you paid a fortune for is well used up here. A real winner, this pizza makes most others seem just plain ordinary.

To make the dough, pour the water into a large bowl, then tip in the yeast with the sugar. After 10 minutes or so you should find beige foam floating on the water (which may conjure memories of shabbier Mediterranean harbours). Add half the flour and carefully stir it in. Little lumps do not matter. Gradually add the remaining flour with the salt. Mix in the bowl with your hand and, as soon as the contents come together in a soft, spongy lump, turn it out on to a floured work surface and knead for 7 minutes or so. The dough should feel smooth, elastic and not be tacky to the touch.

Wipe oil around a clean, large bowl. Form the dough into a ball, smoothing down the sides so that they are taut and any crinkles and seams are underneath. Place the dough in the bowl and cover loosely with clingfilm that has been greased with oil to stop the rising dough sticking to it. Leave the dough in a warm place until it has doubled in size (about 45 minutes–1 hour). Oil a large baking sheet on which to cook the pizza.

Preheat the oven to 220°C fan/240°C/Gas 9. When the dough has risen, turn it out on to a lightly floured work surface and knock it back with a few gentle blows. Roll it out very finely (there may be more of it than you need, according to the size of your oven) into a large rectangle and place it on the baking sheet. Brush the top with more oil and cover loosely with clingfilm. Leave the dough to rest for a further 15 minutes. Preheat the oven to full capacity.

Just before cooking the pizza, slice the potatoes lengthways with a mandolin or knife. It is essential that the potato be very finely cut or it will not cook in time. Pat the potato slices dry on kitchen paper, then, leaving a 1cm margin around the edge, lay the potato slices on to the dough, overlapping them about halfway. Season well and pass over with a good drizzle of oil.

Slice the mozzarella, patting it dry on kitchen paper (otherwise it will leak water on to your pizza). Arrange it on top of the pizza. Sprinkle over the Parmesan. Finally, scribble over the pizza with one more hit of oil. Bake in the oven for 15–18 minutes until the cheese is totally melted and just beginning to colour. The dough should be a rich orange brown and crispy.

If feeling luxurious, now grate over some fine feathers of truffle or dribble over some truffle oil. *Buon appetito!*

Autumn macaroni with button onions, pancetta, hazelnuts & Fontina cheese

Serves 2

12 small button onions, skins left on
50g butter
1½ teaspoons caster sugar
1 tablespoon balsamic vinegar
flaked sea salt
60g macaroni
4 thin slices of pancetta
100ml double cream
50g Fontina cheese,
   rind removed, grated
½ handful of whole, toasted and
   barely chopped hazelnuts

I visited the Valle d'Aosta, a wonderful part of northern-most Italy that nestles right up against the Swiss border and is the country's smallest region. Full of many delicious foods, it is the proud home of Fontina cheese. This creamy yellow stinker, made with summer cows' milk, is the result of happy days spent munching wild flowers and herbs among the high peaks. Treated with unwavering seriousness and respect, the cheeses are regularly washed in brine, turned and stored in around eight large, deep caves, kept under lock and key. Obsessively enjoyed by every resident, Fontina seems to be included in a good majority of the Aostan culinary repertoire, melted into everything from beef stews to pasta dishes. One feels that should the Fontina Co-operative's collection ever be stolen from their guarded caves, then the whole country would go into meltdown. Although Britain is only drip-fed with valuable Fontina, it is easily found in good cheese shops. This was a dish I invented to sum up my snowy winter stay in its homeland.

Drop all the onions into a pan of rolling water and boil for 7 minutes. Drain and allow them to cool. Carefully trim them of any whiskers and a fraction off the root end, as you need to keep them intact. Remove their jackets and tops.

Fill a small saucepan with water for the pasta and put it on to boil. Melt the butter in a frying pan and when it's foaming add the onions and fry for 8–10 minutes. Stir them occasionally and regulate the heat if needs be, as the butter must not burn. The onions should end up richly coloured and tender, and the butter nutty brown. Sprinkle over the sugar and vinegar, then swirl the onions around until the balsamic has reduced and the sugar caramelised and stuck to the onions. Season generously with salt, then turn off the heat.

Drop the macaroni into the boiling water and cook for 8 minutes, or until firm yet tender but not mushy. Just before it is ready, put the onions back over a medium heat. Push them to one side and wipe the empty half clean with kitchen paper. Lay down the pancetta; it will not take long to cook – 3 minutes or so. Turn it once and be careful not to burn it. It should be crisp and brittle. Turn the onions so that they warm through evenly. When the pancetta is done, turn off the heat.

Drain the macaroni and tip it back into the pot. Pour in the cream and scatter in the cheese. Put the pan back over a low heat and gently fold all together until the cheese has melted. Check the seasoning, adding a little salt if necessary. Spoon the macaroni between two warm plates. Nestle six onions in the middle of the pasta, cut each pancetta slice in half and arrange between the onions. Lastly, scatter over the hazelnuts. Eat immediately, as mountain food is better hot.

Bread sauce

Serves 6–8

600ml whole milk
1 small onion, cut in half lengthways,
    root intact and peeled
8 cloves
2 small bay leaves
150g fine white breadcrumbs
    (made from stale bread)
25g butter
1 teaspoon flaked sea salt
black pepper
a grating of nutmeg

Bread sauce is to pheasant what Batman is to Robin: essential. Mashing it up on the plate with gravy and the remains of potato is a pleasurable habit I just can't resist, even though it drives my mother nuts. This sauce is also fabulous with chicken, duck, turkey, goose, grouse, pigeon, hare and venison. I haven't tried it with a quartet of robins yet.

Bread sauce is always better if made in advance and left to mature. I make it the morning before the meal.

Put the milk in a small pan. Stud one half of the onion with the cloves, then put them both in the pan with the bay leaves to bob around in the milk. Heat very gently until the milk barely simmers. Cook for 20–25 minutes until the onion is very soft. Remove from the heat and leave to infuse for a further 30 minutes.

Take the bay leaves and onion pieces out of the milk with a slotted spoon and discard the onion half with the cloves. Chop the other half as finely as you can until minutely minced and add it back to the pot. Stir the breadcrumbs into the milk until completely soaked (I like to use fine breadcrumbs because they result in a more velvety sauce). Add the butter and cook over a low heat for 8–10 minutes, stirring regularly, until the sauce is smoothish and creamy. Add more milk, if necessary, as the sauce should not be too stiff, but more like thin porridge. Season with the salt, black pepper and a generous grating of nutmeg. Put to one side and reheat gently before serving, adding more milk if necessary, since the sauce thickens up when made in advance.

Oatcakes

Makes 8–10 oatcakes

200g fine oatmeal
2 teaspoons melted lard
   or saved bacon fat
a good pinch of flaked sea salt
a pinch of bicarbonate of soda
Swede, Apple and Plum Pickle
   (*see* page 243), to serve

I love oatcakes – they are really easy to make and perfect nibbling food for walks. I like mine thin, made with fine oatmeal, not the coarse ones that clag up the inside of your mouth. Too many cheese biscuits are overly sweet or confused with chile flakes, sesame seeds and so on. Good cheese needs a fairly blank canvas.

Preheat the oven to 160°C fan/180°C/Gas 4. In a bowl, combine the oats with the melted lard or fat, salt and bicarbonate of soda. Dribble in water at intervals, stirring with a spoon. A ball will form naturally. It should be pliable like Play-Doh but not overly sticky, as this makes it hard to work with. Tear off two sheets of baking paper, each about the size of a sheet of A4 paper. Put the dough into the middle of one piece and cover with the other. Take a rolling pin and roll out the dough between the two sheets to a thickness of about 2mm, turning the whole thing over once or twice and making sure you are not rolling through any crinkles from the paper into the dough.

Peel off the upper piece of baking paper. Pick up the bottom sheet with the dough stuck to it and place it on a baking tray. Cut out the biscuits with a 7cm cutter. Maybe with the help of a knife, remove the bits of the dough you don't want; this can be reformed and rolled out again, but you will need to add an extra splash of water to the dough first.

Bake the biscuits for 20 minutes. Cool on a wire rack. Enjoy with Swede, Apple and Plum Pickle. Birds love 'em too.

Toast as a vehicle

Pigeon with blackcurrants & bacon on toast

Serves 2

2 whole wood pigeons
a small bunch of young
   curly-leaf parsley
2 teaspoons sunflower oil for
   cooking the pigeon carcasses,
   plus 1 tablespoon for rubbing
   on the pigeon breasts
½ medium carrot, scrubbed
   and cut into short lengths
½ small onion, skin left on
1 small celery stick,
   cut into short lengths
600ml cold water
flaked sea salt and black pepper
2 slices of good white rustic bread
4 thin rashers of rindless
   streaky bacon
150ml red wine
75g blackcurrants
15g cold butter, diced, plus extra
   for spreading on the bread
watercress salad, to serve (optional)

Pigeons and blackcurrants are a splendid partnership. Seeing pigeons eat the fruit from the bushes has to be a recommendation from the bird itself. A good little dinner for two.

Cut the breasts and legs off the pigeons (or get a butcher to do it) and reserve the carcasses. Put the breasts on a plate skin-side up to help prevent them drying out and cover with clingfilm. Chop each carcass into three with a large, heavy knife and cut the parsley stalks from the leaves. Place a medium saucepan over a high heat. Add the oil and chuck in the pigeon carcasses with the legs, vegetables and parsley stalks. Fry for 6–8 minutes, or until the bones are well browned. Pour over the water. Bring to the boil, then reduce the heat and simmer gently, uncovered, for 40 minutes, skimming when necessary.

Finely chop the parsley leaves and put aside. Preheat the grill to its highest setting. Strain the stock off the bones through a sieve into a clean pan, then add ½ teaspoon of salt and return it to the heat. Simmer hard until the liquid has reduced to around 100ml, then turn off the heat. Spread the bread with a little butter on both sides and place on a baking tray. Cook the slices under the grill for 1–2 minutes, or until golden and crisp around the edges but a little squidgy in the middle. Turn off the heat, leaving the toast within.

Heat a small, nonstick frying pan over a medium–high heat. Rub the pigeon breasts with a little oil and season well, then put them, skin-side down, in the pan and lay the bacon alongside. Cook for 3 minutes, or until well coloured, taking care not to burn the bacon. Turn the pigeon and bacon on to the other side for a further 2 minutes. Transfer the pigeon to a chopping board to rest and give the bacon a little longer if needs be – it should be nice and crispy.

Return the pan to the heat and deglaze with the red wine. Reduce it rapidly to around 2 tablespoons, then pour in the stock followed by the blackcurrants and cook for 2 minutes, or until the fruit is soft but holding its shape and the sauce is syrupy. Season well.

Put the toast on two warmed plates. Diagonally slice each breast into four slices. Arrange two breasts on each toast with two slices of bacon.

Gradually whisk the cold butter bit by bit into the sauce and swirl around the pan until thickened and glossy. Spoon over the pigeon and toasts, sprinkle with the chopped parsley and tuck in. Watercress salad is a very fine accompaniment.

Salmon, chopped egg & spring onion on toast

Serves 1

1 large free-range egg
2 slices of light rye bread
butter, for spreading on the toast
2 slices of smoked salmon
juice of ½ lemon
2 small pert spring onions,
    finely sliced
2 teaspoons baby capers, well rinsed
black pepper

This is great for when it's hard to pull yourself away from the TV. It can almost be made in ad breaks! Make sure that the smoked salmon is good – not the flabby rubbish that weeps grease.

Boil the egg in rapidly rolling water for 7 minutes, then transfer to cold water to cool. Toast the bread. Peel and roughly chop the egg relatively small. Heavily butter the toast, then lay the smoked salmon on top. Squeeze over the lemon juice, then scatter over the chopped egg, spring onion and capers. Bombard heavily with black pepper. Carry the plate towards the television.

Herring milts (soft roes) on toast

Serves 2

2 tablespoons plain flour

flaked sea salt and black pepper

12–16 herring milts

a handful of curly-leaf parsley leaves,
  finely chopped

2 slices of white bread

40g butter, plus extra for spreading
  on the toast

a pinch of cayenne pepper

juice of ½ large lemon

lemon wedges, to garnish (optional)

My mother used to make this often for me and, luckily, I loved it. Herring roes strike me as one of those old-fashioned things that people do not care for any more. This is a great shame, as they are oh-so-properly-tasty, delightfully savoury and creamy with a faint and intriguing bitterness. The Russians may have caviar on blinis, but we have milts on hot toast. You find them in fishmongers and in the deep-frozen section of supermarkets. The word roes implies these come from the females, but these are 'man eggs' so to speak. The Japanese translation for them is 'white children'. Come on, be adventurous!

Sift the flour on to a plate and then sprinkle over a very generous pinch of good flaked sea salt. Work the salt into the flour with your fingers and then shimmy the plate to erase the trails. Roll the milts in the flour so that they are thoroughly but lightly covered. Have the parsley ready to add the minute it is needed and the bread poised for lowering into the toaster.

Heat the butter in the frying pan over a medium heat. The pan should be big enough to ensure that the roes don't touch and that they colour properly. Test the heat by lowering the tip of one into the foaming butter to see if it fizzles straight away. Only when you get the desired reaction should you add the milts; they will curl up slightly in happiness and fry. Plunge the toast, making sure the butter dish is at hand for when it returns with a twang.

When the milts are nicely browned on one side, turn them over and do the other side. The whole cooking process should take approximately 4 minutes for both sides. The trick is not to burn the butter during the cooking. It should be a pale nutty brown by the time the milts are cooked. Just before removing them from the pan, get the toast, butter it and lay it on two plates. Toss the parsley into the pan and scatter over some cayenne pepper. Jostle all the contents a little to combine everything and lift the milts from the pan on to the toasts. Quickly squeeze and swirl the lemon juice into the hot butter, then pour this juice over. Garnish with a lemon wedge, if you like. Eat immediately! A triumph, I hope.

Mussels on toast

Serves 2

500g big fat live mussels, cleaned,
  beards removed

25g butter, plus extra for spreading
  on the toast

1 level tablespoon plain flour

150ml whole milk

2 slices of Irish soda bread,
  or other bread

a grating of nutmeg

flaked sea salt and black pepper

1 tablespoon finely chopped
  curly-leaf parsley

This is a humble treatment of mussels, a recipe learnt from a shellfish farmer on Holy Island that is so simple it does not even contain an onion, although you may happily include it. It's the kind of thing I cook in boxer shorts with my wet trousers on the radiator – a great tea after a long, rainy coastal walk. My preferred bread would be heavily toasted Irish soda bread.

Pick through the mussels, discarding any that are broken or that fail to close when tapped on the side of the sink. Steam the mussels open in a big pan with a lid on, adding a small splash of water first to get them going. (Cooking them in a large pan will help them open faster and not leave you with half open and half closed.) Cook the mussels for approximately 3 minutes until they have just presented themselves and can be lifted quivering from the shell. Collect the juice in a small bowl. Discard any mussels that have failed to open.

Melt the butter in a small saucepan, then scatter in the flour. Whisk it into the butter well, then cook gently for 30 seconds, or until the mixture foams a little. Add the mussel stock bit by bit. The mixture will clag up at first, then loosen as you add more liquid. When the mussel stock is gone, start adding the milk, bit by bit. When all the milk has been stirred in, let the sauce gently simmer for 7 minutes or so, stirring occasionally.

Toast the bread, then butter it and put it on two plates. Grate a little nutmeg into the white sauce followed by a grinding of black pepper. Lastly, add the mussels and parsley, season with a little salt if necessary and cook for a further 30 seconds until the mussels are hot. Spoon them on to the toast and eat accompanied with a mug of tea.

Chicken or duck livers with tarragon & lemon

Serves 4

leaves from 1 sprig of thyme
250g chicken or duck livers
1 level teaspoon flaked sea salt
black pepper
1 fat hard garlic clove, peeled
2 sprigs of tarragon
a good knob of butter
a splash of olive oil
2 teaspoons sherry vinegar
    or balsamic vinegar
juice of ½ lemon
hot buttered toast made with good
    sourdough bread, to serve

The tempting smell of duck cooking in the oven always demands that I quell my Pavlovian urges with a duck-related snack that delivers almost instant gratification. Duck livers are rich and delicious, but hard to come by on their own, so I've also made this recipe with chicken livers, which can be found with ease. This snack is delicious somewhere around 6.00pm, accompanied with a good glass of white wine before dinner.

Finely chop the leaves from the thyme. Spread each liver out flat and, with surgical precision, cut out any sinew that joins the two parts. Lay the livers on a plate and sprinkle over the thyme, salt and a good grinding of black pepper. Chop the garlic very finely and the tarragon less so. Have them waiting.

Heat the butter and oil in a nonstick frying pan. When it is good and hot, but under no circumstances smoking, drop in the livers, making sure they are well spaced. Let them fry without poking, as this will allow them to take on colour. Cook on each side for 1½ minutes (a minute longer for duck livers). If the pan is hot enough, they will be richly browned in this time. Keeping the pan over the heat, splash the livers all over with the vinegar, throw in the garlic and tarragon and toss everything together. The vinegar will evaporate almost immediately and the livers should be removed from the heat the minute it has; they should definitely be pink, but not raw inside. Squeeze over a little lemon juice.

Serve the livers at once on small squares of hot buttered sourdough toast. I try not to reach for the plate too often, but I'm too old for FHB (Family Hold Back).

My cheese on toast

Serves 2

100g very strong Cheddar (the kind
that stings the roof of your mouth),
coarsely grated

1 teaspoon English mustard

2 generous dessertspoons Hellman's
mayonnaise

black pepper

a few drops of Worcestershire sauce

2 large slices of good white
country bread

6 large brown anchovies in oil,
drained (optional)

½ small red onion, finely sliced

Why have I written a recipe for cheese on toast? Pretty boring you might
say. The reason is because this recipe stops the cheese going rubbery when
cooled by using the addition of mayonnaise, which keeps the whole thing
luxurious until finished.

Preheat the grill to its highest setting. In a bowl, combine the grated cheese
with the mustard, mayonnaise, a good grinding of black pepper and the
Worcestershire sauce. Toast the bread on both sides on a baking tray under
the grill. Cover with the cheese mixture so that it's a good 5mm thick on the
toast. Lay over the anchovies, if using.

Pop the slices under the grill, not too close to the element, and cook until
richly coloured and bubbling. Scatter on the raw onion and eat (probably
in front of the telly).

Purple sprouting broccoli with *anchoïade* & fried egg

Serves 1

4 stems of purple sprouting broccoli

1½ tablespoons olive oil

1 slice of good sourdough bread,
  or other rustic loaf

1 free-range egg

3 teaspoons baby capers, well rinsed

2 liberal teaspoons *Anchoïade*
  (*see* page 124)

flaked sea salt and black pepper

1 lemon wedge

When the PSB is in, a real treat has arrived. This is a superb and handsome vegetable, a noble brassica. I would think three stallholder-boxfuls is a fair estimate of my annual spring consumption – it's not around for long and I just don't tire of it. I usually eat it for lunch or, more accurately, lunch three times, as I'm always straight back in the kitchen boiling another plateful. PSB is unquestionably healthy, with its vitamin-rich mineral twang, a food to eat with guilt-free abandon as happily-taken medicine, much needed after long months of roots, cheese, sugar and pork crackling. With soy sauce and lemon, French dressing or anchovy butter – or however it is dressed – it makes me smile from ear to ear. Here is a favourite approach.

Preheat the grill to its highest setting and put a pan of water on to boil. Trim the broccoli of any bits you do not like the look of. If the base of any of the stems are a bit woody, cut them off and discard them.

Put a small frying pan on the heat and in it get the oil hot without burning. Put the bread under the grill, remembering to turn it over (or use a toaster). Drop the broccoli in the water to boil for 2 minutes. Break the egg in the frying pan, where it should start going 'splut splut' immediately, and scatter the capers around it, but not on top. Cook the egg so the white is slightly crispy underneath while the yolk remains runny. Thoroughly drain the broccoli.

When the toast is done, spread it with the *anchoïade* and then lay the PSB on top, seasoning it lightly with salt. Crown all with the egg and promptly spoon over the now crispy capers with a little oil from the pan. A brief grinding over with black pepper will complete the exercise nicely. Squeeze over the lemon. Ace!

Tomatoes with Dijon mustard & cream on toast

Serves 2

4 good fat ripe tomatoes

a little red wine vinegar

3 teaspoons demerara sugar

flaked sea salt and black pepper

1 tablespoon thyme leaves

30g butter, plus extra for spreading
  on the toast

2 slices of good wholemeal bread

2 teaspoons Dijon mustard

2 tablespoons good double cream

chopped tarragon (optional)

This is a perfect dinner for a Sunday night. Make sure that your chosen tomatoes are good ones.

Preheat the grill to just under its highest setting. Slice the tomatoes in half and lay them on some baking paper on a baking tray. Splash over a little red wine vinegar. Scatter over the sugar, some salt, a really good grinding of black pepper and the thyme. Cut the butter into slices and divide between all the tomatoes. Place under the grill, relatively far from the element. Cook them for 15–20 minutes, or until the tomatoes are obviously soft yet no longer watery, the tops well coloured with burnt areas.

Put the bread in the toaster and when done butter heavily. Over the butter spread the Dijon mustard. Put the tomatoes on the toasts and spoon the cream over. Chopped tarragon can be a wonderful addition.

Puddings

Rhubarb & stem ginger fool

Serves 4

500g pink (forced) rhubarb
3 dessertspoons icing sugar
2 dessertspoons stem ginger syrup
2 dessertspoons water
275ml double cream, well chilled
2 stem ginger bulbs in syrup, finely
  chopped
Swedish ginger thin biscuits,
  to serve (optional)

Early rhubarb is such a wondrous thing. Startling in its tartness and colour, flirting from the market barrows, it shocks me from my slow winter stasis and has me sniffing around for spring. If you can't be bothered to make even this simplest of puddings, you'll find satisfaction by just pouring some cream over the poached rhubarb.

Trim the rhubarb of any leaf tops or undesirable bits and chop it into 5cm lengths. Put it in a pan big enough for all the pieces to lay flat. Scatter over 2 dessertspoonfuls of the icing sugar followed by the syrup from the ginger jar and finally the water. (It doesn't seem like much water, but a lot will exude from the rhubarb.) Put the pan on a medium–low heat with a lid on top and cook for about 10 minutes, or until the rhubarb is totally soft.

Spoon the rhubarb into a sieve over another saucepan, then press out as much juice as possible into the pan – really work the rhubarb for every last drip. Allow the pulp to cool in the sieve. Put the juice pan back on the heat and reduce the liquid by three-quarters; do this gently so as not to burn the syrup. Take it off the heat and allow it to cool totally; folding hot syrup (or hot pulp) into the cream will melt it and have you muttering: 'I am a fool!'

In a large mixing bowl, whip the last spoonful of sugar with the cream until stiff, but only just so. The peaks should certainly stand proud with a lovely eggshell varnish to them, but must not have that over-whipped and grainy look as it also makes a poor fool. Gently fold the rhubarb pulp and chopped stem ginger into the cream, occasionally dribbling in some of the syrup until all has been used up save for 4 teaspoonfuls.

Divide the fool among four glasses, or make one large one, and drip the remainder of the syrup over the top. Chill in the fridge for at least 1 hour before serving. Swedish ginger thins (the biscuits that are so delicate that it's hard not to break half the pack when opening them) are excellent with this simple and elegant pudding.

Lemon possets

Serves 12

1.2 litres double cream
140g caster sugar
juice of 5 lemons
finely grated zest of
   3 unwaxed lemons
ginger thins or cat's tongue biscuits,
   to serve (optional)

This is a very easy pudding for a large number of people and a time-saver from heaven. You can do the cooking bit in 10 minutes and the setting period needs doing in advance anyway. If you wish to, add a good glug of elderflower cordial with the lemon juice; this makes a very nice combination.

Heat the cream and sugar over a medium heat and bring it briefly to a definite boil, being careful that it doesn't spill over the side of the pan. Pour in the lemon juice, followed by the zest. Whisk for 30 seconds or so before removing from the heat and dividing among 12 × 125ml ramekins. The lemon juice will set the hot cream.

Put the ramekins in the fridge for at least 2 hours before serving. These are delicious served with ginger thins or cat's tongue biscuits.

Gooseberry crumble ice cream

Serves 10

450ml double cream
450ml whole milk
1 vanilla pod
10 medium free-range egg yolks
100g caster sugar

Gooseberries

500g gooseberries
3 tablespoons water
50–75g caster sugar, to taste

Crumble mix

50g demerara sugar
60g butter, chilled, cut into
    small cubes
75g plain flour

Gooseberries are a wonderful fruit and here is an ice cream to get Ben and Jerry looking over their shoulder.

To make the ice cream, pour the cream and milk into a large saucepan. Cut the vanilla pod in half lengthways and scrape out the seeds with the point of the knife. Add the seeds and pod to the pan. Bring to the boil, then immediately turn off the heat.

In a large bowl, whisk the egg yolks and caster sugar together until pale. Pour in the milk and cream mixture, whisking immediately. When thoroughly combined, return the liquid to the saucepan and set over a low heat.

Cook the mixture for 15–20 minutes, stirring constantly, until the custard is thick enough to coat the back of the spoon. This custard stage needs your full attention and continuous stirring. It is also important to make sure the mixture does not overheat, otherwise the eggs will begin to scramble. (Sometimes this can be salvaged by pouring the mixture through a fine sieve, but if it is still grainy after sieving, you will have to start again.) Remove the pan from the heat, take out the vanilla pod and pour the custard into a clean bowl. Cover the surface with clingfilm to stop a skin from forming. Leave to cool for 30 minutes.

While the custard is cooling, prepare the gooseberries. Rinse the fruit and put it into a large saucepan with the water. Bring to the boil, then simmer rapidly for about 10 minutes until the fruit has totally collapsed. Put a fine sieve over a large jug or bowl, tip in the contents and press the fruit with a ladle to squeeze through as much of the fruit pulp as possible. This should give you 500ml thick gooseberry purée. Sweeten to taste with the sugar, leaving the mixture a little more sour than you normally would. Leave the fruit to cool.

For the crumble, preheat the oven to 200°C fan/220°C/Gas 7. Blend all the ingredients together in a food processor until the mixture starts to come together in little clusters. Shake on to a baking tray lined with baking paper and spread out. Bake for 15 minutes, or until golden. Leave to cool. (The crumble will crisp up further as it cools.)

Stir the gooseberry purée into the cooled custard. Transfer to a freezerproof container. Cover and freeze for 3 hours, then remove and scrape with a fork to break up the ice crystals that will have formed around the edge. Return to the freezer for 2 hours, then repeat forking and return to the freezer for 2 hours more. Remove, scrape once again with a fork, add the crumble until evenly distributed but remaining in little clusters, then return to the freezer for a further 2–3 hours, or until solid. (Alternatively, churn the cooled custard in an ice-cream maker, then transfer to a freezerproof container, add the crumble mixture and freeze until solid.)

Remove the ice cream from the freezer and leave to stand at room temperature for 10 minutes before serving.

Apricot custard tart

Serves 8–10

20–24 fresh apricots (depending on size), halved and stoned

2 medium free-range eggs

3 medium free-range egg yolks

50g caster sugar, plus 2 tablespoons extra for the apricots

450ml single cream, plus extra to serve

½ vanilla pod

Sweet pastry

250g plain flour, plus extra for dusting

1 tablespoon caster sugar

150g butter, chilled, cut into 1cm cubes

2 medium free-range eggs, beaten

Gazing upon a yellow custard-filled tart, shot with fiery little apricot halves, makes me think of the summer sun. Cutting a slice of this gives me that urgent need to bite the sharp end off before it bends and the fruit falls, and to taste that wonderful thing apricots become when cooked.

To make the pastry, put the flour, sugar and butter in a food processor and blend on the pulse setting until the mixture resembles fine breadcrumbs. With the motor running, slowly add one egg and pulse again for just long enough for the mixture to form a ball.

Turn the contents out on to a lightly floured work surface. Roll out the pastry to the thickness of a £1 coin; you need a circle roughly 30cm in diameter. Use the pastry to line a 23cm deep, nonstick, loose-based fluted quiche tin. Make sure the pastry is tucked into the corner of the tin and leave some overhang all the way round. It is imperative that there are no cracks; if there are, you will not be able to pour in the custard without having a minor disaster on your hands. Reserve a small piece to patch any holes or cracks after baking.

Chill the tart case for 30 minutes. Preheat the oven to 180°C fan/200°C/Gas 6. Very lightly prick the case with a fork. Line with a large piece of crumpled baking paper and fill with a generous amount of baking beans.

Bake on a sturdy baking tray in the centre of the oven for 30 minutes. Remove the paper and beans. Patch any cracks or holes with the reserved pastry. Glaze the inside of the pastry case by using a brush to paint it with the remaining beaten egg. Pop the tart case back in the oven and cook it for a further 5–6 minutes, or until the base of the tart has darkened in colour and looks crisp and dry. Remove from the oven and allow to cool. Gently, using a small paring knife, cut round the lip of the tart case to remove the pastry overhang. Reduce the oven temperature to 140°C fan/160°C/Gas 3.

Preheat the grill to its highest setting. Place the apricots, cut-side up, on a grill pan lined with foil. Sprinkle with the 2 tablespoonfuls of sugar. Grill until the sugar has caramelised and the apricots are lightly scorched. Remove from the heat and leave to cool. Place the apricot halves in concentric circles within the pastry case, leaning each half at an angle on the one before. In a bowl, lightly whisk the whole eggs and egg yolks with the sugar until pale. Pour the cream into a saucepan. Split the vanilla pod half lengthways, scrape out the seeds into the cream and stir them in. Heat gently for 4–5 minutes, stirring, then remove from the heat and beat into the eggs and sugar. Transfer to a jug.

Carefully pour most of the custard mixture around the apricots (not over the top, as the exposed fruit should not be covered in overcooked custard). Place the tart in the oven and pour in as much of the custard as the tart case will take. Cook for 50–60 minutes. The custard should be only just set, as it will go on cooking when removed from the oven. Tap the edge of the tart case with a finger; there should be only the faintest wobble in the middle. Allow to cool.

Just before serving – no earlier, as the custard could crack – lift the tart carefully out of the tin and slide on to a serving plate. Serve with more cream.

Blackcurrants with lemon & cinnamon shortbread

Serves 6

400g blackcurrants
3 tablespoons caster sugar, or to taste
double cream, to serve

Shortbread

250g plain flour
50g semolina
100g caster sugar
a good pinch of flaked sea salt
1 teaspoon ground cinnamon
finely grated zest of 2 unwaxed
    lemons
200g unsalted butter, chilled

Blackcurrants are great in Ribena, dried in Eccles cakes or turned into fool, but I enjoy them best of all when they are fresh and uncooked. Here they are with lemon and cinnamon shortbread (just leave out these flavourings if you prefer it plain).

When baking, I often have to scurry back to books, as it is a numbers game and I have no head for them. Shortbread, however, has an easy rule to remember: 3-2-1: 3 flour, 2 butter, 1 sugar – brilliant! Apart from the fact that I can't help being reminded of Dusty Bin, that irritating automated garbage can from the particularly perplexing Eighties game show 3-2-1.

Start with the shortbread. Preheat the oven to 150°C fan/170°C/Gas 3½. In a large bowl, mix the flour, semolina, sugar, salt, cinnamon and lemon zest. Grate in the chilled butter on the side of the grater you would use to do the kiddies' Cheddar. (Grating the butter means you need to finger it less and the mixture won't be hand-warmed and pudgy.)

With a spoon, thoroughly mix the ingredients together, pulling the dough against the side of the bowl. When it's pretty much one lump, lift it from the bowl and form it into a block about 10cm × 6cm with your hands. Wrap in clingfilm and refrigerate for 30 minutes.

Cut the shortbread in slices about 8mm thick and arrange them on a baking tray lined with baking paper. Bake for 40–50 minutes until pale golden. Cook for a little longer if needs be. Leave to cool completely, then remove from the baking tray and cut into slices.

While the shortbread cooks, turn the blackcurrants with the sugar into a serving bowl (I like 3 tablespoons for this quantity, but you may want more), then chill in the fridge, covered. I like them slightly cold when served, but if you don't, skip the fridge step. Eat with the shortbread and plenty of cream.

Fresh blackcurrant jelly

Makes 3 jars (roughly 1kg)

1kg blackcurrants
1 litre cold water
450g caster sugar per 600ml
    liquid collected
2 tablespoons lemon juice

This old-fashioned preserved jelly is great for spreading on fresh bread, toast, scones and for filling cakes and pastries. It is easy to do half a jar in one sitting.

Pick over the fruit and remove any damaged berries, but don't worry about the soft green stalks. Wash the blackcurrants and drain well. Put the fruit in a large pan with the water and bring to the boil. Reduce the heat and simmer for 20–30 minutes, or until very soft.

Strain through a sieve lined with a new J Cloth, folded in half, or through a jelly bag, for 3–4 hours into a large bowl. You want to collect as much juice as possible. One is told not to squeeze the bag, but I've found that as long as you

» are gentle, the juice presses through the tiny holes in the fabric and doesn't become cloudy. Discard the pulp.

Measure the blackcurrant liquid in a jug and then return to the saucepan. Add 450g of sugar for every 600ml of liquid collected.

Place over a low heat, add the lemon juice and stir until the sugar dissolves. Bring to the boil. Skim off any scum that rises to the surface of the liquid and boil for 15–20 minutes. Put a saucer in the fridge ready for testing the jelly.

While the jelly is boiling, sterilise the jars (*see* page 259). Test the jelly for setting after 15 minutes. Spoon a little on to the cold saucer and leave for a minute or so. Run your finger through the centre. If the jelly wrinkles either side of your finger, it is ready; if not, continue boiling for a further 2–3 minutes and then test again.

Pour the hot jelly carefully through a wide, clean funnel into three warm jelly jars. Screw on the lids, and allow to come down to room temperature. Store in a cool, dark place and eat within 6 months.

Chocolate roulade with redcurrants

Serves 8

butter, softened, for greasing
6 large free-range eggs, separated
150g caster sugar
60g cocoa powder, plus extra
   for dusting
icing sugar, for dusting

Filling

250ml double cream
1 tablespoon icing sugar
250g redcurrants

Chic, rich and delicious, I hope chocolate roulade acknowledges her poor Swiss and Arctic cousins. I, certainly, will always defend both cousins from taunts of being low-brow, as I like them as well. This recipe contains no flour, so is perfect for those who avoid gluten. It is very light indeed, so I suggest you cut a big slice.

Preheat the oven to 160°C fan/180°C/Gas 4. Line a 23cm × 33cm Swiss roll tin with baking paper. Grease with a little butter and set aside.

Put the egg yolks and caster sugar in a large bowl and whisk until thick and creamy. Sift the cocoa powder over the egg mixture and whisk it in thoroughly. Wash and dry the beaters, then, using a clean bowl, whisk the egg whites until stiff but not dry. Fold a third of the egg whites into the cocoa mixture, then gently fold in the rest until evenly distributed. Pour into the prepared tin and spread gently with a spatula.

Bake in the centre of the oven for 20 minutes, or until well risen and just beginning to shrink away from the sides of the tin. Remove from the oven, loosen the edges with a round-bladed knife and leave to stand until cold. The cake will sink down into the tin and this is fine.

To make the filling, whip the cream with the icing sugar until thick enough to stand in soft, floppy peaks. Remove the redcurrants from their strings by sliding the stalks through a fork. (Keep a couple of the prettier strings whole for decorating the finished cake.) Place a large piece of baking paper on the work surface and gently turn out the cake on to the paper.

Spread the cream over the cake and dot with the redcurrants. Roll up gently from one of the short sides and transfer to a serving plate with the outer edge end face down on the plate in order to present a smooth top. Dust with icing sugar and cocoa powder. Decorate with the reserved redcurrants and cut into thick slices to serve. This is good chilled as well, but dust with cocoa and sugar only after you have taken it out of the fridge and are ready to serve it.

Gingersnap horns, whipped cream & summer berries

Serves 10

175g butter
175g granulated sugar
115g golden syrup
a capful of brandy
2 teaspoons ground ginger
175g plain flour
600g fresh summer berries
  (try to include blackcurrants)
2 tablespoons icing sugar, or to taste
450ml whipping cream

This is a favourite pudding of mine – a) because the gingersnaps taste like Dime bars and b) because you get to smash them. Of course, the berries and cream are great too. I have done quite a lot of snap mix here, as every time I have made them I have burnt some and been smoked out of the kitchen. If you are nimbler than me, this recipe will leave you with extra snap mix, which freezes well, or you can make extra for the biscuit tin.

Preheat the oven to 170°C fan/190°C/Gas 5. In a saucepan, melt the butter gently with the granulated sugar, syrup and brandy. Turn off the heat, then sift in the ginger with the flour and stir until all are thoroughly incorporated.

Let the mixture cool until you can handle it, then roll it into 10 balls. Put a ball in the centre of a baking tray lined with baking paper. Flatten it slightly and bake for 12 minutes, or until flat, bubbling and a uniform deep golden brown. Leave it to cool on the tray for 1 minute, then lift it off with a palette knife and lay it along the size of a horizontal wine bottle to achieve a curve. While still warm and pliable, take it from the bottle and quickly manipulate it to resemble a cone. Continue like this to make the rest of the gingersnap horns. Cool on a wire rack.

In a blender, blend a third of the fruit to a purée with enough icing sugar to suit your taste. Tip the remaining fruit into the purée and stir through. In a bowl, beat the whipping cream until semi-stiff peaks are formed, again adding icing sugar to taste. Hold each cone and fill it, alternating the fruit and cream, until the horn is plentiful. Serve immediately. The cream can be whipped and the fruit prepared in advance, but these horns must be put together just before serving, as they will suffer if left to sit around. Absolutely smashing!

Fresh raspberry jelly

Serves 2

750g raspberries, plus extra
   for decorating
200ml cold water
3 heaped tablespoons caster sugar,
   plus extra if necessary
a squeeze of lemon juice (optional)
4 sheets of gelatine (about 8g)
2 tablespoons *crème de menthe*
   (optional)
double cream, to serve (optional)

Writing about jelly makes me think of my childhood, a happy fraction of which was spent throwing licked Chivers jelly cubes on to the ceiling, where they would stick fast. Oh happy days! No such luck with this recipe, I'm afraid, as it is made with fresh fruit. Mint and raspberries always go well together, even in this *crème de menthe*-splashed version, which has a slightly ghoulish colour combo.

Put the raspberries in a saucepan with the water and sugar. Stir over a low heat until the sugar dissolves, then bring to the boil. Reduce the heat slightly and simmer briskly for 6–8 minutes, or until the raspberries are very soft, stirring occasionally.

Take the pan off the heat and pass the purée through a fine sieve into a large jug (do not push it through too hard, as grinding the pips will result in a cloudy jelly). Make the liquid up to 600ml with cold water. Sweeten with a touch more sugar, if necessary, and add a squeeze of lemon if you think it needs sharpening just a little. Return to the saucepan and heat gently. It should not be boiling hot when you add the gelatine.

Soak the gelatine sheets in a bowl half-filled with cold water for 4 minutes until soft. Lift out with your fingers and squeeze over the bowl to remove as much of the water as possible. Whisk the gelatine into the warm raspberry mixture until melted, then pour into a 600ml jelly mould or individual ramekins. Cover with clingfilm and chill in the fridge for around 8 hours, or until set. When ready to eat, slide a knife gently around the outside of each jelly, then dip the mould or moulds into a bowl of just-boiled water and hold for the count of five. Turn the jelly out on to a large plate, or individual plates, and decorate with extra raspberries. If it's not too left-field for you, pour over a little *crème de menthe* just before serving with cream, if you like.

Mint granita

Serves 8–10

300ml elderflower cordial
300ml water
a large bunch of mint (about 80g)
100ml freshly squeezed lemon juice
   (about 2 lemons)
2 tablespoons caster sugar

This is cooling and icy for a hot summer's day – and curiously pink. I am not a molecular cook and can't for the life of me work out why it goes this beautiful colour. Any thoughts, Heston?

Put the cordial and water in a saucepan. Put the mint on a board and shred through the whole bunch roughly. Chop the stalks as well, save for the ends.

Put the mint in the pan and then stir in the lemon juice and sugar. Heat together until certainly warm, but not hot. The sugar needs to melt, but don't bring it up to even a simmer; make the water too hot and the mint flavour will become unpleasant. Turn off the heat and leave the mint to infuse for 2 hours. Strain through a fine sieve into a freezerproof container. Attach a lid and freeze for 2 hours.

Remove and distress the partially frozen mixture by scraping it with a fork. Return it to the freezer. Repeat every 1–2 hours until the mixture takes on a snow-like consistency.

Spoon into low glasses or teacups. Eat immediately.

Watermelon with lime, chile & salt

Serves 8

2 teaspoons flaked sea salt
2 teaspoons chile powder
(ancho is good, but any will do)
1 medium fridge-cold watermelon
1–2 big juicy limes, plus lime wedges
to decorate (optional)

In the hot, grimy, sticky, thick air of Mexico City, this comes as a refreshing saviour on nearly every street corner. This combination might strike you as odd at first, but I tell you it's thirst-quenching beyond belief.

On a small plate, combine the salt with the chile powder, then pinch it together with your fingers. Cut as much of the watermelon as you want to serve, slicing it from the skin into shards about 2cm wide and 10cm long.

Upend the melon pieces into plastic or paper cups, squeeze over some lime juice, adding lime wedges to decorate, if you like, and pinch over a good amount of the chile and salt. Eat and feel cooled.

Poached peaches in lemon syrup with almond biscuits

Serves 4–8

4 good large ripe (not mushy)
   peaches
600ml white wine
juice of 1 lemon
75g caster sugar
finely grated zest of 1 unwaxed lime
sprigs of basil and mint, to decorate
dollops of crème fraîche, to serve
   (optional)

Almond biscuits

2 medium free-range egg whites
100g caster sugar
35g butter, melted and cooled
¼ teaspoon vanilla extract
100g plain flour
25g flaked almonds

Does a perfect peach really need the interference of heat? Probably not, but this is a simple pudding I make when the fruit bowl plonked on the table seems lazy. Serve chilled.

First make the almond biscuits. Preheat the oven to 180°C fan/200°C/Gas 6. Line a large baking tray with baking paper.

Whisk the egg whites lightly in a bowl to break up the albumen, but not so that they are too frothy. Whisk in the sugar, melted butter and vanilla extract. Sift the flour on top and stir to make a smooth batter.

Put the mixture in a piping bag fitted with a plain nozzle and pipe eight strips of the batter, each about the length and thickness of your middle finger, on to the baking tray, spaced well apart. Spread with a palette knife until roughly 12cm × 4cm and the thickness of a £2 coin. If you're not concerned with uniformity, just spread them out with a palette knife and skip the piping stage.

Sprinkle with half the flaked almonds. Bake for 8–10 minutes until firm and golden brown around the edges. Cool for a few minutes on the tray, then transfer to a wire rack. Repeat with the remaining batter and almonds.

Meanwhile, cut the peaches in half and remove the stones. Do not worry about removing the skin. Combine the wine, lemon juice and sugar in the bottom of a large, shallow pan. Place in the peach halves, flat-side down. Bring the peaches up to a simmer and cook them like this for about 15 minutes or so, skimming occasionally, until totally soft; when you place the point of a small knife on the peach it should very easily slide in.

Lift the peaches carefully from the pan and place them in a big, shallow bowl. This is a good time to pinch off the skins – they should come off in one go. (Alternatively, I don't mind eating the skin.)

Turn up the heat a little and reduce the liquor for a further 15 minutes until only marginally runnier than cough mixture. Allow the syrup to cool and stir in the lime zest. Pour the liquor over the peaches and either chill or leave at room temperature. Decorate with basil and mint sprigs, and serve with the almond biscuits, and crème fraîche if liked.

Fresh blackberry & lemon sponge

Serves 8

225g margarine or spreadable butter, plus extra for greasing

225g caster sugar

4 medium free-range eggs

250g self-raising flour

1 teaspoon baking powder

½ teaspoon vanilla extract

sifted icing sugar, for dusting

finely grated zest of 1 unwaxed lemon, to decorate (optional)

Filling

125g butter, softened, cut into small cubes

250g icing sugar, sifted

finely grated zest of 1 unwaxed lemon

2 teaspoons lemon juice

½ jar (about 150g) good-quality blackberry jam

250g blackberries

I love this cake; it's one to make when the blackberries are out in force (be quick with your basket, as it's not the blackbirds that are cause for concern but nimble-fingered little old ladies). I never skimp on the filling; so often it seems just a mean smear for so much sponge. You may look askance at my use of marge, but it makes for a fluffier sponge.

This is a big cake, Cakezilla, but it should just about fit inside an old biscuit or sweetie tin – a storage method that makes me think lovingly of my dear friend Elaine, guardian of the great English teatime.

Preheat the oven to 170°C fan/190°C/Gas 5. Grease two 20cm, loose-based sandwich tins and line the bases with discs of baking paper.

Put the margarine or butter, caster sugar, eggs, flour, baking powder and vanilla extract in a food processor and blend on the pulse setting until well combined and creamy. You may need to remove the lid once or twice and push the mixture down with a spatula in order to help it combine thoroughly.

Spoon the mixture evenly into the tins and smooth the surface. Bake on the same shelf in the centre of the oven for about 20–25 minutes, or until the sponge is well risen and just beginning to shrink back from the sides of the tins. Leave to cool for 5 minutes before running a knife around the cakes and turning them out on to a wire rack. Peel off the baking paper and leave the cakes to cool completely.

To make the filling put the butter, icing sugar and lemon zest and juice in a food processor or mixing bowl and blend or whisk until smooth and creamy.

Place one of the sponges on a plate or cake stand and spread with the jam, then dot with the blackberries. Spread the flat side of the other sponge with the lemon filling, then carefully sandwich the cakes together. Leave to stand for 30 minutes or so to allow the filling to become a little firmer.

Dust the cake with sifted icing sugar. Finely grate a little more lemon zest on top, if you like, and serve in large wedges with Lapsang Souchong, a delightful tea that rather has the smell of ridden horses (in a good way).

Queen of plums

Serves 6

6 large firm ripe plums, halved
   and stoned
275g caster sugar
juice and finely grated zest of
   ½ small unwaxed lemon
4 medium free-range eggs
15g butter, softened, plus extra
   for greasing
125g fresh white breadcrumbs
300ml whole milk
200ml double cream
½ teaspoon vanilla extract
single cream, chilled, to serve

Queen of puddings is one of my favourites, but when clusters of plums make the boughs hang heavy, the raspberry jam can move over and make way. Then plums can move over for apples when the time comes.

Place the plum halves in a medium saucepan with 100g of the sugar and the lemon juice. Cover and cook gently for 15 minutes until the sugar has dissolved and the plums are sitting in their juice, then remove the lid and increase the heat. Simmer the plums for a further 8–10 minutes until they are very soft and have collapsed in a thick syrup – similar to a fruit compote. Stir regularly as they cook so that they do not stick. Spoon into a well-buttered 2-litre ovenproof pie dish. Leave to cool for 30 minutes.

While the plums are cooling, separate three of the eggs and beat the three yolks with one whole egg in a large bowl until smooth. Reserve the whites. Stir in 25g of the remaining sugar along with the lemon zest, softened butter, breadcrumbs, milk and cream. Leave to stand for 15 minutes to allow the breadcrumbs to swell. Spoon the bread mixture gently on top of the cooled plums, spread evenly and allow to stand for a further 15 minutes. Meanwhile, preheat the oven to 160°C fan/180°C/Gas 4.

Bake the pudding on a sturdy baking tray in the centre of the oven for about 35–40 minutes until faintly browned around the edges and only just set – it should still wobble in the middle. It is very important that the bread filling remains very soft and giving as when cooked to 'cakey' the pud is not such a treat. Whisk the egg whites until stiff and gradually whisk in the remaining sugar until the meringue is thick and glossy. Beat in the vanilla extract at the end. Remove the dish from the oven, increase the oven temperature to 170°C fan/190°C/Gas 5 and pile the meringue on top. Return to the oven for a further 18–20 minutes until the meringue is set and lightly browned. Serve hot with single cream for pouring. Dive in.

Toffee apples

Serves 6

6 small Cox's apples
250g caster sugar
100ml water

Fireworks, bonfires, the rustle of autumn leaves, fairgrounds and scarves all deserve a toffee apple. You will need six chopsticks.

Snap the stalks off each apple and ram a chopstick into the bottom of each, halfway up into the fruit. Lay a piece of baking paper on a flat work surface, then put the sugar with the water in a medium-sized saucepan over a medium heat and bring up to a brisk simmer. It's essential that the pan is clean and there are no foreign bodies in the bottom of it, as the sugar will crystalise instead of turning to caramel. After 10 minutes or so you will notice that the sugar is beginning to brown in patches. This means you will need to swirl the syrup so that it colours evenly; do not stir it. The desired colour is that of a pale hazelnut (cooked darker, it will become very bitter and children do not like these tastes). You will need to cook it for a further 3–4 minutes to achieve the required colour.

Turn off the heat and tilt the pan so that the caramel goes to one side. You have to work quickly now, as the caramel will still keep on cooking, its taste changing all the time. Holding each apple by the stick, twist it to cover it with a layer of caramel, then hold it upright and twist it slowly a few times; keep twisting so that the caramel doesn't slide off. Upend it on the baking paper. Repeat with all the apples. The last one might be a bit lumpy – more sugar for some lucky blighter. They are ready the minute the caramel makes a hard sound when tapped with a spoon.

Apple fritters with chestnut honey & grappa cream

Serves 4

225g gluten- and wheat-free plain
  flour blend, such as Doves Farm
½ teaspoon flaked sea salt
225–250ml dry cider, chilled
olive oil, for frying
3 good hard tart dessert apples
chestnut honey, or other honey

Grappa cream

150ml whipping cream
  or double cream
1–2 dessertspoons icing sugar
1–2 teaspoons grappa

These apple fritters are a little off-piste from the norm, as they are fried in olive oil and slathered in bitter chestnut honey. If you are not one for bitter tastes, use any runny honey you please. On a skiing trip I ate these by the plate-load, thinking that my committed attack of the slopes warranted such joyful energy replacement. It made no more sense than eating a family box of Krispy Kremes after climbing the stairs. Easy does it! I have changed the original batter mix for a winning tip-off from Mr Mark Hix.

To make the grappa cream, whip the cream with the icing sugar, adding the grappa as it starts to thicken. Continue whisking until firm peaks have formed. Take care not to over-mix the cream. Leave to one side, covered, in the fridge. If using whipping cream, it is important to whip it until it is fairly thick or it will collapse quickly.

In a large bowl, mix the flour and salt together. Slowly add the cider while whisking lightly with a balloon whisk until the batter is smooth and thick. The batter should only be mixed just enough to incorporate the ingredients.

Heat a wok or deep frying pan filled with 2cm oil to 170°C (don't allow the oil to overheat and don't leave it unattended). Peel, core and thickly slice the apples into rounds, or cut chunks that warrant two large mouthfuls. Drop them into the batter and toss all together until thoroughly but lightly coated.

When the oil is at the correct temperature, lift some of the apple pieces one by one with tongs and gently drop them into the pan. The oil must be hot enough or the apples will be greasy and soggy.

Cook the fritters in two or three batches for 3½–4 minutes until crisp and golden, turning once or twice. Drain the apples on kitchen paper while you cook the next batch. Arrange them all on a plate and spoon over some honey. Serve with the boozy cream.

Floating islands with espresso caramel sauce

Serves 4–6

1 litre whole milk
6 large free-range eggs, separated
125g caster sugar
½ teaspoon vanilla extract
1 vanilla pod, split in half lengthways

Caramel

100g caster sugar
4 tablespoons cold water
4 tablespoons very strong coffee
  (ideally espresso)

This is one of my all-time favourite puddings, with clouds of fluffy sweet meringue hanging low over a sunshine sea of custard. I realised that, as a coffee lover, I had not included it anywhere in the book, so timidly decided to smuggle it into this classic pudding. The result works well. My father used to serve the custard warm and poach the islands in front of us, so you can also cook the dish this way – hot.

Heat the milk in a large, wide-based nonstick saucepan until it is gently simmering (but do not let the milk boil). Whisk the egg whites in a large, clean mixing bowl until stiff but not dry. Gradually, whisk in 50g of the sugar, a tablespoon at a time, until all is incorporated. Whisk in the vanilla extract.

Using 2 dessertspoons, form a little of the egg white mixture into a quenelle, a little larger than an egg, and slide it into the simmering milk. Make and cook two more quenelles in the same way. Cook the meringues for 2 minutes, then turn over and cook on the other side for a further 2 minutes. The meringues will expand as they cook. Lift out of the milk with a slotted spoon and drain on a plate lined with several sheets of kitchen paper. Working quickly, continue making the meringues until you have prepared a further nine in exactly the same way. Leave to stand, then cover and chill for up to 2 hours before serving.

Strain the milk into a measuring jug – it should now measure around 600ml (add a little extra milk if not). Pour into a clean saucepan. Scrape out the vanilla seeds from the pod with the point of a knife and stir into the milk. Bring to a gentle simmer.

Whisk the egg yolks and the remaining 75g sugar together in a large bowl until pale and thick. Whisk in the hot milk, then return to the pan. Place over a medium–low heat and cook for about 15 minutes, stirring constantly, until the custard is smooth and thick enough to coat the back of a spoon. Do not allow it to get too hot or the eggs will scramble. Remove from the heat, cover the surface with clingfilm to prevent a skin forming and leave to cool.

Just before serving, put the sugar and water for the caramel in a small saucepan and place over a medium heat until the sugar dissolves, swirling occasionally. Continue cooking until the caramel turns a deep golden brown, then remove from the heat and immediately pour in the coffee. Take care, as it will splatter. Stir until the caramel and coffee combine to make a thick syrup.

Spoon or pour the custard into four or six deep plates, top with the meringues and drizzle with the coffee syrup.

Pear & chocolate frangipane tart

Serves 8

150g dark chocolate

175g unsalted butter, softened

175g caster sugar

125g ground almonds

75g plain flour

½ teaspoon flaked sea salt

½ teaspoon baking powder

2 medium free-range eggs, beaten

¼ teaspoon vanilla extract

3 ripe (but not squishy) Conference pears

juice of ½ lemon

15g flaked almonds

crème fraîche or cream, to serve

Sweet pastry

250g plain flour, plus extra for dusting

150g unsalted butter, chilled, cut into small cubes

2 tablespoons caster sugar

1 medium free-range egg, beaten

1 tablespoon cold water

Pears and chocolate first came to my attention at school. Canned pears, that is, with lumpy chocolate custard. It was my favourite pudding and I'd try to blend back into the dinner queue to lots of jostling elbows and shouts of 'Warner, sod off, you've already had some!' If you like this recipe, by all means have some more.

Preheat the oven 180°C fan/200°C/Gas 6. To make the pastry, put the flour, butter and sugar in a food processor and pulse until the mixture resembles fine breadcrumbs. Mix together the egg and water (this helps to prevent streaky pastry), then, with the food processor motor running, slowly add this to the flour mixture. Turn off the motor as soon as the dough forms a ball. Wrap the pastry in clingfilm and pop it in the fridge for an hour or so.

Roll out the pastry on a well-floured work surface to the thickness of a £1 coin, lifting and turning after every few rolls, then use it to line a 25cm deep, fluted tart case. Don't worry if the pastry tears a little; simply repair any gaps with the trimmings. Really tuck the pastry down into the corner. Place on a sturdy baking tray and prick the base lightly with a fork. Line the pastry case with crumpled baking paper and fill with baking beans. Bake blind for 22 minutes, then remove the paper and beans and cook for a further 3 minutes, or until the base is dry. Remove from the oven and put to one side while the filling is prepared. Reduce the oven temperature to 150°C fan/170°C/Gas 3½.

For the filling, slam the chocolate, in its wrapper, on to the table to break it up into big chunks or, if feeling more peaceful, snap it into pieces instead. Personally, I prefer a little drama. In a food processor, blend the butter and sugar until pale and soft. Add the ground almonds, flour, salt, baking powder, eggs and vanilla extract. Blend well. Remove the blade and stir in three-quarters of the chocolate pieces with a spatula.

Spread the almond mixture evenly over the cooled pastry case, starting around the edge before heading into the centre. Peel the pears and cut into quarters. Remove the cores, put all the pear quarters into a large bowl and dress with a little squeeze of lemon juice. Arrange the pear quarters pregnant-side upwards and, with the narrow ends towards the middle, press them gently into the almond batter. Press the remaining chocolate pieces well into the batter.

Bake the tart on a tray in the centre of the oven for 30 minutes. Remove from the oven, sprinkle all over with the flaked almonds, then return to the oven for a further 35–40 minutes, or until the pears are tender and the frangipane filling is well risen and golden brown. Leave to stand for 15 minutes before lifting from the tin. Ideally, time this so that the tart is served warm. Mind you, it's good cold too, or at room temperature. It is an offence to serve this without crème fraîche or cream.

Autumn trifle

Serves 8

6 medium Comice or Conference
   pears (ideally just ripe), peeled
700ml red wine
juice of 1 orange
125g caster sugar
4 cloves
1 bay leaf
a good grating of nutmeg
25g flaked almonds
5 sheets of gelatine
300ml sweet sherry
100–125g Savoiardi biscuits
   (about 12–18)
300ml whipping cream
icing sugar, to taste
finely grated zest of 1 unwaxed lemon
dark chocolate, for grating (optional)

Custard

1 vanilla pod
300ml double cream
300ml whole milk
6 medium free-range egg yolks
100g caster sugar
2 tablespoons cornflour

Gotta love a trifle.

Place the pears in a snug-fitting saucepan and pour over the wine so that they are covered. Add the orange juice, sugar, cloves, bay leaf and nutmeg. Bring the pears up to a simmer and poach them like this until they are utterly tender – a knife rested on the pear flesh should slide in without much prompting. Meanwhile, toast the flaked almonds in a dry frying pan over a medium–high heat, swirling them continuously, until they are golden brown. Leave to cool.

Remove the pears from the liquor and allow them to cool. Remove the cloves and bay leaf from the liquor. Soak the gelatine sheets in a bowl half-filled with cold water for 5 minutes until soft. Lift them out with your fingers and squeeze them over the bowl to remove as much of the water as possible. Whisk the gelatine into the warm wine until melted. Transfer to a jug and set aside to cool (don't take so long to come back to it that it sets).

Pour the sherry into a wide-based bowl and, taking one biscuit at a time, dunk them so that they soak up the booze but not for so long that they fall apart. Lay them at the bottom of a large glass serving dish. Cut the pears into quarters and remove and discard the cores. Arrange the pears on top of the biscuits.

Now make the custard. Split the vanilla pod lengthways and scrape out the seeds with the back of a knife. Pour the cream and milk into a saucepan and drop in the vanilla seeds and the scraped-out pod. Place over a medium–low heat and bring up to a faint simmer. In the meantime, whisk the egg yolks, sugar and cornflour together until smooth and thick. Tip the hot cream and milk into the eggs and sugar, whisking all the time, then pour the contents back into the saucepan. Remove the vanilla pod. Stir over a low heat, keeping the mixture moving all the time, until it starts to thicken (this will take about 15 minutes); you will know this when faint ribbons start forming behind the spoon. Put the custard in its pan into a basin of cold water to cool; it needs to be thick enough to coat the back of a spoon. Pour it slowly and evenly over the pears. It is imperative that the custard be in one solid layer and go right up to the edge of the bowl so that when the jelly is poured in it does not infiltrate the lower layers. Leave to cool, then put it in the fridge for a couple of hours to set.

Pour the wine jelly very slowly and carefully on to the custard (keeping close to the surface of the custard) and return to the fridge for 4–6 hours, or until set.

Finally, whip the cream with the desired amount of icing sugar to just sweeten it. In good dollops, spoon the cream over the jelly, pulling your hand up at the end of each movement to make nice little peaks. Scatter the toasted almonds over the whipped cream. Finish by grating over lemon zest followed by some dark chocolate, if you desire.

Poached quinces & cream

Serves 6

5 tablespoons caster sugar
750ml white wine
3 medium quinces, split in half
   lengthways
crème fraîche or double cream,
   to serve (optional)

A woefully betrayed fruit, quinces are seldom seen any more either in the greengrocer or supermarket and this is a shame, for they are truly delicious in a different way to their cousins the apple and pear. The Spanish and Portuguese love them reconfigured as membrillo, a delicious sweet, dense quince jelly that is a good accompaniment to cheese.

Quinces do require cooking and maybe this is why the taste for them has disappeared in this 'I simply don't have the time to cook' age. It is why I would say, again, 'Have a go, as good things come to those who wait'. I find the quince's faintly grainy/gritty texture very enjoyable and the colour of their flesh and syrup once cooked is a stunning glossy, brown maroon. Wild duck is a good meat to eat with them, as is most red-fleshed game, such as venison. They do well under a roof of crumble and make an excellent ice cream. Eat more quinces.

In a pan wide enough to fit the halved quinces in a single layer lying flat, mix the sugar and wine together. Lay in the quinces, flesh-side down. Bring the wine up to the faintest simmer and place a lid on the pan. Simmer them ever so gently like this for 2 hours. As the timing nears the end, the pectin in the quinces will thicken the syrup to jelly, and if there is not enough liquid in the pan, then burning the sugary syrup is dismayingly easy. Add water carefully if at any point you feel it necessary. Watch it like a hawk as – hell's teeth! – I had to cook this three times on the day we shot it for the photograph. If the quinces are ready before the wine is syrupy, remove with a slotted spoon and continue to simmer the liquid gently until well reduced.

Serve the quinces with dollops of crème fraîche or a drizzle of double cream, if you like.

Lemon meringue pie

Serves 12

Sweet pastry

250g plain flour, plus extra
for dusting
1 tablespoon caster sugar
150g butter, chilled, cut into
1cm cubes
1 medium free-range egg, beaten

Lemon curd

6 large free-range eggs
9 large free-range egg yolks
250g unsalted butter
250g caster sugar
finely grated zest of 4
unwaxed lemons
250ml lemon juice

Meringue

5 large free-range egg whites
250g caster sugar, plus 1 teaspoon
extra for sprinkling
½ tsp vanilla extract

cream, to serve

This recipe is in honour of Dame Marguerite Patten, whom I had the good fortune to meet and work with on a programme about war-time food rationing. In 1953, sugar rationing came to an end and she made a lemon meringue pie for the hungry households of the nation on BBC Television to show her pleasure at its return. Although this is not her actual recipe, whenever I eat the pudding now I think of her. I appreciate that it contains a lot of eggs, but this is not the kind of dish you eat every day, nor is it for one.

To make the pastry, put the flour, sugar and butter in a food processor and blend on the pulse setting until the mixture resembles fine breadcrumbs (the pulse button should be used when making pastry in a food processor, as it can become overworked if blended in one long, continuous run). With the motor running, slowly add the egg and pulse again for just long enough for the mixture to form a ball.

Turn the contents out on to a lightly floured work surface. Roll out your pastry to the thickness of a £1 coin; you need a circle roughly 28cm in diameter. Use the pastry to line a 26cm deep, nonstick, loose-based fluted tart tin. Make sure the pastry is tucked into the corner of the tin and leave some overhang all the way round.

Chill the tart case for 30 minutes. Preheat the oven to 180°C fan/200°C/Gas 6. Very lightly prick the case with a fork, ensuring you don't completely pierce the base. Line with a large piece of crumpled baking paper and fill with a generous amount of baking beans.

Bake on a sturdy baking tray in the centre of the oven for 30 minutes. Remove the paper and beans. Pop the tart case back in the oven and cook it for a further 5–6 minutes, or until the base of the tart has darkened in colour and looks crisp and dry. Remove from the oven and allow to cool. Gently, using a small paring knife, cut around the lip of the tart case to remove the pastry overhang.

For the lemon curd, beat the whole eggs with the yolks. Drop the butter, sugar, eggs and lemon zest and juice into a saucepan over a medium–low heat and start whisking with a balloon whisk. This will require your total concentration for the next 20 minutes. The butter will start to break up and the mixture will not look too appealing for a while. Keep on whisking and before long you will be looking at a delicious deep-yellow mixture. The minute you see wisps of steam rising from the pan, you are getting close to the desired moment. Do not stop whisking and make sure the corner of the pan is explored with the whisk. Suddenly things will start to thicken. When reasonably distinct ribbons trail behind the whisk, pour the hot curd into the tart case. The mix should be very smooth and velvety, and have no scrambled lumps in it. If you left it a little too late, pour the mix into the tart case through a fine sieve (sadly, you will lose the zest, but better a tart than no tart). Leave it to set for a couple of hours or so.

Preheat the oven to 160°C fan/180°C/Gas 4. For the meringue, put the egg whites in a large, clean bowl and beat with an electric whisk until the mixture

» forms stiff peaks; it is ready when the bowlful turned upside down over your head does not empty into your hair. Add the sugar a few tablespoons at a time, really whisking it in each time. Whisk in the vanilla extract once all the sugar has been added. The meringue should be very glossy and is ready when the sugar is all used. Dollop large spoonfuls of meringue on to the tart, pulling the spoon up to leave a lovely peaky crown all over the top of the tart. Sprinkle with the 1 teaspoon of sugar.

Bake for 12–15 minutes, or until the stiff peaks are nicely browned. (Do not overcook the tart, as this is the second opportunity to scramble the curd.) Leave to cool for 10–15 minutes, but no longer, as the meringue may begin to weep, before removing from the tin. Serve immediately with cream and thank your lucky stars you did not have to endure rationing.

Chocolate lime fondants

Serves 6

175g dark chocolate (minimum 70% cocoa solids)
150g butter, cut into small cubes, plus extra for greasing
3 large free-range eggs
3 large free-range egg yolks
finely grated zest of 3 unwaxed limes
50g caster sugar
25g self-raising flour
icing sugar, for dusting
crème fraîche, to serve

There are a lot of fondant puddings around – which is a good thing – but I wanted mine to be slightly different. I was thinking about my favourite sweets as a child, which were the lime éclairs, those green ones with the little chocolate centre. This is my explanation for putting lime in my fondants.

Butter six 175ml metal dariole moulds and line each base with a small disc of baking paper. Break the chocolate into pieces and put in a heatproof basin with the butter. Place over a pan of gently simmering water until melted, stirring occasionally. Remove from the heat and leave to cool for 10 minutes.

Use an electric whisk to whisk the whole eggs, egg yolks, lime zest and caster sugar together until pale and thick. Gently fold in the melted chocolate and butter. Sift the flour over the chocolate mixture and fold in lightly. Spoon into the prepared moulds and place in the fridge for at least 30 minutes (and up to 8 hours) before cooking.

Preheat the oven to 180°C fan/200°C/Gas 6. Remove the puddings from the fridge 15 minutes before serving. Bake for 10–11 minutes until well risen but still wobbly in the middle. (Add a minute to the cooking time for each hour that the puddings are chilled, up to 3 minutes extra.)

Remove from the oven and loosen the side of each pudding with a round-bladed knife. Turn out on to six dessert plates and remove the lining paper. Dust the puddings with icing sugar and serve with crème fraîche.

Citrus yoghurt & black sugar pudding

Serves 6–8

1kg Greek-style yoghurt
finely grated zest of 3 large
   unwaxed limes
finely grated zest of 2 large
   unwaxed oranges
finely grated zest of 2 large
   unwaxed lemons
150g dark muscovado sugar

This is about the easiest pudding in the world to make, a real winner for dinner if you have left everything to the last minute, people are coming over and you're in a flap. Mum used to make it all the time. Use full-fat yoghurt, as it will taste twice as good as the half-fat nonsense.

Put the yoghurt in a bowl and mix in all the zest. Take a glass serving dish and put just under half the citrus yoghurt in the bottom, then evenly scatter over half the sugar. (Muscovado tends to get hard little lumps in it, so really try to crumble them out between your thumb and finger.)

Add the rest of the yoghurt in dollops over the sugar and then gently spread it out with the back of a spoon so as not to drag the first layer of sugar around too much. Scatter the rest of the sugar on the top and place the pudding, covered, in the fridge for up to a couple of hours but no more. Serve alone, or with biscuits, or poached fruit – or both, God damn it!

Iced orange loaf

Serves 8

2 medium–large unwaxed oranges
1 unwaxed lemon
100ml cold water
175g golden caster sugar
175g unsalted butter, softened,
   plus extra for greasing
175g self-raising flour
½ teaspoon baking powder
3 large free-range eggs
100g icing sugar, sifted

I very much approve of mid-afternoon tea, especially during the grim winter months. Eating cake as the rain patters against the windows, and mist hangs in the hedges, gives such a cosy feeling. A good pot of Ceylon tea would go well on the tray next to this cake.

Peel the oranges with a potato peeler and cut each strip into long, thin shreds. Finely grate the zest of the lemon and set aside. Cut the oranges and lemon in half and squeeze out the juice. Reserve 4 teaspoonfuls and put the rest in a small saucepan with the orange shreds. Add the water and bring to the boil, then reduce the heat slightly and simmer for about 30 minutes, or until well softened. Stir 50g of the caster sugar into the pan and boil for another 4 minutes until the liquid is syrupy and reduced to around 3 tablespoons, stirring occasionally. Lightly drain and reserve a third of the orange shreds in a small bowl. Pour the orange syrup and remaining shreds into a large bowl and leave to cool for 10 minutes.

Preheat the oven to 160°C fan/180°C/Gas 4. Line the base of a 1.2-litre nonstick loaf tin with baking paper, so that the liner sticks 2–3cm over the ends of the tin (these will help lift the cake out once cooked). Butter the inside of the tin well.

Put the remaining caster sugar with the butter, flour, baking powder, eggs and lemon zest in a food processor and blend on the pulse setting until just combined, thick and smooth. Transfer to the large bowl and gently fold in the orange syrup, including the orange shreds.

Spoon the cake batter into the prepared tin and level the surface. Bake for 35–40 minutes, or until well risen and pale golden brown. Cool in the tin for 5 minutes, then transfer to a wire rack until cold.

To make the icing, blend the reserved 4 teaspoons of citrus juice with the icing sugar until smooth. Put a plate under the cake while on its cooling rack. Drizzle the icing over and leave to set for 10 minutes. Scatter the reserved orange shreds on top of the icing and serve in thick slices with tea.

Orange & butterscotch pudding

Serves 6–8

2 small unwaxed oranges

225g butter, plus extra for greasing

125g dark muscovado sugar

100g caster sugar

265g self-raising flour

4 large free-range eggs

100g walnut halves, roughly broken

double cream, for serving

2 small oranges, skins left on,
  very finely sliced

Butterscotch sauce

250g caster sugar

50g butter, chilled, cut into
  small cubes

3 capfuls of whisky

6 tablespoons double cream

Hark the herald angels sing, glory to this steamed pudding! I love my Christmas pud, but stick a few pennies in this one instead if you are open to change.

Butter a 1.7-litre pudding basin and line the base with a small circle of baking paper. Start making the butterscotch sauce. Put the caster sugar in a small frying pan over a low heat and pour over just enough cold water to cover. Heat until the sugar dissolves, swishing the contents around the pan occasionally, without stirring. Add the orange slices and bring to a gentle simmer. Cook the oranges in the sugar syrup for 6–8 minutes until just softened, then remove with a slotted spoon and drain on a plate. Reserve the syrup and slices for later. Now make the pudding. Finely grate the zest from one orange. Slice one end off each orange and place the whole fruits on a chopping board, flat-side down. Using a small, sharp knife, cut off the peel and pith all the way round. Next, cut between the membranes to release the segments. Cut each segment into three pieces and put the pieces in a sieve over a bowl to drain off excess juice.

Put the butter, sugars, flour, eggs and orange zest in a food processor. Blitz on the pulse setting until smooth and thick. You may need to remove the lid and push the mixture down a couple of times with a spatula. Transfer to a large mixing bowl. Stir in the broken walnuts and reserved orange segments until thoroughly mixed. Drink any juice from the bowl.

Choose the best slices of the softened orange and arrange around the inside of the pudding basin. Spoon the batter into the prepared basin and smooth over the surface. Cover the dish with a large circle of baking paper, with a pleat in the middle to allow for expansion. Cover the paper with a circle of foil, again with a pleat. Tie both tightly in place with string. Create a handle by taking the excess string across the top of the basin and tying to the string on the other side – this will help you lift the pudding once it's cooked.

Place the basin on an upturned heatproof saucer or small trivet in a large, deep saucepan and add enough just-boiled water to come halfway up the side of the basin. (Alternatively, cook in a hob-top steamer.) Cover the pan with a tight-fitting lid and place over a medium heat. Allow to steam in simmering water for 2 hours, adding more water if necessary.

Meanwhile, continue making the sauce. Return the pan with the sugar syrup to the heat and bring to the boil. Simmer, without stirring, until the sugar caramelises. It should be a deep golden-brown colour. Remove the pan from the heat and carefully add the chilled butter, piece by piece (the caramel will spatter furiously), whisking vigorously between additions until the sauce is thick and smooth. Gradually whisk the whisky and cream into the butterscotch mixture and return to the heat for 1–2 minutes until gently bubbling.

When the pudding is done, turn off the heat and carefully lift the basin from the water. Stand for 5 minutes. Reheat the sauce if necessary. Cut the string, foil and paper off the basin. Loosen the side of the pudding with a round-ended knife and invert on to a deep plate. Remove the lining paper and pour over a little of the butterscotch sauce. Serve the pudding in generous wedges with more butterscotch sauce for pouring.

Barbecued pineapple
with white rum

Serves 4

1 pineapple
a splash of double demerara rum
  or white rum
lime juice
a sprinkling of demerara sugar

Generally, I am not a one for barbecuing fruit (save for bananas in foil with chocolate buttons in the middle), but here is one way I do like it. Modern pineapples can be a bit confusing in that, although bright green on the outside and unripe-looking, they can be sweet and totally ripe within. A good way to choose your pineapple is to pull one of the central leaves from the crown; if it comes away easily, your pineapple is probably ripe. Shop attendants don't tend to like you doing this though!

Cut the stalk, skin and studs away from the pineapple flesh and cut away four large, long pieces round the core. (The core, then, tends to get tossed in the bin, but this is a shame; cut it into big chunks and chew it up to get as much juice out of it as possible, discreetly spitting out the roughage left behind into the bin.)

Choosing a place on your barbecue away from fish fat or beef grease, lay down your pineapple pieces and give them a good hammering over some fierce heat, turning occasionally. Each side should pick up some good black lines and lovely browning where the dripping sugars have started to caramelise. I can't give you precise timings here, as I don't know what stage your barbecue is at, or what kind it is, but try not to fiddle with the pineapple too much. Colour, colour, colour is what you want.

Lift the pieces from the grill, chop them roughly and splash with the rum. Finish with some lime juice and a sprinkling of demerara sugar. Let everything soak together a bit and make sure that before eating your chosen chunk you give it one last proper roll in the booze. Follow with cold beers or more rum and the afternoon will suddenly turn into evening.

Nut clusters

Makes a happy bagful

300g hazelnuts
300g caster sugar
1 teaspoon flaked sea salt

Be prepared for a cold-weather snack-attack with a small pile of this rubble in your pocket.

Preheat the oven to 200°C fan/220°C/Gas 7. Tip the hazelnuts into a baking tray and pop in the oven. They should take about 6 minutes to toast. What you are looking for is a deep goldenness to the flesh when the skin has been removed. Check them, as I have burnt thousands of pounds worth of nuts throughout my career to the frustration of my employers (I'm surprised Alistair Little didn't start docking my wages). When the nuts are done, tip them into a tea towel and fold it up. Rub the tea towel together. This will take off the majority of the skins, though a little left is no great matter. Pick out the hazelnuts and put in a bowl.

Put a piece of baking paper on the baking tray. Pour the sugar into the bottom of a medium-sized saucepan, along with enough water so that the sugar is thoroughly soaked but not swimming. Heat and bring up to a brisk simmer. Make sure there are no foreign bodies in the bottom of the pan, as this will mess up the caramel-making process. When it starts to colour, after 10 minutes or so, swirl the pan, as this will prevent the sugar from burning in one place and help the caramel to colour evenly. Do not stir it. When it is approaching the colour of hazelnut shells (after a further 3–4 minutes), turn off the heat and pinch in the salt. You have to work very quickly here, as the caramel will colour super-fast and quickly become bitter and inedible.

Tip in the nuts and stir them through before immediately turning it all out on to the baking paper and pressing it out into one rough layer. Allow to cool for 40 minutes before smashing with a rolling pin that you don't mind denting, or with an alternative blunt object.

Prune & brandy crème brûlée

Serves 6

150g pitted soft prunes
150ml orange juice
4 tablespoons brandy

Custard

600ml double cream
1 vanilla pod, split lengthways
4 large free-range egg yolks
100g caster sugar

When I was small, I was sometimes taken out for dinner by my parents, where I often fell asleep at the table, head down on the starched cloth. If still awake, though, I would always order crème brûlée, with its hard caramel, excited by any opportunity to smash something. I always associate it with grown-up restaurants and evening time, and really wanted to exaggerate this by adding prunes and brandy to make it serious.

Preheat the oven to 130°C fan/150°C/Gas 2. Put the prunes in a small saucepan with the orange juice and cook over a low heat for about 6–8 minutes, or until the prunes soften and become plump, stirring occasionally. Tip into a food processor and add the brandy. Blitz to a smooth, spreadable purée. If the mixture looks too stiff, add a little more orange juice and blitz again. Spread into the base of six 125ml ramekins.

To make the custard, pour the cream into a medium saucepan and into it scrape out the vanilla seeds from the pod and add the pod too. Heat the cream over a very low heat for about 10 minutes, stirring occasionally. Do not allow to boil. Whisk the egg yolks and half the sugar in a jug until well combined. Strain the eggs through a fine sieve into the cream. Stir well. Remove the vanilla pod.

Set the ramekins in a roasting tin and divide the cream mixture between them. Pour enough just-boiled water into the roasting tin to rise halfway up the outsides of the ramekins. Carefully transfer to the oven and bake for 30 minutes, or until the custard is very lightly set and still wobbles slightly in the middle. Do not allow them to overcook or they will split; separated brûlée is no fun. Remove from the oven, take the ramekins out of the water and leave to cool. Once cold, transfer the dishes to the fridge and leave to chill overnight.

About an hour before serving, sprinkle the custards with the remaining sugar and either pop under a very hot preheated grill or use a chef's blowtorch to caramelise the sugar. Refrigerate and then serve.

Treacle tart

Serves 10–12

4 medium free-range eggs

907g can golden syrup

juice and finely grated zest of
1 small unwaxed lemon

225g white breadcrumbs, made from
a 1–2 day-old loaf (crusts removed)

clotted cream, to serve

Pastry

250g plain flour, plus extra
for dusting

1 tablespoon caster sugar

150g butter, chilled, cut into 2cm dice

1 medium free-range egg, beaten

The sight of a treacle tart, clotted cream beside it, is a beloved British landscape in my eyes. Deep-filled and with that hint of lemon are my two unarguable rules. The pudding is cheap to make and serves loads of people.

To make the filling, put the eggs in a large bowl and whisk lightly. Stir in the syrup and lemon juice and zest, followed by the breadcrumbs. Set aside while the pastry case is prepared. This will give the breadcrumbs time to absorb the syrup.

To make the pastry, put the flour, sugar and butter in a food processor and blend on the pulse setting until the mixture resembles fine breadcrumbs. With the motor running, slowly add the beaten egg and blend for just long enough for the mixture to form a ball.

Transfer to a lightly floured work surface and roll out to around 3mm thick, turning the pastry and flouring the surface regularly. Use to line a 25cm loose-based fluted tart tin. Make sure the pastry is tucked into the corner of the tin. Trim the edges neatly, prick the base lightly with a fork and chill the pastry for 30 minutes. Preheat the oven to 180°C fan/200°C/Gas 6.

Put the pastry case on a baking tray and line with crumpled baking paper. Fill with baking beans. Bake blind for 20 minutes, then carefully take out of the oven and remove the baking paper and beans. Return to the oven for a further 5–6 minutes, or until the base of the tart has darkened in colour and looks crisp and dry. Remove from the oven and reduce the temperature to 160°C fan/180°C/Gas 4.

Pour the syrup mixture into the tart case. Bake for 35–40 minutes, or until the filling is pale golden brown. Leave in the tin for 30 minutes, then remove. Cut into slender wedges to serve with clotted cream.

Dundee cake

Serves 10

200g self-raising flour

1 teaspoon ground mixed spice

25g ground almonds

175g butter, at room temperature,
  plus extra for greasing

100g golden caster sugar

75g orange marmalade

3 large free-range eggs, beaten

175g currants

175g sultanas

75g undyed glacé cherries, halved

finely grated zest of 1 unwaxed lemon

3 tablespoons whisky or whole milk

50g blanched almonds, to decorate

A heavy slice of Dundee cake is an exceptional comrade when you're out in the field or on a long walk in the cold. However, I never seem to get it right as I either show no resolve and eat my ration far too early in the day, or happily rediscover it all clingfilm-bound and squidged up in my coat pocket two months later. Delicious with hard British cheeses, such as Lancashire.

Preheat the oven to 160°C fan/180°C/Gas 4. Grease and double-line a 20cm loose-based cake tin with baking paper. Sift the flour and spice into a bowl. Stir in the ground almonds.

Beat together the butter, sugar and marmalade in a large bowl with an electric whisk until very light and fluffy. Add a third of the beaten eggs, a little at a time, beating well after each addition. Stir in 2 heaped tablespoons of the flour mixture. Gradually beat in another third of the egg, followed by 2 more tablespoons of the flour mixture. Finish by beating in the remaining egg and stirring in the rest of the flour mixture.

Add the dried fruits and glacé cherries, grated lemon zest and whisky or milk to the cake batter, stirring until evenly distributed. The mixture should have a soft dropping consistency, so add a little extra whisky or milk if necessary.

Spoon the mixture into the cake tin, smooth the surface and arrange the blanched almonds in circles on top. Bake for about 1 hour, or until well risen and golden brown. A skewer inserted into the centre of the cake should come out clean. If the cake begins to overbrown before it is ready, cover the surface with some foil.

Leave the cake to cool for 5 minutes, then remove from the tin and place on a wire rack until cold. Store in a cake tin and eat within a week.

Drinks

Raspberry daiquiri

Serves 1

75ml raspberry purée, from fresh
    fruit whizzed and then sieved
50ml white rum
25ml sugar syrup
15ml lime juice
ice cubes
crushed ice

Strictly speaking, a true daiquiri has no fruit in it, but having endured a lot of strictness in the first half of my life, I can do without it now. I like my daiquiri to err on the sweet side, but please alter the sugar syrup as you see fit. Buying sugar syrup in branded bottles is a pointless waste of money. Simply dissolve unbleached white sugar with an equal amount of water and let it cool. If keen on your cocktails, make more than you need, as it keeps.

In a cocktail shaker, rattle all the ingredients (bar the crushed ice) energetically for 10 seconds or so. Pour through the nozzle into a Martini glass half-full with crushed ice. Sip before the ice allows the drink to become too watery.

Dick's rum shack punch

Serves 1

25ml Wray & Nephew overproof
    white rum
25ml Wood's 100 Old Navy Rum,
    or other double demerara rum
25ml freshly squeezed lime or
    lemon juice
20ml grenadine
2 dashes of Angostura bitters
50ml exotic juice (from a carton),
    such as passion fruit, mango
    or pineapple
ice cubes
a grating of nutmeg

The Colony Room was a notorious drinking club, a melting pot of creativity and booze that is sadly no more. A place to chat with strangers as much as friends, it was full of artists, musicians, odd bods and the outspoken, a hub in London's smoky lung that is Soho.
In my brief membership, Dick was the barman towards the end and this was the drink he normally made me, and I rarely deviated. This is his recipe in his own words, as he texted them.

'The rum shack punch is an attempt to copy the drink people enjoy on their Caribbean holiday. The secret is in the petrol flavour of Wray & Nephew overproof white rum.

Shake all with ice, then strain over fresh ice in a tall glass. Dust with nutmeg and hope that helps.'

Mango milkshake

Serves 4

300g Alfonso mango flesh, halved
   and stoned
50g condensed milk
300ml whole milk
ice cubes (optional)

Small, vividly yellow Alfonso mangoes from India, lovingly packed in a box with gaudy shredded paper, are one of the high points of the year when they come into season in late spring. Sticky-chinned and grinning, I love to suck the pulp through a cut in the skin, having massaged the contents to mush. If this is all a bit too messy, here is a delicious alternative that I grew fat on in Delhi. The addition of condensed milk is essential.

Remove the mango pulp from the skins and flop it straight into a blender. Follow with the condensed milk and whole milk and blitz until completely smooth. Either serve after chilling in the fridge or immediately pour it over ice. Drink in the sun holding a black umbrella in the other hand for shade.

Gin & tonic with cucumber

Serves any number

2 large cucumbers, peeled
good gin, such as Hendrick's,
   Sipsmith, Plymouth or
   Bombay Sapphire
tonic water
very thin slices of lime, to serve

Something different, and certainly refreshing.

Put the cucumbers into a food processor and blitz until totally turned to slush. Over a measuring jug, place a fine sieve, covered with a fresh J Cloth. Pour the cucumber mixture in and push all the liquid through until only the sediment is left. Pour the juice into an ice tray and place it in the freezer until frozen.

Mix your gin and tonic as you normally would, then pop in a couple of cucumber cubes and a very thin slice of lime.

Army & navy

Serves 1

50ml Beefeater or Sipsmith gin
25ml freshly squeezed lemon juice
15ml orgeat syrup (almond syrup)
ice cubes

So the story goes that there was a bar in London's Orange Street called Ciros. This place was reputed to be frequented by a bunch of foppish folk who for one reason or another were able to drink their way through the World War I while their fellow countrymen suffered the trenches in France or the waters of the Atlantic. Certain people thought poorly of this establishment, so in an attempt to show some tact, its members invented this cocktail in honour of the forces and carried on drinking.
This is one of my favourite cocktails and thankfully almond syrup is fairly easily found in larger supermarkets and good bottle shops. I like the Monin and Teisseire brands. This recipe is courtesy of the most excellent barman Paul Mant, one of the few who can serve a drink to suit even the most unexplainable mood.

Vigorously rattle the ingredients in a cocktail shaker briefly with some ice. Pour from the nozzle into a tumbler over more ice.

Hot spiced cider

Serves 2–8

1 litre good interesting medium cider

2 thumb-sized pieces of root ginger, peeled and finely sliced

1 cinnamon stick

a grating of nutmeg

1 heaped tablespoon dark muscovado sugar, or to taste

a few sprigs of thyme

5 cloves

200ml brandy

Deep and mellow, this is also a rousing drink that I brew regularly for back-of-the-year festivities, from Hallowe'en to New Year's Eve (although I wouldn't recommend it to those lighting fireworks). A couple of cups and I get a pleasant chuckly feeling; it's like being in a little warm room of your own, volume turned down, but interrupted by moments of wild abandon. Don't boil away the alcohol to syrup; make it in batches instead.

Pour the cider into a pan. Add the ginger, cinnamon, nutmeg, sugar, thyme and cloves (crush the little crowns of the cloves with your fingers first to get the max out of them). Heat the cider until it's hot, with wisps of steam rising from it, then simmer gently for 4 minutes and pour in the brandy. Goodbye!

Bloody Maria

Serves 2

1 tablespoon flaked sea salt

½ juicy lime

150ml orange juice

½ small red onion, grated

1½ teaspoons Worcestershire sauce

Tabasco, to taste

clamato juice (tomato and clam), or tomato juice, to taste

2 double shots (about 100ml) tequila blanco

ice cubes

2 slices of lime

I love the standard-issue Sunday Bloody Mary bolstered with sherry and some celery, but occasionally I want to move left-field and Mexico is the right place. Tequila blanco is a young tequila, under a year old.

Wet the lip of two large, heavy-based tumblers, then turn upside down and press on to a side plate scattered with the salt. The lip of the glass should now be white-rimmed and salted.

Into a small jug squeeze the lime and orange juices through a small sieve and then press through the juice from the grated onion. Add the Worcestershire sauce, Tabasco and as much clamato or tomato juice as you like. Stir all together and doctor according to your preference.

Into each glass pour the tequila over ice and top up with the tomato mix. Finish with a slice of lime.

Clementine cooler

Serves 1

crushed ice
50ml vodka
15ml *crème de cassis*
100ml freshly squeezed
   clementine juice

This is a really nice drink for the Christmas period.

Shove some crushed ice in the bottom of a glass and pour over the vodka, followed by the cassis. Pour in the clementine juice. Swizzle. Get swizzled.

Tinto con limon

Serves 1

3 ice cubes
a slice of lemon
Spanish red wine
Fanta Limon or bitter lemon

This is a drink I absolutely fell for in Spain, as it was incredibly cooling under the blistering hot Andalucian sun. It can go down a little too easily, so make sure when you nap off that your lounger is under an umbrella. The point of the lemonade is that it's not the white lemonade like Sprite or 7 Up, but the misty variety. Fanta Limon would be the first choice, or bitter lemon if this proves difficult.

Take one nice high tumbler, drop in the ice cubes and slice of lemon. Fill to halfway up with red wine, top up with the lemonade and drink through a straw.

Port cup

Serves 6

400ml Port
200ml red wine
juice of 2 oranges
juice of 1 lemon
1 tablespoon orgeat almond syrup
1 tablespoon caster sugar
crushed ice
a grating of nutmeg
6 thin slices of lemon

Let the Christmas cooking start with a drink. This is delicious and fresh, and should not be thought of as a cold mulled wine. Orgeat syrup is made with almonds combined with orange-flower or rose water. Monin and Teisseire are good brands.

Combine the Port, wine, juices and orgeat syrup. Stir in the sugar until it has dissolved. Add crushed ice to six glasses and pour over the wine cocktail. Stir briefly, then pass over with a dusting of nutmeg and slip in a thin slice of lemon.

Dark & stormy

Serves any number

ice cubes
dark rum, such as Lamb's
Angostura bitters
ginger beer
lime wedges

Dark and stormy is a fine drink. Its name would rightly imply that it is the perfect drink to be handed on making it back to the harbour from a chunky sea.

For each person, fill a tumbler with ice and pour in a double shot (50ml) of dark rum. Add a splash of Angostura bitters and top up with ginger beer. Finish with a squeezed wedge of lime and a quick stir.

Coconut, lime & pineapple drink

Serves 1–2

200g pineapple, skin and core
   removed
100ml coconut milk
juice of ½ small lime
1 heaped teaspoon demerara sugar
rum, to taste (optional)
ice cubes

On gloomy days, I might mix this up for breakfast, as it transports me to sandy beaches, turquoise water and fluttering palm fronds.

Combine all the ingredients apart from the ice cubes in a blender and hit go. Blitz it to death. (Alternatively, do it all in the bottom of a measuring jug with a stick blender.) You now have two choices. Version one is unstrained and full of roughage; good for the gut. Version two, for which you will need to push the contents through a sieve, is smooth and luxurious.

Pour into a glass, or glasses, and plop in a couple of cubes of ice and maybe a wee paper umbrella if you have any. Feel free to add a good splash of white rum to the ice first if you want to head more towards a Piña Colada.

The best hot chocolate ever

Makes 2 small teacups

50ml double cream
200ml whole milk
70g good dark chocolate
1 heaped teaspoon good
    cocoa powder

Whenever I visited Paris as a child to see my Godfather, we would go to Les Deux Magots or Café de Flore (two undeniable tourist traps, incidentally) in order to enjoy this most luxurious hot chocolate. When poured, I seem to remember having to wait a while before it finally oozed slowly from the spout, but perhaps this is a little over-imaginative. Anyway, it was thick and rich, and here it comes.

In a small saucepan, heat the cream and milk together until the mixture just begins to foam around the edges. Give it a stir so as to make sure it is hot in the middle of the pan as well as around the edge.

Smash the chocolate thoroughly in the packet either with a rolling pin or by slapping it very hard on the table a couple of times. Alternatively, remove it from the packet and chop on a chopping board with a knife. Put it into a ceramic bowl that you have pre-warmed with hot water from the kettle. Scatter over the cocoa powder. Using a whisk, dribble in the hot cream and milk, swishing all the time. When all the chocolate has melted, pour the contents of the bowl back into the pan and give it one last warming through; this thick, it doesn't stay hot for long.

Pour into a small teapot that has also been warmed with hot water. Pour into teacups. *Vive la France*!

Chai

Serves 4

800ml whole milk
3 tablespoons caster sugar

Spice bag

8 green cardamon pods, smashed
4 large thin slices of unpeeled
   root ginger
1 cinnamon stick, broken in half
1 teaspoon fennel seeds, bruised
3 cloves, heads pinched to release
   their flavour
2 black peppercorns
1 large bay leaf, bruised to release
   the flavour
2 Darjeeling or Assam tea bags,
   or the equivalent amount
   of loose-leaf tea

This deeply wonderful cup of hot milk, drunk from battered enamel mugs, was our saviour in the Northern Indian jungle when the night-time temperature would suddenly plummet. The sweetness of the chai we drank was illustrated by our guide's teeth, but it is a drink that should be sweet. When not warmed enough by this, a shot of whisky was our preferred chaser.

Tie up all the spices, the bay leaf and the tea bags or loose-leaf tea in a little piece of muslin cloth. Bring the milk and sugar up to a simmer with the spice-and-tea bag in a small saucepan. Turn off the heat and leave to stew for a further 5 minutes. If not to strength, gently press the bag against the side of the pan with a spoon. (Alternatively, dump all the ingredients into the pot and pour the chai through a sieve when serving.) Drink with both hands gripping all the way round the cup.

Index

Love & wild garlic to...

Denise Bates and all at Mitchell Beazley – I really enjoy working for you. Thank you for letting me have a hand in everything.

Becca Spry – A true original. Thank you for your loyalty, fun and adjustable deadlines.

Jonathan Lovekin – Excellent photographer and excellent company, may your lens be demisted of duck fat. Thank you for always being there when the egg yolk ran or the leaf curled just so.

Hattie Ellis – Thank you for your wisdom and for standing your ground. I really love talking with you.

Justine Pattison – I take it that because you're still working with me, this is a good sign. You are a great wing woman.

Pene Parker – For your cool head, great eye, total understanding of the point, and making smoking look cool in front of boys.

Fiona Smith – Friend and tolerator of my music on our many long journeys. You make a gruelling thing enjoyable.

Grainne Fox – For once again talking about the sensitive things on my behalf.

Sarah O'Keefe – For your bottomless magic dressing-up box. Thanks are also due to Summerill & Bishop.

Leanne Bryan – For tidying up my afterthoughts.

Miranda Harvey – For your inspiring flash in the pan.

Lauren Spicer – A great help. I think you investigated every known lane in West Dorset.

Jane Gwillim – For your hurrying, scurrying, borrowing, buying and sugar-sweet temperament.

Richard, Kay and Amy – For eating everything that organic pigs are not allowed to. Amy, thanks for your vegetable back-up.

The pigs – Most helpful of waste recyclers, sorry I threw some of the bin on your backs in haste. You were just a little scary sometimes. I look forward to you feeding me in return.

Simon at the Old Watch House – You're as nice as the fish that you sell.

Mother Nature – Can happily live with you, can't live without you.

Mark Hix – For being such a good and generous friend to have in Dorset when these busy weeks were finished.

The burglars who stole my lap-top – A grudging thank you for teaching me the valuable lesson of *backing up*. I hope you tried some of the recipes.

Kitty and Cooper – As always.

My dear sister Alexa – For lending us your wonderful house, a beautiful, peaceful and concentrated environment. I don't think we broke anything.

My darling wife – For turning round this easily distracted fellow and sending him back to work and for telling me when potentially embarrassing bits of writing were less than funny.